THE
EVERYTHING®
CHINESE COOKBOOK
2ND EDITION

Dear Reader,

I fondly remember the Chinese restaurant that my family ran in Denver in the 1970s and '80s. It was one of the first in the area, and a true reflection of the Chinese-American experience, a blending of our ethnic heritage with the tastes of the region to which we had immigrated. We served the dishes familiar to most people—egg foo yung, sweet and sour pork, sesame chicken, various kinds of fried rice. The recipes in this book reflect that menu. In addition, it includes dishes particular to our restaurant, such as Chicken Cantonese, and some family favorites served only at home back in that era, such as Pork Riblets in Black Bean Sauce.

These days, Chinese food has become so commonplace that anyone who has ever had dim sum will likely recognize the Pork Riblets. People's understanding of Chinese cuisine has stretched far beyond the Comfort Classics from menus of the '70s and '80s—those dishes that some might critique as not being "authentic" while secretly craving them. The recipes here will satisfy both urges. They span the range from old-school "Polynesian"-style dishes to fresh, new interpretations of Chinese cooking, with many vegetarian and vegan options. Be inventive. Have fun preparing an entire Chinese meal, or mix and match with different cuisines.

Manyee Elaine Mar

Welcome to the EVERYTHING® Series!

These handy, accessible books give you all you need to tackle a difficult project, gain a new hobby, comprehend a fascinating topic, prepare for an exam, or even brush up on something you learned back in school but have since forgotten.

You can choose to read an Everything® book from cover to cover or just pick out the information you want from our four useful boxes: e-questions, e-facts, e-alerts, and e-ssentials.

We give you everything you need to know on the subject, but throw in a lot of fun stuff along the way, too.

We now have more than 400 Everything® books in print, spanning such wide-ranging categories as weddings, pregnancy, cooking, music instruction, foreign language, crafts, pets, New Age, and so much more. When you're done reading them all, you can finally say you know Everything®!

QUESTION

Answers to
common questions

FACT

Important snippets
of information

ALERT

Urgent
warnings

ESSENTIAL

Quick
handy tips

PUBLISHER Karen Cooper

MANAGING EDITOR, EVERYTHING® SERIES Lisa Laing

COPY CHIEF Casey Ebert

ASSISTANT PRODUCTION EDITOR Alex Guarco

ACQUISITIONS EDITOR Lisa Laing

SENIOR DEVELOPMENT EDITOR Brett Palana-Shanahan

EVERYTHING® SERIES COVER DESIGNER Erin Alexander

Visit the entire Everything® series at *www.everything.com*

THE
EVERYTHING®
CHINESE COOKBOOK

2ND EDITION

Manyee Elaine Mar

Aadamsmedia
Avon, Massachusetts

For my family, and especially my father, who died a year ago,
July 4, 2012. With thanks, too, to my brother, who cared for him
the last years of his life.

An Everything® Series Book.
Everything® and everything.com® are registered trademarks of F+W Media, Inc.

Published by Adams Media, a division of F+W Media, Inc.
57 Littlefield Street, Avon, MA 02322 U.S.A.
www.adamsmedia.com

ISBN 10: 1-4405-6819-7
ISBN 13: 978-1-4405-6819-0
eISBN 10: 1-4405-6820-0
eISBN 13: 978-1-4405-6820-6

Printed in the United States of America.

10 9 8 7 6 5 4 3 2 1

Library of Congress Cataloging-in-Publication Data
Mar, Manyee Elaine.
  The everything Chinese cookbook / Manyee Elaine Mar. -- 2nd edition
     pages cm
  Includes index.
  ISBN-13: 978-1-4405-6819-0 (paperback)
  ISBN-10: 1-4405-6819-7 (paperback)
  ISBN-13: 978-1-4405-6820-6 (electronic)
  ISBN-10: 1-4405-6820-0 (electronic)
1. Cooking, Chinese. I. Lauret Parkinson, Rhonda. Everything Chinese cookbook. II. Title.
  TX724.5.C5L376 2013
  641.5951--dc23
                              2013030960

Always follow safety and common-sense cooking protocol while using kitchen utensils, operating ovens and stoves, and handling uncooked food. If children are assisting in the preparation of any recipe, they should always be supervised by an adult.

Many of the designations used by manufacturers and sellers to distinguish their products are claimed as trademarks. Where those designations appear in this book and F+W Media was aware of a trademark claim, the designations have been printed with initial capital letters.

Photos by Nam Nguyen.
Nutritional stats by Leah Traverse, RD, LDN.
Cover image © Nam Nguyen; © istockphoto/ dionisvero.

This book is available at quantity discounts for bulk purchases. For information, please call 1-800-289-0963.

Contents

Introduction

WHAT MAKES CHINESE CUISINE so appealing? Mu Shu Pork and Kung Pao Chicken have become restaurant classics. Even the idea of Sweet and Sour Sauce has its own unique appeal.

What is it that makes the food so special? It is no longer a sense of surprise in vegetables and seasonings that we might consider exotic. Chinese takeout is now as familiar as delivery pizza, and a skilled cook can prepare a meal that epitomizes the best of Chinese cuisine using only locally obtained ingredients. Nor is specialized equipment necessary. A standard kitchen knife may take the place of a cleaver; a stir-fry can be done in a sauté pan rather than a wok.

So why aren't more people steaming pork buns and boiling dumplings? One misconception is that it takes a skilled chef working with state-of-the-art kitchenware to prepare good Chinese food. Fortunately, that's not true. Stir-frying, steaming, and deep-frying—the three primary Chinese cooking techniques—are all easily mastered with practice, often using equipment already at hand.

Another common complaint is that the recipes are too complex. The sight of a lengthy ingredient list can be daunting. But it doesn't take long to learn how to break down that list into understandable components—flavorings for a marinade, vegetables to stir-fry, seasonings, stock, garnishes, and so on. After that, the basic recipe is frequently quite simple.

As for time involved, most of the work lies in preparation. Time spent actually cooking can be mere minutes, especially if you're stir-frying. And once you've cooked a few dishes you'll find yourself falling into a routine—cutting vegetables while the meat is marinating, preparing a sauce while waiting for the oil to reach the required temperature for deep-frying. Other handy time-savers include washing vegetables in the morning—giving them all day to dry—and marinating meat ahead of time and refrigerating it until you're ready to cook.

What are the pluses of cooking Chinese food at home? Besides the obvious economic advantage, homemade meals are often more healthful than restaurant fare, since you control the fat and calorie count. You can let your own creativity come into play, adjusting a recipe to add favorite foods or seasonal local ingredients. Cooking Chinese food at home also allows you to modify a recipe to suit your family's tastes; substituting parsley for cilantro, for example.

An added bonus is that there is something about cooking Chinese food that brings families together. Many pleasurable evenings can be spent filling dumplings or making pancakes. Appetizers such as egg rolls can often be baked as well as deep-fried, making it easier to involve young children.

This book is designed to help you incorporate home-cooked Chinese meals into your daily life. Tips on purchasing equipment, cooking techniques, and stocking the pantry are all here. Recipes include popular favorites such as Mu Shu Pork, and less well-known dishes such as Cheong Fun, a stuffed dim sum noodle. Information on cooking with more exotic ingredients such as Szechwan peppercorns and fermented black beans is provided, along with suggestions for substitutes where possible.

CHAPTER 1

Let's Get Started

It may seem like a daunting task to try and create your favorite dim sum dishes or restaurant menu items, with their array of choices and flavors, but it's easy to prepare many Chinese recipes at home. All it takes is a good wok, mastery of a few simple cooking skills, and stocking the pantry with basic ingredients, many of which are available on local supermarket shelves.

At the Asian Market

To supplement your regular shopping, you may want to visit the local Asian grocery store. To the uninitiated, a visit to the Asian market can seem like a trip to a foreign land, minus a map or guidebook. But structure and organization do exist. Unlike the typical large supermarket, Asian groceries share much in common with the shops of days gone by, when several businesses shared the same general space. Most groceries have a butcher shop, where slabs of glazed barbecued pork hang from hooks. A fishmonger sells the freshest fish possible, preferably caught earlier that day. Most stores have a bakery that offers fresh-baked bread and buns. All of these businesses normally operate independently from the main grocery store.

FACT

In Chinese cooking, the fresher the better! It is quite possible that the fish you see on a slab of ice was killed mere hours before being delivered to the market. Freshness is particularly important in Cantonese cuisine. It is a point of pride with Cantonese cooks to create dishes that retain as much of the natural flavor and texture of the food as possible.

As for the main grocery area, the most important thing to remember is that the space allocation for various products is different from that in Western supermarkets. One aisle may be set aside for the myriad sauces and seasonings used in Chinese cooking, while another contains a varied assortment of noodles, flour, and starch. And where else would you find an entire aisle devoted to tea, China's national drink?

Two areas that may prove challenging are spices and fresh vegetables. It is very common for grocers to provide only the Cantonese names for produce. Similarly, bags of spices may have Chinese writing on the label, leaving you unsure of their English equivalent. However, it shouldn't be difficult to find a store employee or manager to help you figure it out.

An added plus to shopping at the Asian market is that you can stock up on ingredients and purchase the tools you need to begin cooking Chinese food at the same time. While most supermarkets carry only a few cooking tools, in Asian markets it is very common for several aisles to be stocked with everything from woks to harder-to-find accessories such as cooking chopsticks.

Is monosodium glutamate (MSG) necessary for Chinese dishes?
You don't need to add MSG to home-cooked dishes; fresh ingredients will provide plenty of flavor. However, since many restaurants use MSG, you may find it difficult to reproduce the taste of your favorite restaurant dish without it.

Staple Ingredients

Certain flavors such as ginger and garlic feature prominently in Chinese cooking. While on occasion you may find yourself scouring Chinatown for a seldom-used ingredient such as shark's fin, keeping the pantry stocked with a few basics will allow you to whip up a stir-fry any night of the week, using whatever combination of meat and vegetables you have on hand.

In southern China the day begins and ends with a bowl of steaming rice. While noodles are the grain of choice in China's colder northern regions, rice is consumed there as well. Long-grain rice is favored for main dishes, but medium-grain rice is an acceptable substitute. Short-grain rice is used primarily in desserts.

Chinese noodles are not much different from Italian pasta. Most types of noodles are very user-friendly, often requiring only a quick soaking to soften before use.

COOKING CHINESE NOODLES		
Noodle Type	**Cooking Method**	**Cooking Time**
Cellophane/Bean Thread Noodles	Soak in Hot Water	15 minutes
Egg Noodles, Fresh	Boil	3–5 minutes
Egg Noodles, Dried	Boil	4–5½ minutes
Rice Noodles	Soak in Hot Water	15–20 minutes
Rice Paper	Soak in Hot Water	1 minute
Wheat Flour, Fresh	Boil	3–5 minutes
Wheat Flour, Dried	Boil	4–5 minutes

Fresh Is Best

Always use the freshest ingredients possible; nothing can replace the bite of freshly ground white pepper, or ginger that has gone straight from garden to kitchen, bypassing the market.

- *Ginger:* Used for everything from seasoning oil to complementing flavors in seafood dishes. Be sure to use fresh instead of powdered.
- *Garlic*: The mainstay of northern Chinese dishes, where cooks rely on hardy vegetables that can tolerate cold winters and a short growing season. Like ginger, it is also used to flavor hot oil before stir-frying.
- *Green onions:* Also called spring onions and scallions, these are used in cooked dishes and as a garnish.
- *Celery:* Celery's crisp texture makes a nice contrast with other vegetables in stir-fries.
- *White pepper:* Freshly ground white pepper lends a sharp bite to soups and stir-fries. Use sparingly at first or according to taste.

ESSENTIAL

The Chinese also use hundreds of dried ingredients, from tangerine peel to lily buds. The most commonly used are dried black mushrooms—you'll frequently find these stacked in bins at the entrance to Asian markets. Don't worry about purchasing the most expensive brands, but do look for mushrooms with a nice curl to them.

Sauces and Oils

A good sauce is a key component in Chinese cooking. Savory sauces like oyster and hoisin sauce add their own intriguing blend of flavors to a sauce or marinade, while soy sauce is used both to flavor and color the food. Here are some of the sauces most commonly used in Chinese cooking:

- *Dark soy sauce:* This sauce is used primarily to lend a darker color to marinades, sauces, and heavier dishes. The recipe will state if dark soy sauce is required.

- *Light soy sauce:* Saltier and aged for a shorter period of time, light soy sauce makes a frequent appearance in soups, stir-fries, and deep-fries. When a recipe calls for soy or soya sauce, use light soy sauce.
- *Oyster sauce:* This rich sauce adds a savory flavor to dishes.
- *Hoisin sauce:* Made from seasoned soybean paste, the sweet and savory flavor of hoisin sauce is an indispensable tool of northern Chinese cooks.
- *Chili paste and chili sauce:* Fiery Szechwan cuisine wouldn't be the same without hot chilies. Just remember that a little goes a long way!

FACT

Versatile cornstarch has many uses, from binding liquid ingredients in meat marinades to coating food during deep-frying. Mixed with water, it's frequently used to thicken sauces during the final stages of cooking.

Both stir-frying and deep-frying require oils with a high smoking point. While Chinese cooks favor peanut oil, it can go rancid if there is too long a period between stir-fries. Vegetable oils such as canola and corn oil are an acceptable substitute. Sesame oil is used to add a unique nutty flavor to soups and fried dishes—just drizzle a few drops into the dish in the final stages of cooking.

You will also need to get Chinese rice wine, which is valued for its sweet flavor and ability to temper strong odors in marinades and stir-fries. (Generally, pale dry sherry is an acceptable substitute.) In marinades and special sauces where the flavor of each ingredient counts more, stick with Chinese rice wine or make sure to use a higher-quality pale dry sherry.

Cooking Equipment

You don't need to splurge on a bunch of fancy gadgets to cook Chinese food. All it takes is a wok and a few basic utensils. The versatile wok is a steamer, frying pan, deep-fryer, and roasting pan all rolled into one. A good chef's knife can be used instead of a Chinese cleaver, and you don't need a rice cooker to boil rice, but a wok is the one piece of equipment that you should definitely consider purchasing before you begin cooking Chinese food.

It would be stretching the truth to say that you absolutely must have a wok to cook Chinese food. If using a sauté pan, the main thing to remember is to use a heavy skillet that can take the high heats required for stir-frying. Cast-iron and hard-anodized aluminum pans are both good choices. Still, if it's possible, a wok is preferable.

Material Matters

Originally, woks were large round vessels made of cast iron, with handles on either side for easy lifting in and out of the conventional Chinese oven. Over the centuries, woks have evolved to meet changing needs. Today, most Asian cooks favor woks made of carbon steel. Inexpensive and easy to handle, carbon steel woks can take the high heat needed for stir-frying and deep-frying. Properly seasoned and cleaned, they will last for years—and develop their own nonstick surface.

Still, modern technology has provided other options. It's now possible to purchase woks made with a nonstick coating. There are some advantages to cooking with a nonstick wok. It can be more healthful from a caloric standpoint, since you will not need to use as much oil. Another advantage is that there is less cleanup. It can be frustrating to interrupt cooking dinner to wash the remains of a meat marinade from the wok before starting to stir-fry the vegetables. A nonstick coating means less immediate fuss and muss.

However, the kind of coating used may have its own health drawbacks. Investigate carefully. One other potential drawback with nonstick woks is that the coating may warp under higher temperatures. Be prepared to pay extra for hard-anodized aluminum or carbon steel woks with a nonstick coating that can take the high heats needed for stir-frying.

Wok Design

As a general rule, the type of stove you have will influence your choice of wok design. Traditional round-bottomed woks don't sit properly on an electric stove element. Originally, wok manufacturers tried to solve the problem by devising a round "collar" to sit on the burner and hold the wok in place. However, a better solution for an electric stove is a wok with a flat bottom.

In addition to being safer, flat-bottomed woks ensure that the food cooks quickly and evenly. Both round and flat-bottomed woks work on gas stoves.

FACT

Purchase a wok that is too small, and you'll be spending extra time in the kitchen, stir-frying and deep-frying in batches. While fascinating to look at, the mammoth woks favored by Chinese restaurant chefs are designed to feed a crowd, and aren't necessary for home cooking. For most families, a 14" wok is a good choice.

Pay Attention to the Cover

Be sure that the wok you purchase comes with a lid. Unlike the conventional frying pan cover, wok lids are bowl-shaped, with a handle on top. Use them to cover foods during braising and steaming, and as a large bowl for tossing food prior to cooking.

Other Kitchen Accessories

Just as Chinese cooks have adapted techniques for cooking dishes that originated hundreds of years ago, you also can take advantage of modern technology. Here are a number of handy tools and gadgets that will make your cooking go more smoothly.

- *Cleaver or chef's knife:* It doesn't need to be a Chinese cleaver, but it must be sharp and able to cut everything from meat to mushrooms.
- *Mandoline:* Great for cutting potatoes and other root vegetables julienne style. There are also miniature mandolines that do a nifty job of shredding garlic and ginger.
- *Food processor:* Invaluable for mixing sauces and crushing ingredients.
- *Wire mesh skimmer:* A large wire mesh spoon that makes transferring deep-fried food from wok to plate much easier.
- *Cooking chopsticks:* Longer than regular chopsticks, these are great for lightly beating eggs, mixing marinade ingredients, and maneuvering individual pieces of food in the wok.

- *Cutting board:* Chinese chefs favor thick wooden cutting boards, but acrylic is also acceptable. Avoid plastic, as it can damage your knife.
- *Chinese spatula:* With a wide handle shaped like a child's toy shovel, this utensil is the perfect size and shape for moving large quantities of food through the wok while stir-frying, ensuring that the food lands back in the pan and not on the stove or floor.

Cooking Techniques

While anyone can learn to prepare Chinese food, it helps to master a few basic techniques. Whether you're stir-frying chicken for four or making egg rolls for twenty, here are a few general tips to keep in mind when cooking Chinese food:

- *Start small.* Try preparing a stir-fry entrée accompanied by steamed rice, or a vegetable side dish to serve with your main meal. Later, you can work up to an entire Chinese meal complete with appetizer, soup, and dessert.
- *Try to create meals that provide an interesting variety of textures, colors, and flavors.* The goal of Chinese cooking is to strike a pleasing balance, with no one ingredient overpowering the others.
- *Use fresh ingredients wherever possible.* If a recipe calls for a certain ingredient that is out of season, substitute whatever is available locally.
- *Think about texture as well as color when making substitutions.* Zucchini stands in nicely for a Chinese gourd, while crisp broccoli makes a good substitute for bok choy.
- *Be creative with leftovers.* Leftover vegetables can be used for fried rice, and chicken bones can be stored in the freezer until you are ready to make chicken stock.
- *Leaving the meat partially frozen will make it easier to cut.*
- *Always marinate fresh meat before cooking.* Use the time while the meat is marinating to cut vegetables and mix sauces.
- *Keep a supply of paper towels on hand to drain stir-fried and deep-fried food.*
- *Don't use dark soy sauce unless the recipe specifically calls for it.* Light soy sauce has a higher salt content than dark; substituting one for the other will affect the flavor of the dish. Taste each to know your own preference.

- *Never use more cornstarch than the recipe calls for; a little goes a long way.*
- *Trust your judgment.* Something as minor as varying salt levels between different brands of soy sauce can affect the flavor of a dish. Always do a taste test at the end of cooking and adjust the seasonings if you think it is necessary.

Stir-Frying

It may look daunting when you watch a television chef skillfully maneuvering food in a wok, but anyone can learn to stir-fry. The key to successful stir-frying is high heat combined with vigorous stirring.

Make sure all your ingredients are prepared ahead of time. The average stir-fry takes less than seven minutes, leaving little time for last-minute slicing and dicing. Always leave stir-frying until the end of cooking. Stir-fries are meant to go straight from wok to table.

Cut all the ingredients to a uniform size to ensure that they cook at the same rate. If you're improvising instead of following a recipe, a good rule of thumb is to cut everything into bite-size pieces.

If you are using a carbon steel wok, preheat the wok for 1 minute before adding oil. If you are using a wok made out of a different type of material, or a wok or frying pan with a nonstick coating, check the manufacturer's instructions first to ensure that preheating will not cause any damage.

When adding oil, pour it so that it swirls around the sides of the wok before reaching the bottom. Test to see if the oil is hot by standing a cooking chopstick straight up in the wok's center. If the oil sizzles all the way around the chopstick, you can start cooking. If you don't have a chopstick, a small piece of bread works also.

ESSENTIAL

When it comes to cooking temperatures for stir-frying, be prepared to do a bit of experimenting. Every stove is different, and it may take a few attempts before you find the optimum temperature for stir-frying on your make and model.

Before adding other ingredients, try flavoring the oil with a few slices of ginger and/or garlic. Stir-fry until they are aromatic. Then, add other ingredients. To stir-fry, simply move the spatula through the wok and stir the ingredients every few seconds.

When you cook meat, sear it briefly before stir-frying. To make sure all of it comes into contact with the pan, it's important not to overcrowd the wok. Cook meat in batches, if necessary.

Never pour a cornstarch-and-water mixture directly over the food in the wok. Instead, push the food up to the sides of the wok and add the cornstarch and water in the middle. Turn up the heat and stir vigorously to thicken. Once the mixture has thickened you can mix it with the other ingredients.

Most importantly, don't panic. If you feel things are moving too fast, just take the wok or frying pan off the heat and give yourself a moment to relax and refocus. Stir-frying is a very forgiving art.

Deep-Frying

Deep-frying seals-in meat's juices and adds a crispy coating to dishes. The trick is keeping the temperature constant during cooking. Too low temperatures will lead to greasy food loaded with extra fat and calories. The following tips will help you prepare deep-fried dishes that are crisp and full of flavor.

ALERT

As you cook, continue to monitor the oil temperature while deep-frying. The easiest way to do this is with a deep-fry thermometer with a clamp that can attach to the side of the wok. That way, your hands remain free for cooking while you're checking the temperature.

First of all, make sure the wok is securely attached to the stand. Next, pour in enough oil to completely cover the food being cooked, while leaving a couple of inches of room at the top of the wok. Unless the recipe states otherwise, the temperature of the oil should rise to about 350–375°F.

Slide the food in carefully, so that it doesn't splatter when it meets the hot oil. Leave plenty of room in the wok for the food to move around. Deep-fry in batches, if necessary. As soon as the food is added, check the temperature of the oil. Turn and separate the individual pieces of food while they are cooking.

Use a slotted spoon or a mesh skimmer to carefully remove the deep-fried food from the wok. Drain the deep-fried food on paper towels. If the recipe calls for food to be deep-fried twice, retest the temperature and make sure the oil is hot enough before you begin deep-frying the second time.

To reuse cooked oil, let it cool and then strain and store it in a sealed container in the refrigerator. Cooked oil can be reused up to five times. Throw it out if the color darkens or it begins to smell rancid.

Even with these tips, you may find that using a wok to deep-fry is not for you. Wok deep-frying demands your undivided attention. If you have small children at home, or frequent interruptions are the norm, consider using a deep-fat fryer instead.

Steaming

Steaming, or cooking food by placing it over boiling or simmering water, is the third and the simplest Chinese cooking technique. The key to successful steaming lies in ensuring that the hot water never touches the food.

When it comes to equipment, a set of bamboo steamers is ideal. Bamboo steamers allow you to prepare multiple layers of food at the same time. In contrast to aluminum steamers, the natural texture of bamboo acts to prevent condensation from getting into the food. The cooked food can move straight from wok to table, with the steaming baskets doing double duty as cooking utensil and serving dish.

Steaming is the least intrusive cooking technique; the flavor, color, and texture of the steamed food remain closer to what nature intended. Nutritionally speaking, steamed food retains more nutrients and vitamins, and is generally lower in fat and calories, than food cooked by other methods.

Steaming with bamboo is easy if you keep the following tips in mind:

- Before placing the food in the bamboo steamer, line the steamer with cabbage leaves, bamboo or banana leaves, or cheesecloth. This prevents the food from sticking.

- Be sure to leave approximately 1" between the water and the food to be steamed.
- For smaller items such as dumplings, place the bamboo base or trivet in the water, with the steaming basket on top. Place the food in the basket, cover, and cook. For larger items such as meat and seafood dishes, either use a larger set of bamboo steamers or substitute a heat-proof dish. Also placed on the bamboo base, the heatproof dish can be anything from a dinner plate to an aluminum pie plate. The wok lid makes an ideal cover.
- When choosing a bamboo steamer, inspect it carefully to make sure none of the parts are connected with staples. If you find staples, choose another brand.
- Prior to its first use, give the steamer a thorough washing with soap and hot water. Dry completely before using.
- For best results, always use the freshest ingredients possible.

Tea Time

Dine at a Chinese restaurant, and chances are that before you've placed your order, the waitress will appear at your table with a steaming pot of tea. In China, tea is more than merely a hot drink. Over centuries, tea drinking has gone from being a refined pastime stretching several hours to an essential part of every meal.

A Brief History of Tea in China

According to a charming legend, tea was discovered when an emperor fell asleep underneath a tea bush and awoke to find that a brown leaf had drifted into his cup of boiled water. This legend places the discovery of tea to 2737 B.C. Whether or not the story is true, there is no doubt that the Chinese were cultivating tea by A.D. 350.

However, it took the publication of a scholarly work to transform tea from merely a hot brew into China's national drink. Late in the eighth century, Lu Yu published *The Classic Art of Tea Drinking*. A poet and performer who had been educated by Buddhist monks, Lu Yu attempted to provide a complete overview of the history, cultivation, processing, and drinking of tea. The result was a definitive tome that is still consulted by tea experts today.

ALERT

Brewing the perfect cup of green tea is a tricky process. With improper handling, those same polyphenols that protect the body against cancer and other diseases can ruin the tea's flavor. Allow boiled water to cool to a temperature of no more than 175°F before pouring over the tea. Steep for 2–3 minutes before drinking. Plan on using 1–2 teaspoons of green tea per cup.

Tea's popularity skyrocketed following the publication of Lu Yu's work. Buddhist monks introduced tea to the Japanese, although its use in Japan didn't become widespread until the 1200s. Today, teahouses are scattered throughout cities in China. Each has its own atmosphere; you can play chess at one, or listen to music played on ancient Chinese instruments at another. The one thing that remains constant is the quality of the tea.

Types of Tea

When you consider the different types of teas available, it's easy to believe that they come from different plants. In fact, all tea comes from the *Camellia sinensis* plant. In general, tea is categorized both by the way it is processed and its country of origin.

There are literally hundreds of varieties of Chinese teas, many named after the region where they were first cultivated. However, the majority fall into one of these five categories:

- *Green tea:* Probably the most famous Chinese tea due to its reputed health benefits, green tea is made from unfermented tea leaves. The leaves are dried immediately after picking. This prevents oxidation, leaving the chemical properties of the tea intact.
- *Oolong tea:* Made from larger tea leaves, this is a tea that has been partially fermented, so that full oxidation of the leaves does not take place. After drying in the sun, the leaves are heated to stop the oxidation process. This gives them a greenish-black color. Because

fermentation can be stopped at any point, the flavor of different types of oolong tea varies.

- *Black tea:* Black tea consists of tea leaves that have been rolled and then fully dried and fermented, giving them a darker color. Black tea is more popular in the West than in Asia.
- *Scented teas:* These are made by adding flowers to the tea leaves during the fermentation process. The most popular scented teas are jasmine and chrysanthemum.
- *White tea:* Like green tea, white teas are unfermented. However, instead of steam drying, the tea leaves are dried naturally in the sun. White tea is believed to have even more health benefits than green tea.

ESSENTIAL

When it comes to tea, not all water is created equal. Tea just won't taste the same if it is made with water that contains impurities or has been treated with chlorine. A good water filter helps here, and bottled water is always preferable. According to the sage of Chinese tea, Lu Yu, pure water from natural springs is best for making tea, followed by river water and well water, in that order.

Health Benefits of Tea

In recent years, scientists have been paying a great deal of attention to the health benefits of drinking green tea. What sets green tea apart from other teas? Green teas contain a polyphenol called epigallocatechin gallate (EGCG), which is known to be a powerful antioxidant.

Since antioxidants inhibit the growth of free radicals found in cancer cells, it's not surprising that most of the research on green tea has focused on its ability to prevent cancer. However, EGCG has other health benefits as well. Green tea has been shown to lower blood pressure and reduce high cholesterol levels. It is also believed to lower the risk of stroke.

QUESTION

Which is better, tea bags or loose-leaf tea?
Loose-leaf teas are preferable to bagged tea. Made with a lower grade of tea leaves known as "fannings," bagged teas tend to have less flavor. Many higher-quality teas aren't available in bags. Still, bagged tea does have its advantages if you're in a hurry or want a quick cup of tea at the office.

While most of the research has focused on green tea, scientists are discovering that there are also health benefits to be derived from drinking black tea. Black teas contain another type of polyphenol called theaflavin-3'-monogallate (TF-2). Like EGCG, TF-2 is believed to inhibit the growth of cancer cells. Research is also being conducted on the use of black tea to treat arthritis.

CHAPTER 2

Popular Chinese Sauces

Ginger Scallion Sauce

This is perhaps the most common sauce for Cantonese cuisine. Its bright, fresh flavors pair well with traditional New Year's dishes like salted steamed chicken or fish.

INGREDIENTS | MAKES 1 CUP

½ cup thinly sliced scallions
¼ cup finely minced fresh ginger
¼ cup neutral-flavored oil
Pinch of salt

Combine all ingredients in a small bowl. Let sit for 15–30 minutes for the flavors to combine. May be stored for several days in the refrigerator.

PER SERVING (1 TABLESPOON) Calories: 33 | Fat: 3 grams | Protein: 0 grams | Sodium: 30 milligrams | Fiber: 0 grams | Carbohydrates: 0 grams | Sugar: 0 grams

Black Bean Chili Sauce

This is an intense sauce that can be used in cooking or sparingly for dipping. If served as a dipping sauce, you may want to dilute it with peanut oil.

INGREDIENTS | MAKES ½ CUP

2 tablespoons peanut oil
2–3 small red chili peppers, finely minced
⅓ cup fermented black beans, rinsed and chopped
1 tablespoon Xiaoshing wine
1 teaspoon sugar

1. Heat the oil in a saucepan over medium heat. Add the chilies and fermented black beans. Cook for about 1 minute.

2. Add the wine and cook, stirring, for another 2–3 minutes. Add the sugar; stir to combine.

3. Turn off the heat. Let sit to cool. Use immediately or store refrigerated.

PER SERVING (1 TEASPOON) Calories: 15 | Fat: 1 gram | Protein: 0 grams | Sodium: 42 milligrams | Fiber: 0 grams | Carbohydrates: 1 gram | Sugar: 0.5 grams

Black Bean Garlic Sauce

This is an earthy sauce for salt and garlic lovers, a great addition to flavor a quick stir-fry.
It can also be used as a dipping sauce, diluted with oil according to taste.

INGREDIENTS | MAKES 2 CUPS

¾ cup vegetable oil, divided

⅓ cup fermented black beans, roughly chopped

½ cup minced garlic

½ cup Shaoxing rice wine

1. Preheat a wok over high heat. Swirl in ¼ cup of the oil. Add the beans and garlic and stir-fry 2–3 minutes.

2. Add the wine, decrease the heat to medium, and cook until the mixture is reduced by ¾, about 2–3 minutes.

3. Remove from the heat and allow to cool. Transfer half the mixture to a blender or food processor and purée at high speed while adding the remaining ½ cup oil.

4. Stir the purée back into the remaining mixture. Use immediately or store in the refrigerator for up to 7 days.

PER SERVING (1 TABLESPOON) Calories: 60 | Fat: 5 grams | Protein: 0 grams | Sodium: 169 milligrams | Fiber: 0 grams | Carbohydrates: 3 grams | Sugar: 1 gram

Hot Mustard Dip

Hot mustard's bite makes a great combination with Egg Rolls (see recipe in Chapter 3) and less highly spiced appetizers such as Traditional Gow Gees (see recipe in Chapter 3).

INGREDIENTS | MAKES ⅓ CUP

3 tablespoons hot mustard

3 tablespoons water

1 teaspoon rice vinegar

½ teaspoon sugar

Combine all the ingredients in a small bowl. Use immediately.

PER SERVING (1 TABLESPOON) Calories: 19 | Fat: 0 grams | Protein: 0 grams | Sodium: 81 milligrams | Fiber: 0 grams | Carbohydrates: 3 grams | Sugar: 0 grams

What Makes Hot Mustard Hot?

A better question would be, why aren't all mustards hot? The secret behind hot mustard's fiery flavor lies in the chemical reaction that occurs when mustard seeds come in contact with a liquid such as water or salad oil. Commercially prepared mustards tone down the reaction by adding ingredients such as flour. The strength and flavor of mustard also depends on the type of mustard seeds used.

Hot Mustard Sauce

*This sauce is a little runnier than a paste. Use in a salad like
Chinese Potato Salad (see recipe in Chapter 4).*

INGREDIENTS | MAKES ¼ CUP

2 tablespoons mustard powder

2 tablespoons rice vinegar

1 teaspoon brown sugar

1 tablespoon vegetable oil

3 drops sesame oil

Mix all the ingredients in a small bowl and use immediately.

PER SERVING (1 TABLESPOON) Calories: 62 | Fat: 4 grams | Protein: 1 gram | Sodium: 2 milligrams | Fiber: 0 grams | Carbohydrates: 2 grams | Sugar: 1 gram

Plum Sauce

*For best results, prepare the plum sauce several hours ahead
of time to give the flavors a chance to blend.*

INGREDIENTS | MAKES ⅔ CUP

1 (12-ounce) can plums, drained, juice reserved

2 tablespoons brown sugar

4 tablespoons rice vinegar

1 slice ginger

1 clove garlic

½ cup juice from the drained plums

½ cup water

1. Remove the plum pits. In a medium saucepan, bring all the ingredients to a boil. Reduce the heat to low and simmer, covered, for about 2 hours, or until the plums are soft.

2. Remove the ginger and garlic. Process the sauce in a blender or food processor until smooth. Cool and chill in the refrigerator. Use within a few days.

PER SERVING (1 TABLESPOON) Calories: 28 | Fat: 0 grams | Protein: 0 grams | Sodium: 1 milligram | Fiber: 0 grams | Carbohydrates: 7 grams | Sugar: 6 grams

Brown Sauce

Out of cornstarch? You can substitute flour as a thickener in this recipe— just double the amount to 2 tablespoons.

INGREDIENTS | MAKES ⅔ CUP

1 tablespoon plus 1 teaspoon oyster sauce

3 teaspoons hoisin sauce

1 teaspoon Xiaoshing wine

1 teaspoon soy sauce

½ teaspoon sugar

½ cup beef broth or juices from cooked meat

2 tablespoons water

1 tablespoon cornstarch

1. Combine all the ingredients, adding the cornstarch last, in a small saucepan. Bring to a boil.

2. Reduce the heat to medium-low and cook, stirring constantly to thicken mixture. The sauce should be neither too thin nor too runny, but thick enough to use as a dip, if desired. Serve immediately or refrigerate up to 3 days.

PER SERVING (2 TABLESPOONS) Calories: 21 | Fat: 0 grams | Protein: 0 grams | Sodium: 305 milligrams | Fiber: 0 grams | Carbohydrates: 4 grams | Sugar: 1 gram

Vegetarian Brown Sauce

For a more aromatic sauce, you may heat up 1 teaspoon of oil and fry the garlic and ginger for about 30 seconds before adding the other ingredients.

INGREDIENTS | MAKES ¾ CUP

3 teaspoons hoisin sauce

1 teaspoon Xiaoshing wine

1 teaspoon soy sauce

½ cup vegetable stock or ¼ cup vegetable stock and ¼ cup liquid from soaking dried shiitake mushrooms

1 clove garlic, minced

1 teaspoon minced ginger

¼ teaspoon ground white pepper

1 tablespoon cornstarch mixed with 2 tablespoons water

1. In a small saucepan, mix together the hoisin sauce, wine, soy sauce, stock, garlic, ginger, and pepper. Bring to a boil over high heat.

2. Reduce the heat to medium and pour in the cornstarch mixture. Cook, stirring, until the sauce has thickened. Serve immediately or refrigerate up to 3 days.

PER SERVING (2 TABLESPOONS) Calories: 16 | Fat: 0 grams | Protein: 0 grams | Sodium: 195 milligrams | Fiber: 0 grams | Carbohydrates: 3 grams | Sugar: 1 gram

Peanut Sauce

Use this spicy sauce with the Chinese-Style Gado Gado Salad
(see recipe in Chapter 4) or to liven up a plain garden salad.

INGREDIENTS | MAKES 1 CUP

½ cup chicken broth

½ cup peanut butter

2 garlic cloves, minced

2 tablespoons minced red onion

2 teaspoons brown sugar

4 tablespoons soy sauce

½ teaspoon chili sauce

2 tablespoons plus 2 teaspoons rice vinegar

2 tablespoons water

1 teaspoon chopped cilantro

1. Combine all the ingredients except for the cilantro and purée in a food processor.

2. Bring the mixture to a boil in a small saucepan over high heat. Remove from the heat and stir in the cilantro. Use immediately.

PER SERVING (2 TABLESPOONS) Calories: 108 | Fat: 8 grams | Protein: 5 grams | Sodium: 606 milligrams | Fiber: 1 gram | Carbohydrates: 5 grams | Sugar: 3 grams

Szechwan Salt and Pepper Mix

For variety, try using this flavorful mix in place of plain salt and pepper,
even when you're not eating Chinese food.

INGREDIENTS | MAKES ⅓ CUP

2 tablespoons Szechwan peppercorns

1 teaspoon black peppercorns

½ teaspoon white peppercorns

¼ cup salt

Don't Let the Name Fool You

Szechwan peppers aren't peppers at all! They are distinctive reddish-brown berries that come from the prickly ash native to the Szechwan province.

1. In a heavy skillet on medium to medium-low heat, brown the peppercorns and salt, shaking the pan occasionally, until the Szechwan peppercorns are fragrant and the salt turns a light brown color.

2. Grind the cooled mixture in a spice grinder or blender. Store in a sealed jar.

PER SERVING (½ TEASPOON) Calories: 1 | Fat: 0 grams | Protein: 0 grams | Sodium: 945 milligrams | Fiber: 0 grams | Carbohydrates: 0 grams | Sugar: 0 grams

Hoisin Satay Sauce

Orange marmalade lends flavor to a traditional hoisin-based sauce in this fusion recipe. For a different taste, substitute 1 tablespoon of honey. Serve with Beef Satay (see recipe in Chapter 7).

INGREDIENTS | MAKES ⅓ CUP

3 tablespoons hoisin sauce

2 teaspoons dark soy sauce

1 teaspoon rice vinegar

1 teaspoon orange marmalade

Up to ¼ teaspoon cayenne pepper flakes

1 clove garlic, chopped

¼ cup peanuts, crushed

In a small bowl combine all the ingredients. Serve immediately or refrigerate up to 5 days.

PER SERVING (2 TABLESPOONS) Calories: 136 | Fat: 8 grams | Protein: 4 grams | Sodium: 552 milligrams | Fiber: 2 grams | Carbohydrates: 13 grams | Sugar: 7 grams

Quick and Easy Sweet-and-Sour Sauce

Adjust the thickness by increasing or reducing the amount of cornstarch.

INGREDIENTS | MAKES ½ CUP

½ cup vinegar

1 tablespoon plus 1 teaspoon sugar

1 large clove garlic, minced

1 teaspoon cornstarch

4 teaspoons water

In a medium saucepan over high heat, bring all the ingredients to a boil, stirring to thicken. Remove from the heat and let cool. Serve immediately or refrigerate up to 5 days.

PER SERVING (2 TABLESPOONS) Calories: 14 | Fat: 0 grams | Protein: 0 grams | Sodium: 1 milligram | Fiber: 0 grams | Carbohydrates: 2 grams | Sugar: 1 gram

Sweet-and-Sour Sauce with Ketchup

For extra flavor, add red and green bell pepper and pineapple chunks to the sauce after stirring in the cornstarch.

INGREDIENTS | MAKES ¾ CUP

⅓ cup rice vinegar

¼ cup brown sugar

2 tablespoons ketchup

1 tablespoon soy sauce

¼ cup water

4 teaspoons cornstarch mixed with 4 teaspoons water

1. In a small saucepan, combine the rice vinegar, brown sugar, ketchup, soy sauce, and water and bring to a boil over high heat.

2. Stir in the cornstarch-and-water mixture, stirring vigorously to thicken. Remove from the heat and let cool. Serve immediately or refrigerate up to 5 days.

PER SERVING (2 TABLESPOONS) Calories: 51 | Fat: 0 grams | Protein: 0 grams | Sodium: 228 milligrams | Fiber: 0 grams | Carbohydrates: 12 grams | Sugar: 10 grams

Hot Chili Oil

Hot Chili Oil makes an excellent dipping sauce for any dish. Use it whenever you want to add heat to your meal.

INGREDIENTS | MAKES 1 CUP

6 red chili peppers

1 tablespoon sesame oil

1 cup vegetable oil

Handling Hot Chilies
When handling chili peppers, it's important to make sure that none of the chemical gets in your eyes. For extra safety, wear rubber gloves.

1. Cut the chili peppers in half and remove the seeds. Chop coarsely.

2. Mix the oils and heat in a wok or heavy skillet over medium heat.

3. Add the chopped chili peppers and reduce the heat to low. Cook for about 5 minutes, or until the oil turns red.

4. Cool the oil and strain into a sealed jar. Store in the refrigerator for up to 7 days.

PER SERVING (1 TABLESPOON) Calories: 135 | Fat: 14 grams | Protein: 0 grams | Sodium: 1 milligram | Fiber: 0 grams | Carbohydrates: 0 grams | Sugar: 0 grams

Spicy Szechwan Peanut Sauce

Use as a dipping sauce or in Szechwan dishes such as Bang Bang Chicken
(see recipe in Chapter 9). For best results, use within a few days.

INGREDIENTS | MAKES ½ CUP

3 tablespoons peanut butter

3 tablespoons soy sauce

4 teaspoons sugar

3 tablespoons black rice vinegar

1 tablespoon sesame oil

1 clove garlic, chopped

2 tablespoons Hot Chili Oil (see recipe in this chapter)

Place all the ingredients in a food processor and process until smooth. Serve immediately or refrigerate up to 5 days.

PER SERVING (2 TABLESPOONS) Calories: 194 | Fat: 16 grams | Protein: 4 grams | Sodium: 809 milligrams | Fiber: 1 gram | Carbohydrates: 8 grams | Sugar: 6 grams

Soy Vinegar Dressing

This dressing takes mere minutes to make. Drizzle over vegetables and rice, or use
as a dipping sauce for Mini Spring Onion Pancakes (see recipe in Chapter 3).

INGREDIENTS | MAKES ¼ CUP

3 tablespoons soy sauce

2 teaspoons rice vinegar

¼ teaspoon minced ginger

Combine all the ingredients in a small bowl. Serve immediately or refrigerate up to 5 days.

PER SERVING (2 TABLESPOONS) Calories: 17 | Fat: 0 grams | Protein: 2 grams | Sodium: 1,520 milligrams | Fiber: 0 grams | Carbohydrates: 1 gram | Sugar: 0 grams

Mild Szechwan Peanut Sauce

Want to enjoy Szechwan cooking without experiencing the extreme heat?
Use this sauce instead of Spicy Szechwan Peanut Sauce (see recipe in this chapter).

INGREDIENTS | MAKES ⅓ CUP

3 tablespoons peanut butter

3 tablespoons soy sauce

4 teaspoons sugar

3 teaspoons black rice vinegar

1 teaspoon sesame oil

1 clove garlic, chopped

2 teaspoons chili sauce

Place all the ingredients in a food processor and process until smooth. Serve immediately or refrigerate up to 5 days.

PER SERVING (2 TABLESPOONS) Calories: 172 | Fat: 11 grams | Protein: 7 grams | Sodium: 1,300 milligrams | Fiber: 1 gram | Carbohydrates: 12 grams | Sugar: 9 grams

Hot Food Antidote

Tempted to reach for a glass of water after tasting fiery Szechwan food? Try a forkful of rice instead. Oil and water don't mix, and a glass of water will roll right over the chili oils that add heat to Szechwan cooking. Rice, milk, or even beer all provide more immediate relief than a glass of water.

Soy Hoisin Dressing

This savory dressing makes a great dip and adds flavor to vegetable and noodle salads.

INGREDIENTS | MAKES ⅓ CUP

2 teaspoons Chinese rice wine or dry sherry

1 teaspoon minced ginger

2 teaspoons hoisin sauce

2 tablespoons soy sauce

2 tablespoons dark soy sauce

Combine all the ingredients in a small bowl. Serve immediately or refrigerate up to 5 days.

PER SERVING (2 TABLESPOONS) Calories: 34 | Fat: 0 grams | Protein: 2 grams | Sodium: 1,645 milligrams | Fiber: 0 grams | Carbohydrates: 6 grams | Sugar: 3 grams

Soy Ginger Dressing

The clean flavor of ginger gives this dressing a sharp bite. Use as a dip with Chinese dumplings such as Traditional Gow Gees (see recipe in Chapter 3).

INGREDIENTS | MAKES ⅓ CUP

2 tablespoons soy sauce

2 teaspoons rice vinegar

1 teaspoon grated ginger

⅛ teaspoon sesame oil

Combine all the ingredients in a small bowl. Serve immediately or refrigerate up to 5 days.

PER SERVING (2 TABLESPOONS) Calories: 12 | Fat: 0 grams | Protein: 1 gram | Sodium: 812 milligrams | Fiber: 0 grams | Carbohydrates: 1 gram | Sugar: 0 grams

Worcestershire Sauce

It may have been invented by two British chemists in the 1800s, but Worcestershire sauce wouldn't be the same without an Asian influence. The secret ingredient in Worcestershire sauce is tamarind, an acid-tasting fruit that gives many Thai sauces their sharp bite. Today, Worcestershire sauce makes a frequent appearance in Chinese dipping sauces.

Asian Vinaigrette

This dressing nicely complements a simple tossed green salad.
Stored in a sealed container and refrigerated, it will keep for a few days.

INGREDIENTS | MAKES ½ CUP

4 tablespoons salad oil

2 tablespoons black rice vinegar

2 teaspoons soy sauce

½ teaspoon sugar

⅛ teaspoon sesame oil

Combine all the ingredients in a jar and shake to mix thoroughly. Serve immediately or refrigerate up to 14 days.

PER SERVING (2 TABLESPOONS) Calories: 132 | Fat: 13 grams | Protein: 0 grams | Sodium: 169 milligrams | Fiber: 0 grams | Carbohydrates: 2 grams | Sugar: 1 gram

Northern Noodle Sauce

This spicy sauce adds bite to noodle and tofu dishes. For a milder sauce,
leave out the chili oil. It can also be served as a dipping sauce.

INGREDIENTS | MAKES ⅓ CUP

1 small clove garlic, chopped

½ green onion, mainly white part, thinly sliced

¼ cup dark soy sauce

2 teaspoons black rice vinegar

1 teaspoon Hot Chili Oil (see recipe in this chapter)

½ teaspoon sugar

¼ teaspoon sesame oil

1 teaspoon cornstarch mixed with 4 teaspoons water

1. In a blender or food processor, combine garlic clove and green onion with the dark soy sauce, black rice vinegar, Hot Chili Oil, sugar, and sesame oil. Process until smooth.

2. Add the mixture to a small saucepan and bring to a boil over high heat.

3. Reduce the heat to medium and add cornstarch mixture to the sauce, stirring vigorously to thicken. Cool. Serve immediately or refrigerate up to 5 days.

PER SERVING (1 TABLESPOON) Calories: 25 | Fat: 1 gram | Protein: 1 gram | Sodium: 802 milligrams | Fiber: 0 grams | Carbohydrates: 2 grams | Sugar: 0 grams

Sweet Green and Red Chili Sauce

This dip will give a burning sensation in the back of your mouth,
but without the sweating and watery eyes associated with hotter peppers.

INGREDIENTS | MAKES ⅔ CUP

3 jalapeño peppers
¼ red bell pepper
¼ cup rice vinegar
4 tablespoons sugar
1 teaspoon cornstarch
4 teaspoons water

1. Cut the jalapeño peppers in half lengthwise. Remove the seeds and chop. Wash the red bell pepper and cut into squares.

2. Place the rice vinegar, sugar, jalapeño peppers, and red pepper in a blender or food processor and process until smooth.

3. In a small saucepan, bring the mixture to a boil over high heat. Reduce the heat and simmer for 5 minutes.

4. In a small bowl, mix the cornstarch and water together. Stir the cornstarch mixture into the saucepan and continue to cook until the sauce thickens. Serve immediately or refrigerate up to 7 days.

PER SERVING (1 TABLESPOON) Calories: 23 | Fat: 0 grams | Protein: 0 grams | Sodium: 0 milligrams | Fiber: 0 grams | Carbohydrates: 5 grams | Sugar: 5 grams

Sweet Soy Sauce

*Serve this sauce with Cheong Fun (see recipe in Chapter 3)
or Vegan Turnip Cake (see recipe in Chapter 3).*

INGREDIENTS | MAKES 1 CUP

1 cup soy sauce
⅓ cup crushed Chinese rock sugar

In a small saucepan, heat the soy sauce and rock sugar over moderately low heat until the sugar dissolves completely. Let the sauce cool before serving. May be stored in the refrigerator for up to 14 days.

PER SERVING (1 TABLESPOON) Calories: 25 | Fat: 0 grams | Protein: 1 gram | Sodium: 1,005 milligrams | Fiber: 0 grams | Carbohydrates: 4 grams | Sugar: 4 grams

Pot Sticker Dipping Sauce

This sauce may be served with pot stickers or other Chinese dumplings.

INGREDIENTS | MAKES ⅓ CUP

2 tablespoons soy sauce
¼ teaspoon sesame oil
2 teaspoons black rice vinegar
1 teaspoon Hot Chili Oil (see recipe in this chapter)
1 teaspoon cilantro leaves, finely chopped

Combine all the ingredients in a small bowl. Serve immediately or refrigerate up to 3 days.

PER SERVING (2 TABLESPOONS) Calories: 31 | Fat: 2 grams | Protein: 1 gram | Sodium: 823 milligrams | Fiber: 0 grams | Carbohydrates: 1 gram | Sugar: 0 grams

Intriguing XO Sauce

For an interesting twist, try adding a teaspoon of XO sauce to your favorite dipping sauce recipe. First served at Hong Kong Chinese restaurants, this flavorful sauce is an intriguing mix of seafood and spicy seasonings such as hot chilies and garlic.

CHAPTER 3

Appetizers and Dim Sum

Egg Rolls

While peanut butter may seem an unusual ingredient for egg rolls, its creamy texture and nutty flavor combines well with the shredded chicken and crunch of the bean sprouts.

INGREDIENTS | SERVES 15

1 tablespoon soy sauce

¼ cup chicken stock

4 cups plus 2 tablespoons vegetable oil, divided

1 teaspoon minced ginger

1 stalk celery, thinly sliced on the diagonal

1 cup fresh mung bean sprouts

2 green onions, thinly sliced on the diagonal

1 teaspoon ground white pepper, or more to taste

1 teaspoon sesame oil

⅓ cup smooth peanut butter

1 cup shredded cooked chicken

15 egg roll wrappers

1 egg, beaten

1. In a small bowl, combine the soy sauce and chicken stock. Set aside.

2. Add 2 tablespoons of oil to a preheated wok or skillet. When the oil is hot, add the ginger and stir-fry about 30 seconds. Add the celery and stir-fry until it starts to become translucent. Add the bean sprouts and green onions. Stir-fry about 1 minute. Add the pepper and sesame oil. Stir to combine.

3. Pour in the chicken stock mixture. As it begins to boil, stir in the peanut butter and mix well to form a thick sauce. Add the shredded chicken and heat everything through. Turn off the heat, transfer the mixture to a bowl, and allow it to cool.

4. Clean the wok and pour in 4 cups of oil. Heat to 375°F. While the oil is heating, assemble the egg rolls: Place a wrapper on a work surface with one corner pointing at you. Place 2 tablespoons of filling near the bottom of the wrapper. Fold the corner up. Now fold in the two side corners. Brush the top corner of the wrapper with egg. Roll the filled portion of the wrapper up to the top corner, applying gentle pressure so that the egg roll is compact. Press the top seam to seal. Continue until you have used all the filling and wrappers.

5. Deep-fry the egg rolls until they turn golden brown (2–3 minutes). Drain on paper towels.

PER SERVING Calories: 228 | Fat: 13 grams | Protein: 7 grams | Sodium: 304 milligrams | Fiber: 1 gram | Carbohydrates: 20 grams | Sugar: 1 gram

Spring Rolls

Spring rolls use a thinner wrapper than egg rolls, and thus fry up more crisply.

INGREDIENTS | SERVES 12

½ pound pork tenderloin, shredded

2 tablespoons oyster sauce, divided

½ teaspoon baking soda

6 dried mushrooms

1 tablespoon chicken broth or stock

½ teaspoon sugar

4 cups plus 3½ tablespoons vegetable oil, divided

1 cup mung bean sprouts, rinsed and drained

1 cup grated carrot

2 green onions, thinly sliced on the diagonal

¼ teaspoon sesame oil

12 spring roll wrappers

2 tablespoons cornstarch mixed with 1 tablespoon water

1. In a medium bowl, marinate the pork in 1 tablespoon oyster sauce and baking soda for 30 minutes.

2. Soak the dried mushrooms in hot water for 20 minutes to soften; drain and thinly slice.

3. In a separate bowl, combine the remaining 1 tablespoon oyster sauce, chicken broth, and sugar. Set aside.

4. Add 2 tablespoons of oil to a preheated wok or skillet. When the oil is hot, add the marinated pork. Stir-fry briefly until it changes color and is nearly cooked through, 2–3 minutes. Remove from the wok.

5. Add 1½ tablespoons of oil to the wok. When the oil is hot, add the dried mushrooms. Stir-fry for 1 minute, then add the bean sprouts, carrot, and the green onions. Add the prepared sauce in the middle of the wok and bring to a boil. Add the pork and mix through. Drizzle with the sesame oil. Cool.

6. In the wok, heat 4 cups of oil to 375°F. While the oil is heating, prepare the spring rolls: To wrap, lay the wrapper in a diamond shape. Place a tablespoon of filling in the middle. Coat all the edges with the cornstarch-and-water mixture. Roll up the wrapper and tuck in the edges. Seal the tucked-in edges with cornstarch and water. Continue with the remainder of the spring rolls. (Prepare more cornstarch and water as necessary.)

7. Deep-fry the spring rolls, 2 at a time, until they turn golden. Drain on paper towels.

PER SERVING Calories: 253 | Fat: 14 grams | Protein: 7 grams | Sodium: 375 milligrams | Fiber: 1 gram | Carbohydrates: 23 grams | Sugar: 1 gram

Wild Mushroom Spring Rolls

Experiment with a variety of different mushrooms in these spring rolls: shiitake, oyster, chanterelle, or any others you see in your local market. Serve with Hot Mustard Sauce (see recipe in Chapter 2).

INGREDIENTS | SERVES 12

1 bundle rice vermicelli

4 cups plus 2 tablespoons peanut oil

1 tablespoon minced garlic

½ tablespoon grated fresh ginger

2 scallions, sliced thin

1 pound mixed mushrooms

2 cups shredded Chinese cabbage

1 carrot, grated

1 tablespoon hoisin sauce

1 tablespoon oyster sauce

2 tablespoons finely chopped cilantro

1 teaspoon salt

1 teaspoon ground white pepper

1 package spring roll wrappers

1 egg, beaten

1. Soak the vermicelli in warm water to soften for 15 minutes. Drain and set aside.

2. Heat 2 tablespoons of peanut oil in wok over high heat. Add garlic, ginger, and scallions. Stir-fry 1 minute. Add the mushrooms. Stir-fry 1 minute. Add the cabbage and carrot. Cook, stirring, until the cabbage begins to wilt, about 2 minutes. Add the hoisin and oyster sauce. Stir to coat.

3. Remove the mixture from the heat. Mix in the vermicelli, cilantro, salt, and pepper.

4. Set a spring roll wrapper on a work surface with one corner facing you. Place 2 tablespoons of the filling near the bottom. Fold up the corner. Fold in the two side corners. Brush the top corner of the wrapper with beaten egg. Roll up the spring roll to meet the top corner. The spring roll should be packed fairly tightly.

5. Heat the remaining oil in the wok. Fry the egg rolls until they are golden brown on all sides. Drain on paper towels.

PER SERVING Calories: 285 | Fat: 12 grams | Protein: 5 grams | Sodium: 513 milligrams | Fiber: 2 grams | Carbohydrates: 38 grams | Sugar: 1 gram

Bao Dough

Char Siu (Chinese barbecued pork) and red bean paste are the traditional fillings for bao, but the possibilities are endless. Have fun experimenting.

INGREDIENTS | SERVES 10

2 teaspoons active dry yeast
¾ cup lukewarm water
2 tablespoons plus 1 teaspoon sugar
2 teaspoons baking powder
3 cups flour
2 tablespoons canola oil

1. Proof the yeast in water with 1 teaspoon sugar.

2. In a large bowl, combine the remaining sugar, baking powder, and flour. Make a well in the center, and pour in the yeast mixture. Stir with a wooden spoon to combine the wet and dry ingredients. Once the dough begins to form into a ball, add the oil. Using your fingers, gather up the dough and knead in the oil. Transfer the dough to a work surface and continue kneading about 5 minutes, until it is smooth and slightly elastic.

3. Place the dough in a lightly oiled bowl, turning to coat completely. Cover with plastic wrap or a clean towel and place in a warm, draft-free place to rise until doubled, about 45 minutes.

4. Punch down the dough. Knead again gently until it is in one smooth ball again. It is now ready for use.

PER SERVING Calories: 175 | Fat: 3 grams | Protein: 4 grams | Sodium: 99 milligrams | Fiber: 1 gram | Carbohydrates: 32 grams | Sugar: 3 grams

Char Siu Bao

The pork filling may be diced or shredded, according to personal preference.

INGREDIENTS | SERVES 10

Bao Dough (see recipe in this chapter)

1½ cups diced or shredded Char Siu (see recipe in Chapter 8)

10 (3") squares of parchment paper

1. Divide the dough into 10 equal pieces. Flatten a piece of dough between your hands to form a circle about 5"–6" in diameter. Place 2 tablespoons of Char Siu in the center of the circle. Bring up the edges of the dough and twist together to form a pouch around the filling. Place the bun on a square of parchment paper.

2. Once you have finished forming all the buns, cover them with a clean towel and place in a warm, draft-free place to rise for 30 minutes.

3. Heat several inches of water to simmer in a wok and set a rack on top. Place the buns inside a bamboo steamer or on a plate, about 1" apart, and steam with the lid on for 15 minutes. Do not lift the lid to check. Serve hot.

PER SERVING Calories: 230 | Fat: 5 grams | Protein: 9 grams | Sodium: 253 milligrams | Fiber: 1 gram | Carbohydrates: 35 grams | Sugar: 6 grams

Bao with Red-Cooked Tofu

This is a rich and savory vegetarian twist on a dim sum staple.

INGREDIENTS | SERVES 10

Bao Dough (see recipe in this chapter)

1½ cups Red-Cooked Tofu (see recipe in Chapter 11)

10 (3") squares of parchment paper

1. Divide the dough into 10 equal pieces. Flatten a piece of dough between your hands to form a circle about 5"–6" in diameter. Place 2 tablespoons of tofu filling in the center of the circle. Bring up the edges of the dough and twist together to form a pouch around the filling. Place the bun on a square of parchment paper.

2. Once you have finished forming all the buns, cover them with a clean towel and place in a warm, draft-free place to rise for 30 minutes.

3. Heat several inches of water to simmer in a wok and set a rack on top. Place the buns inside a bamboo steamer or on a plate, about 1" apart, and steam with the lid on for 15 minutes. Do not lift the lid to check. Serve hot.

PER SERVING Calories: 207 | Fat: 5 grams | Protein: 6 grams | Sodium: 231 milligrams | Fiber: 1 gram | Carbohydrates: 34 grams | Sugar: 4 grams

Bao with Bok Choy and Mustard Greens

The crunch and smoky flavor of the vegetables pairs nicely with the soft, slightly sweet buns.

INGREDIENTS | SERVES 10

Bao Dough (see recipe in this chapter)
1½ cups Stir-Fried Bok Choy and Mustard Greens (see recipe in Chapter 12)
10 (3") squares of parchment paper

1. Divide the dough into 10 equal pieces. Flatten a piece of dough between your hands to form a circle about 5"–6" in diameter. Place 2 tablespoons of vegetable filling in the center of the circle. Bring up the edges of the dough and twist together to form a pouch around the filling. Place the bun on a square of parchment paper.

2. Once you have finished forming all the buns, cover them with a clean towel and place in a warm, draft-free place to rise for 30 minutes.

3. Heat several inches of water to simmer in a wok and set a rack on top. Place the buns inside a bamboo steamer or on a plate, about 1" apart, and steam with the lid on for 15 minutes. Do not lift the lid to check. Serve hot.

PER SERVING Calories: 192 | Fat: 4 grams | Protein: 4 grams | Sodium: 261 milligrams | Fiber: 2 grams | Carbohydrates: 34 grams | Sugar: 3 grams

Tea Eggs

This snack puts a new spin on plain hard-boiled eggs.
Watch for the "fault" lines traveling down the cooked egg.

INGREDIENTS | SERVES 6

6 hard-boiled eggs, cooled
½ cup brewed black tea
1 dried tangerine peel
1 cinnamon stick
3½ cups water

Cracked Egg

Don't worry if you crack the egg—the effect of the marbled lines crisscrossing the cooked egg should still be visible.

1. Tap each egg very gently with the back of a spoon, until tiny lines form. Try not to actually crack the eggs.

2. In a large saucepan, add the eggs, black tea, tangerine peel, and cinnamon stick to the water and bring to a boil over high heat. Reduce the heat to low and simmer, covered, for 2 hours. Turn off the heat, and let the eggs sit in the liquid for a few more hours before serving.

3. To serve, remove the shell and cut into quarters.

PER SERVING Calories: 77 | Fat: 5 grams | Protein: 6 grams | Sodium: 62 milligrams | Fiber: 0 grams | Carbohydrates: 0 grams | Sugar: 0 grams

Wonton Wrappers

These wrappers are useful for many dim sum recipes.

INGREDIENTS | MAKES 24

½ teaspoon salt
2¼ cups flour
1 medium egg
1 teaspoon vegetable oil
⅔ cup water

1. Sift the salt into the flour. Add the remaining ingredients, adding the water slowly and not using more than necessary. Form the batter into a dough and knead until smooth. Cover the dough and let it rest for 30 minutes.

2. Cut the dough in half. Form each half into a cylinder. Lightly score the dough into ½" pieces and cut (you should have 12 pieces). Repeat with the other half.

3. On a lightly floured surface, roll each piece out into a 3½" square. Store wrapped in plastic in the refrigerator or freezer until ready to use.

PER SERVING (3 WRAPPERS) Calories: 140 | Fat: 1 gram | Protein: 4 grams | Sodium: 154 milligrams | Fiber: 1 gram | Carbohydrates: 26 grams | Sugar: 0 grams

Deep-Fried Wontons

Have more filled wontons than you need? Freeze and use the next time you're making Wonton Soup (see recipe in Chapter 4). Thaw before adding to the soup.

INGREDIENTS | MAKES 24

3 medium dried mushrooms

1½ cups ground pork

½ cup canned bamboo shoots, shredded

1½ green onions, thinly sliced

1 slice ginger

2 teaspoons black rice vinegar

2 teaspoons soy sauce

1 teaspoon sugar

1 teaspoon sesame oil

Wonton Wrappers (see recipe in this chapter) or store-bought wonton wrappers

4 cups vegetable oil

Maintaining Oil Temperature During Deep-Frying

To prevent greasy food, it's important to keep the oil temperature from dropping substantially during deep-frying. This can be tricky, since it is normal for the temperature to drop when food is first added to the wok. One solution is to heat the oil to a higher temperature than called for in the recipe. For example, if the instructions state the food should be deep-fried at 350°F, wait until the oil temperature reaches 355–360°F before starting to deep-fry.

1. Soak the dried mushrooms in hot water for at least 20 minutes to soften. Drain, remove the stems. In a medium bowl, combine the ground pork, bamboo shoots, green onions, mushrooms, ginger, vinegar, soy sauce, sugar, and sesame oil.

2. Add the vegetable oil to a preheated wok and heat to 375°F. While waiting for the oil to heat, wrap the wontons. Lay a wrapper in a square shape in front of you. Place 1 teaspoon of filling in the middle of the wrapper. Fold the wonton wrapper in half lengthwise, making sure the ends meet. Roll the wonton wrapper over again, being sure to keep the filling centered. Wet the ends. Bring the corners together so that one overlaps the other, and seal. Continue with the remainder of the wontons. Cover the completed wontons with a damp towel to prevent drying.

3. Carefully slide a few wontons at a time into the wok. Deep-fry until they turn golden (about 2 minutes). Remove with a slotted spoon and drain on paper towels.

PER SERVING (3 WONTONS) Calories: 345 | Fat: 19 grams | Protein: 13 grams | Sodium: 260 milligrams | Fiber: 1 gram | Carbohydrates: 28 grams | Sugar: 1 gram

Crab Rangoon

This Chinese restaurant creation, popularized in the 1950s, is still a standard on menus today.

INGREDIENTS | SERVES 24

48 wonton wrappers
1 cup fresh or canned crabmeat
1 cup cream cheese, softened
½ teaspoon Worcestershire sauce
½ teaspoon soy sauce
⅛ teaspoon freshly ground white pepper
2 teaspoons minced onion
1½ green onions, thinly sliced
1 large clove garlic, minced
4 cups vegetable oil

Make-Ahead Crab Rangoon

Want to get a head start on making cocktail appetizers? Crab Rangoon can be prepared ahead of time up to the deep-frying stage and frozen. Thaw the filled wontons before deep-frying.

1. Cover the wonton wrappers with a damp towel to prevent drying. Set aside.

2. If using canned crabmeat, drain thoroughly. Flake the crabmeat with a fork and place it in a medium bowl. Add the cream cheese, then mix in the Worcestershire sauce, soy sauce, white pepper, onion, green onion, and garlic.

3. Lay a wrapper in a diamond shape or circle, depending on the shape of wonton wrappers you are using. Add a heaping teaspoon of filling in the middle, spread out evenly but not too near the edges. Spread the water along all 4 sides. Fold the bottom over the top to form a triangle (round wrappers will form a half moon). Seal the edges, adding more water if needed. Cover the filled wontons with a damp towel to prevent drying.

4. Heat the oil in a preheated wok to 375°F. Slide in the wontons a few at a time, and deep-fry for 2–3 minutes, until they turn golden brown. Remove with a slotted spoon and drain on paper towels. Cool and serve.

PER SERVING Calories: 174 | Fat: 9 grams | Protein: 4 grams | Sodium: 161 milligrams | Fiber: 0 grams | Carbohydrates: 18 grams | Sugar: 0 grams

Lettuce Wraps

Serve Lettuce Wraps as an appetizer, or as a main course with stir-fried rice vermicelli.

INGREDIENTS | SERVES 6

1 pound boneless, skinless chicken breasts

1 head iceberg lettuce

1 tablespoon soy sauce

2 tablespoons oyster sauce

1 tablespoon Chinese rice wine

1 teaspoon sugar

4 tablespoons vegetable oil, divided

1 teaspoon minced garlic

1 teaspoon minced ginger

½ (8-ounce) can water chestnuts, rinsed, drained, and sliced in 1" pieces

1 stalk celery, thinly sliced on the diagonal

1 red bell pepper, seeded and chopped

½ (8-ounce) can bamboo shoots, rinsed, drained, and sliced in 1" pieces

1 tablespoon cornstarch mixed with 2 tablespoons water

2 green onions, thinly sliced on the diagonal

1 teaspoon sesame oil

1. Wash the chicken and pat dry. Pound lightly to tenderize. Cut the chicken into thin slices approximately 2½" long.

2. Wash the lettuce and dry and separate the leaves. Set aside.

3. In a small bowl, mix the soy sauce, oyster sauce, Chinese rice wine, and sugar. Set aside.

4. Add 2 tablespoons of oil to a preheated wok or heavy skillet. When the oil is hot, add the garlic and ginger. Stir-fry briefly, then add the chicken. Stir-fry until it is browned and nearly cooked through, about 3–4 minutes. Remove from the wok and drain on paper towels.

5. Add 2 tablespoons of oil. When the oil is hot, add the water chestnuts and celery. Stir-fry for about 1 minute, then add the red pepper and bamboo shoots. Stir-fry until the vegetables are brightly colored and tender, about 5 minutes.

6. Stir in the soy/oyster sauce mixture. Give the cornstarch/water mixture a quick stir and add in the middle, stirring quickly to thicken. Stir in the green onions. Drizzle with sesame oil.

7. To prepare lettuce wrap, lay a lettuce leaf flat. Place one-twelfth of the chicken combined with the vegetable/sauce mixture in the middle and roll up the lettuce leaf.

PER SERVING Calories: 221 | Fat: 11 grams | Protein: 20 grams | Sodium: 423 milligrams | Fiber: 2 grams | Carbohydrates: 11 grams | Sugar: 5 grams

Paper-Wrapped Chicken

This popular appetizer also makes a satisfying meal when served with green salad.
Cooking parchment or cellophane paper can be used instead of aluminum foil.

INGREDIENTS | SERVES 12

2 (8-ounce) boneless, skinless chicken breasts

4 large Chinese dried mushrooms

1½ green onions

2 tablespoons oyster sauce

2 tablespoons soy sauce

1 slice ginger, shredded

1 teaspoon sesame oil

1 tablespoon Chinese rice wine or dry sherry

2 teaspoons sugar

Salt and pepper, to taste

24 (6") squares of aluminum foil

1. Wash the chicken and pat dry. Cut the chicken into thin slices approximately 2½" long. You want to have 48 strips, or 2 strips for each packet. (With a larger breast you may have more chicken than you need, so you can make more packets.)

2. Soak the dried mushrooms in hot water for 20 minutes, or until they are softened. Squeeze the mushrooms gently to remove excess water, and cut into 24 thin slices, or 6 slices per mushroom.

3. Thinly slice the green onions on the diagonal so that you have 48 pieces, or 2 slices per packet.

4. In a large bowl, combine the oyster sauce, soy sauce, shredded ginger, sesame oil, Chinese rice wine, sugar, salt and pepper, and green onions. Add the chicken and marinate for 45 minutes. Add the mushrooms and marinate for another 15 minutes.

5. Preheat oven to 350°F.

6. To wrap the chicken, lay out a square of foil so that the lower corner is pointing toward you. Place 2 chicken slices, 1 mushroom slice, and 2 green onion slices in the middle. Bring the bottom corner up over the chicken. Roll this corner once. Fold the right corner over toward the middle, and then the left corner, so that one is overlapping the other. Tuck the triangle at the top into the flap.

7. Place the wrapped parcels on a baking sheet and bake for 15 minutes. Allow to cool before serving.

PER SERVING Calories: 55 | Fat: 1 gram | Protein: 9 grams | Sodium: 283 milligrams | Fiber: 0 grams | Carbohydrates: 3 grams | Sugar: 1 gram

Gift-Wrapped Beef

Serve the beef packets piled on a serving dish with a cilantro garnish.

INGREDIENTS | SERVES 12

½ pound flank steak

1 teaspoon oyster sauce

¼ teaspoon baking soda

6 large dried mushrooms

1 head bok choy

2 tablespoons hoisin sauce

2 tablespoons water

12 (6") squares of aluminum foil

½ teaspoon sugar

1 bunch cilantro

2 tablespoons sesame oil

1. Preheat oven to 350°F.

2. Cut the beef into thin slices 2"–3" long. You want to have about 3 slices for each packet. Place the beef in a medium bowl and add the oyster sauce and baking soda. Marinate the beef for 30 minutes.

3. Soak the dried mushrooms in hot water for 20 minutes, or until they are softened. Squeeze the mushrooms gently to remove any water, and cut them into 48 thin slices, or 8 slices per mushroom.

4. Wash the bok choy, drain thoroughly, and shred. You want to have 3–4 pieces for each packet.

5. In a small bowl, mix the hoisin sauce, water, and sugar together and set aside.

6. To wrap the beef, lay out a square of foil so that it forms a diamond shape. Add 3 of the beef slices, 2–3 slices of mushroom, a few shreds of bok choy, and a few sprigs of cilantro in the middle, being sure to keep the filling in the center and not near the edges. Top with ¼ teaspoon of sesame oil and ½ teaspoon of the hoisin and water mixture.

7. Bring the bottom corner up over the beef. Roll this corner once. Fold the right corner over toward the middle, and then the left corner, so that one is overlapping the other. Tuck the triangle at the top into the flap.

8. Place the wrapped parcels on a baking sheet and bake at 350°F for 15 minutes. Allow to cool before serving. Serve wrapped on a platter, unopened.

PER SERVING Calories: 57 | Fat: 2 grams | Protein: 5 grams | Sodium: 138 milligrams | Fiber: 1 gram | Carbohydrates: 4 grams | Sugar: 2 grams

Rumaki

Originally rumaki were made with chicken liver. Here, sea scallops are used.

INGREDIENTS | SERVES 10

20 slices water chestnut

5 large sea scallops, quartered

10 slices bacon, cut in half

20 toothpicks

4 cups vegetable oil

1. Place a water chestnut slice on top of a scallop quarter. Wrap a slice of bacon around the scallop and water chestnut. Spear with a toothpick. Repeat with remaining ingredients.

2. Once you have assembled all the rumaki, heat the oil in a wok to 375°F. Deep-fry the rumaki until the bacon is crisp, about 7–10 minutes. Drain on paper towels and serve.

PER SERVING Calories: 117 | Fat: 8 grams | Protein: 7 grams | Sodium: 229 milligrams | Fiber: 0 grams | Carbohydrates: 2 grams | Sugar: 0 grams

Pot Sticker Dumpling Dough

Handle the dough gently so that it does not become tough.

INGREDIENTS | MAKES 40 ROUNDS

2 cups all-purpose flour

¾ teaspoon salt

1 cup boiling water

1. Place the flour and salt in a bowl. Pour in the boiling water. Mix until the wet and dry ingredients combine into dough. Transfer the dough onto a lightly floured surface and knead with your hands until it is smooth. Cover it with plastic wrap and let it rest at room temperature 20–30 minutes.

2. Divide the dough into 3 or 4 sections. Using your hands, roll each section into a length ¾" in diameter. Cut them into 1"-long pieces. Form these into circles on a lightly floured surface. Roll them out to flatten into circles 4" in diameter. Lay the rounds out on a baking sheet dusted with flour until ready to use. If stacking the dough rounds, separate the layers with floured paper towels.

PER SERVING (3 ROUNDS) Calories: 68 | Fat: 0 grams | Protein: 2 grams | Sodium: 60 milligrams | Fiber: 0 grams | Carbohydrates: 14 grams | Sugar: 0 grams

Pork Pot Stickers with Rice Wine

For a different flavor, try steaming the pot sticker dumplings in chicken broth instead of water. Serve with Pot Sticker Dipping Sauce (see recipe in Chapter 2).

INGREDIENTS | SERVES 15

1½ cups ground pork

3 teaspoons Chinese rice wine or dry sherry

3 teaspoons soy sauce

1½ teaspoons sesame oil

1½ tablespoons chopped onion

Pot Sticker Dumpling Dough (see recipe in this chapter) or 1 package store-bought round wonton wrappers

¼ cup vegetable oil, divided

½ cup water

Pot Sticker Origins

Pot stickers are dumplings that are pan-fried on the bottom and steamed on top. According to legend, they were invented by an imperial court chef who panicked after realizing he'd accidentally burnt a batch of dumplings. With no time to make more, he served them anyway, and the rest is history. When cooking pot stickers, it's important to add enough steaming water. While a crispy brown bottom is desirable, pot stickers aren't supposed to stick too firmly to the bottom of the pot!

1. In a large bowl, combine the pork, rice wine, soy sauce, sesame oil, and onion.

2. Place 1 teaspoon of filling in the middle of a round of Pot Sticker Dumpling Dough or wonton wrapper. Wet the edges of the dough, fold over the filling, and seal, crimping the edges. Continue with the remainder of the dough or wonton wrappers. Cover the completed pot stickers with a damp towel to prevent drying.

3. Add 2 tablespoons of vegetable oil to a preheated wok or skillet. When the oil is hot, add a few of the pot stickers, smooth side down. Do not stir-fry, but let cook for about 1 minute.

4. Add ½ cup of water. Do not turn the pot stickers over. Cook, covered, until most of the liquid is absorbed. Uncover, and cook until the liquid has evaporated. Loosen the pot stickers with a spatula and transfer them to a serving platter. Repeat with the remaining pot stickers.

PER SERVING Calories: 130 | Fat: 8 grams | Protein: 6 grams | Sodium: 121 milligrams | Fiber: 0 grams | Carbohydrates: 5 grams | Sugar: 0 grams

Spicy Shrimp Pot Stickers

Out of round wonton wrappers? Cut square wonton wrappers into a circular shape.
Serve with Pot Sticker Dipping Sauce (see recipe in Chapter 2).

INGREDIENTS | SERVES 15

¼ pound (4 ounces) fresh shrimp

3 medium dried mushrooms

1 cup ground pork

½ cup canned bamboo shoots, shredded

1½ green onions, thinly sliced

2 teaspoons Worcestershire sauce

2 teaspoons soy sauce

1 teaspoon sugar

1 teaspoon sesame oil

Pot Sticker Dumpling Dough (see recipe in this chapter) or 1 package store-bought round wonton wrappers

¼ cup vegetable oil, divided

½ cup water

1. Wash and devein the shrimp, and chop finely. Soak the dried mushrooms in hot water for at least 20 minutes to soften. Drain, remove the stems, and slice finely.

2. In a large bowl, combine the ground pork, shrimp, bamboo shoots, green onions, mushrooms, Worcestershire sauce, soy sauce, sugar, and sesame oil.

3. Place 1 teaspoon of filling in the middle of a round of Pot Sticker Dumpling Dough or wonton wrapper. Wet the edges of the dough, fold over the filling, and seal, crimping the edges. Continue with the remainder of the dough or wonton wrappers. Cover the completed pot stickers with a damp towel to prevent drying.

4. Add 2 tablespoons of vegetable oil to a preheated wok or skillet. When the oil is hot, add a few of the pot stickers, smooth side down. Do not stir-fry, but let cook for about 1 minute.

5. Add ½ cup of water. Do not turn the pot stickers over. Cook, covered, until most of the liquid is absorbed. Uncover, and cook until the liquid has evaporated. Loosen the pot stickers with a spatula and transfer to a serving platter. Repeat with remaining pot stickers.

PER SERVING Calories: 115 | Fat: 7 grams | Protein: 6 grams | Sodium: 95 milligrams | Fiber: 0 grams | Carbohydrates: 6 grams | Sugar: 0 grams

Sticky Rice in Cabbage Leaves

Don't like cabbage? You can also wrap the sticky rice in aluminum foil or waxed paper before steaming.

INGREDIENTS | SERVES 4

1 cup short-grain (sticky) rice

2 cups water

4 large cabbage leaves

4 dried mushrooms

2 tablespoons oyster sauce

2 tablespoons Chinese rice wine or dry sherry

2 tablespoons chicken broth or stock

2 tablespoons oil for stir-frying

1 garlic clove, finely chopped

2 slices ginger, finely chopped

4 Chinese sausages, cut into bite-size pieces

2 green onions, finely chopped

1. Cover the sticky rice in warm water and let soak for at least 2 hours, preferably overnight. Drain well.

2. In a medium-size saucepan, bring the rice and 2 cups of water to a boil. Simmer, covered, for 20 minutes or until the rice is cooked. Remove from the heat and let cool for 15 minutes. Fluff up the rice before removing from the pot. Split the rice into 4 equal portions and set aside.

3. Blanch the cabbage leaves in boiling water. Drain thoroughly. Soak the dried mushrooms in hot water for 20 minutes to soften. Drain, giving a gentle squeeze to remove any excess water. Cut into thin slices.

4. In a small bowl, combine the oyster sauce, rice wine, and chicken broth.

5. Add the oil to a preheated wok or skillet. When the oil is hot, add the garlic and ginger. Stir-fry briefly until aromatic. Add the sausage. Stir-fry for about 2 minutes, then add the mushrooms. Stir in the green onions. Make a well in the middle of the wok and add the sauce, bringing to a boil. Mix everything together, then remove from the heat and allow to cool.

6. Split the filling into 4 equal portions. Take a cabbage leaf and add a quarter of the rice and the filling, layering it so that there is rice at the top and bottom, with the meat and vegetable filling in the middle. Roll up the cabbage leaf. Repeat with the remaining 3 cabbage leaves.

7. Steam the cabbage wraps, covered, on a heatproof plate in a bamboo steamer for 15 minutes, or until done.

PER SERVING Calories: 516 | Fat: 22 grams | Protein: 17 grams | Sodium: 1402 milligrams | Fiber: 2 grams | Carbohydrates: 60 grams | Sugar: 4 grams

Sticky Rice in Lotus Leaves

Steaming imparts the delicate flavor of lotus leaves to the sticky rice in this popular dim sum dish.

INGREDIENTS | SERVES 4

1 cup short-grain (sticky) rice

2 cups water

4 lotus leaves

4 dried mushrooms

2 tablespoons oyster sauce

2 tablespoons rice wine

2 tablespoons chicken broth or stock

2 tablespoons oil for stir-frying

1 garlic clove, finely chopped

2 slices ginger, finely chopped

½ cup thinly sliced chicken (dark or white meat)

2 Chinese sausages, cut into bite-size pieces

2 green onions, finely chopped

1. Cover the sticky rice in warm water and let soak for at least 2 hours, preferably overnight. Drain well.

2. In a medium-size saucepan, bring the rice and 2 cups of water to a boil. Simmer, covered, for 20 minutes or until rice is cooked. Let cool for 15 minutes. Fluff up the rice before removing from the pot. Split the rice into 4 equal portions.

3. Blanch the lotus leaves in boiling water and drain. Soak the dried mushrooms in hot water for at least 20 minutes to soften. Drain, giving them a gentle squeeze to remove any excess water. Cut into thin slices.

4. In a small bowl, combine the oyster sauce, rice wine, and chicken broth and set aside.

5. Add the oil to a preheated wok or skillet. When the oil is hot, add the garlic and ginger. Stir-fry briefly. Add the chicken, and then the sausage. Stir-fry for about 2 minutes, then add the mushrooms. Stir in the green onions. Make a well in the middle of the wok and add the sauce, bringing to a boil. Mix everything together, then remove from the heat and cool.

6. Take a lotus leaf and add a quarter of the rice and the filling, layering it so that there is rice at the top and bottom, with the meat and vegetable filling in the middle. Form a square parcel with the lotus leaf and tie it up with twine. Repeat with the remaining lotus leaves.

7. Steam the lotus leaf wraps, covered, on a heatproof plate in a bamboo steamer for 15 minutes, or until done.

PER SERVING Calories: 326 | Fat: 9 grams | Protein: 27 grams | Sodium: 562 milligrams | Fiber: 1 gram | Carbohydrates: 31 grams | Sugar: 2 grams

Traditional Gow Gees

Serve with soy sauce or your favorite Chinese dipping sauce.

INGREDIENTS | SERVES 15

¼ pound (4 ounces) shrimp

3 medium dried mushrooms

1 cup ground pork

1 napa cabbage leaf, shredded

1½ green onions, thinly sliced

¼ teaspoon minced ginger

2 teaspoons Chinese rice wine or dry sherry

2 teaspoons soy sauce

1 teaspoon sugar

1 teaspoon sesame oil

4 cups oil

1 package round wonton wrappers, or Pot Sticker Dumpling Dough (see recipe in this chapter)

Avoid Drying Out the Wrappers

It's important to cover filled wontons with a damp towel while preparing the rest, as they have a tendency to dry out quickly. For extra protection, also cover wrappers that haven't been used yet.

1. Wash, devein, and finely chop the shrimp. Soak the dried mushrooms in hot water for at least 20 minutes to soften. Drain, remove the stems, and slice finely.

2. In a large bowl, combine the ground pork, shrimp, cabbage, green onions, dried mushrooms, ginger, rice wine, soy sauce, sugar, and sesame oil.

3. Add the oil to a preheated wok and heat to 375°F. Wrap the gow gees while waiting for the oil to heat: Place 1 teaspoon of filling in the middle of a wrapper. Wet the edges of the wrapper with water, fold over the filling, and seal, crimping the edges. Continue with the remainder of the wontons. Cover the completed wontons with a damp towel to prevent drying.

4. Carefully slide the gow gees into the wok, a few at a time. Deep-fry until they turn golden (about 2 minutes). Remove them with a slotted spoon and drain on paper towels.

PER SERVING Calories: 116 | Fat: 8 grams | Protein: 4 grams | Sodium: 87 milligrams | Fiber: 0 grams | Carbohydrates: 5 grams | Sugar: 0 grams

Mini Spring Onion Pancakes

Serve the pancakes alone or with a soy-based sauce such as
Soy Vinegar Dressing (see recipe in Chapter 2).

INGREDIENTS | SERVES 6

1 cup flour
2½ teaspoons salt, divided
½ cup boiling water
2 teaspoons sesame oil
4 green onions, thinly sliced
4 tablespoons vegetable oil, divided

1. Place the flour in a medium bowl. Sift ½ teaspoon of salt into the flour. Stir in a small amount of the boiling water. Add more water and begin forming into a dough. Add the rest of the water and mix in. Cover the dough with a damp towel and let it rest for 30 minutes.

2. Knead the dough until it is smooth. Cut the dough in half.

3. Roll one half of the dough out until it is no more than ¼" thick. Spread 1 teaspoon of sesame oil over the dough. Sprinkle with half the green onion slices.

4. Roll the dough up like a jelly roll and cut into 6 pieces. Take a piece of cut dough, use your fingers to lengthen it a bit, and then form it into an L shape. Push down on the top of the L with the palm of your hand to form a circle. The pancake should be about 2"–3" in diameter. Continue with the remainder of the dough.

5. Add 2 tablespoons of vegetable oil to a preheated wok or skillet. Add half the pancakes and fry until brown on both sides, about 5 minutes each side, watching carefully so that the pancakes do not burn. Sprinkle with the remainder of the salt while cooking. Remove from the pan and repeat with the remaining pancakes.

PER SERVING Calories: 172 | Fat: 11 grams | Protein: 2 grams | Sodium: 965 milligrams | Fiber: 1 gram | Carbohydrates: 16 grams | Sugar: 0 grams

Gow Gees with Ground Turkey

These dumplings taste delicious served with Hot Mustard Dip (see recipe in Chapter 2), Soy Ginger Dressing (see recipe in Chapter 2), or chili paste.

INGREDIENTS | SERVES 15

1½ cups ground turkey

1½ tablespoons oyster sauce

¾ teaspoon sugar

2 teaspoons soy sauce

1 teaspoon sesame oil

1½ green onions, minced

1 tablespoon minced ginger

4 cups vegetable oil for deep-frying

1 package round wonton wrappers or Pot Sticker Dumpling Dough (see recipe in this chapter)

1. In a large bowl, combine the ground turkey, oyster sauce, sugar, soy sauce, sesame oil, green onions, and ginger.

2. Add the oil to a preheated wok and heat to 375°F. Wrap the gow gees while waiting for the oil to heat: Place 1 teaspoon of filling in the middle of the wrapper. Wet the edges of the wrapper, fold over the filling, and seal, crimping the edges. Continue with the remainder of the wontons. Cover the completed wontons with a damp towel to prevent drying.

3. Carefully slide the gow gees into the wok, a few at a time. Deep-fry until they turn golden (about 2 minutes). Remove them with a slotted spoon and drain on paper towels.

PER SERVING Calories: 122 | Fat: 8 grams | Protein: 7 grams | Sodium: 138 milligrams | Fiber: 0 grams | Carbohydrates: 5 grams | Sugar: 0 grams

Shumai

Adding oil before steaming helps prevent the Shumai from sticking to the heatproof plate.

INGREDIENTS | SERVES 8

¼ pound fresh shrimp

3 medium dried or fresh shiitake mushrooms

1 cup ground pork

1½ green onions, thinly sliced

2 teaspoons soy sauce

1 teaspoon sesame oil

Wonton Wrappers (see recipe in this chapter) or store-bought wonton wrappers

1 tablespoon vegetable oil

Fresh versus Dried Mushrooms

Many grocery stores now have fresh shiitake mushrooms, while large bags of dried shiitake mushrooms can be found at Asian markets. What's the difference? Dried shiitake mushrooms will tend to have a stronger, smokier flavor when hydrated. Fresh shiitake are much more delicate. Try each and see which you prefer.

1. Wash and devein the shrimp, and chop finely. If using dried mushrooms, soak them in hot water for at least 20 minutes to soften, then drain. Remove the mushroom stems and slice finely.

2. In a large bowl, combine the ground pork, shrimp, green onions, dried mushrooms, soy sauce, and sesame oil.

3. Place 2 teaspoons of filling in the middle of a wonton wrapper. Do not fold the wrapper over the filling. Gather up the edges of the wrapper and gently pleat the sides so that it forms a basket shape, with the top open.

4. Lightly coat a heatproof plate with vegetable oil. Place the dumplings on the plate. Place the plate on a bamboo steamer in a wok set up for steaming. Steam the dumplings for 5–10 minutes or until they are cooked.

PER SERVING Calories: 265 | Fat: 10 grams | Protein: 14 grams | Sodium: 280 milligrams | Fiber: 1 gram | Carbohydrates: 28 grams | Sugar: 0 grams

Vegan Shumai

Serve with Pot Sticker Dipping Sauce or Hot Chili Oil (recipes in Chapter 2) if you want more of a kick.

INGREDIENTS | SERVES 12

6 ounces firm tofu

2 scallions, minced

¾ cup finely chopped napa cabbage

2 teaspoons grated fresh ginger

3 tablespoons soy sauce

2½ teaspoons sesame oil

1 tablespoon Xiaoshing wine

1 tablespoon cornstarch

24 wonton wrappers

1 tablespoon vegetable oil

1. Crumble the tofu into a large bowl. Add the scallions, cabbage, ginger, soy sauce, sesame oil, wine, and cornstarch, and stir to mix well. Be sure to incorporate the cornstarch thoroughly and evenly, because it is the binder.

2. Brush the edges of a wonton wrapper with water. Place about 1 teaspoon of the filling in the center. Pleat the edges of the wonton skin to create a basket holding the filling, leaving the top exposed.

3. Lightly oil a heatproof plate. Place the shumai on the plate in a single layer. Do not crowd them or they will stick together. Set them in a bamboo steamer if you have one. If not, you can set the plate directly on a steaming rack inside a wok or rice cooker. Steam the shumai, covered, until the filling is set and the wrappers are tender, about 5–10 minutes.

PER SERVING (2 SHUMAI) Calories: 130 | Fat: 3 grams | Protein: 4 grams | Sodium: 198 milligrams | Fiber: 1 gram | Carbohydrates: 19 grams | Sugar: 0 grams

Translucent Dumpling Dough

This dough is used for Har Gow Dumplings (see recipe in this chapter).

INGREDIENTS | SERVES 12

1 cup wheat starch
¼ teaspoon salt
1 cup boiling water
1 tablespoon vegetable shortening

1. Place the wheat starch in a medium-size bowl. Sift in the salt.

2. Slowly pour in the boiling water. Pour in only as much as you need. Stir with a wooden spoon or chopsticks until you have a sticky dough. Let the dough rest and cool for 30 minutes.

3. Add the shortening to the dough, a portion at a time, gradually working it in. Knead the dough until it is smooth and satiny. Make sure the shortening is fully mixed.

PER SERVING Calories: 41 | Fat: 0 grams | Protein: 0 grams | Sodium: 0 milligrams | Fiber: 0 grams | Carbohydrates: 8 grams | Sugar: 0 grams

Pork Riblets in Black Bean Sauce

This dish can also be served with rice and vegetables as a main course.

INGREDIENTS | SERVES 4

1½ pounds pork spare rib, tip ends only, if possible
2 tablespoons fermented black beans, rinsed and mashed with the side of a knife
2 teaspoons cornstarch
½ teaspoon grated fresh ginger
2 cloves garlic, minced
¼ teaspoon ground white pepper
1 teaspoon peanut oil
1 teaspoon sesame oil
1 green chili, chopped finely (optional)

1. Chop the spareribs into 1" segments. In a medium bowl, combine the rest of the ingredients and coat the ribs thoroughly. Marinate at room temperature 30 minutes. Place ribs and sauce into a heatproof dish.

2. Bring several inches of water to boil in a pot or wok with a snug-fitting cover. Set a steaming rack inside, and the dish with the pork mixture on top. Cover. Steam on medium heat for 20 minutes. The pork should be tender and no longer pink.

PER SERVING Calories: 520 | Fat: 42 grams | Protein: 28 grams | Sodium: 573 milligrams | Fiber: 1 gram | Carbohydrates: 4 grams | Sugar: 0 grams

Har Gow Dumplings

These taste delicious with Hot Chili Oil (see recipe in Chapter 2). For variety, replace half the bamboo shoots with 2 tablespoons minced water chestnuts.

INGREDIENTS | SERVES 12

6 ounces raw shrimp

4 tablespoons shredded canned bamboo shoots

1 teaspoon oyster sauce

1 teaspoon sugar

¾ teaspoon Chinese rice wine or dry sherry

¼ teaspoon sesame oil

Translucent Dumpling Dough (see recipe in this chapter)

1. Peel and devein the shrimp. Mince finely. In a medium bowl, combine the shrimp and bamboo shoots with the oyster sauce, sugar, rice wine, and sesame oil. Chill the mixture in the refrigerator.

2. Work the dough if necessary. Cut into quarters. Roll each quarter into a cylinder. Cut into 6 equal pieces (each piece should be approximately 1" thick and 1" wide). You should now have 24 pieces.

3. On wax paper, roll each piece of dough into a circle 2½"–3" in size. Cover with a towel while rolling out the remainder to prevent drying.

4. Prepare the wok for steaming. Place up to 1 teaspoon of the filling in each dumpling. Carefully fold the dough over the filling and pleat the edges.

5. Place the dumplings 1" apart for steaming. Steam, covered, on medium heat for 15–20 minutes, or until the dumplings are done.

PER SERVING (2 DUMPLINGS) Calories: 60 | Fat: 1 gram | Protein: 3 grams | Sodium: 89 milligrams | Fiber: 0 grams | Carbohydrates: 8 grams | Sugar: 0 grams

Shrimp and Chive Dumplings

These dumplings are a simple and flavorful treat for anytime.

INGREDIENTS | SERVES 6

½ cup soy sauce

1 tablespoon rice wine

1 tablespoon sesame oil

1 tablespoon minced fresh ginger

½ pound shrimp, peeled and deveined

½ cup finely chopped chives

12 Wonton Wrappers (see recipe in this chapter) or store-bought wonton wrappers

1½ tablespoons vegetable oil

1. In a medium bowl, combine the soy sauce, rice wine, sesame oil, and ginger.

2. Roughly chop the shrimp and mix with the chives in a separate bowl.

3. Put half the shrimp/chive mixture in a blender or food processor. Add about 1 tablespoon of the soy sauce mixture and pulse to make a smooth paste. Transfer to a bowl along with the remaining shrimp, chives, and soy sauce mixture. Mix well.

4. Place 1 heaping teaspoon of the filling in the center of a wonton wrapper. Brush the edges with water and fold over to make a half circle, pleating the top edges.

5. Heat the oil in a large frying pan and place the dumplings inside, pleated side up. Carefully add enough cold water to reach halfway up the sides of the dumplings, standing back in case of splatter. Cook, covered, about 10 minutes. The tops of the dumplings will be steamed through and the bottoms brown and crispy.

PER SERVING Calories: 182 | Fat: 6 grams | Protein: 12 grams | Sodium: 1,553 milligrams | Fiber: 0 grams | Carbohydrates: 17 grams | Sugar: 1 gram

Cheong Fun (Long Rolled Rice Noodles)

This recipe calls for shrimp, but any filling may be used—beef, pork, even just a sprinkling of chopped scallions.

INGREDIENTS | SERVES 10

⅔ cup rice flour

3 tablespoons wheat starch

2 tablespoons tapioca starch

½ teaspoon salt

1 cup cold water

1½ cups boiling water

1 tablespoon vegetable oil

30 medium shrimp, shelled and deveined

Sweet Soy Sauce (see recipe in Chapter 2)

1. In a large bowl, whisk together the rice flour, wheat starch, tapioca starch, and salt. Pour in cold water, whisking the entire time. Stir in the boiling water. Add the oil and mix well. You should have a smooth, thin batter. Let it rest for 20 minutes at room temperature.

2. Bring several inches of water to a boil in a wok. Set a rack inside for steaming. Lightly oil a cake pan and spread a thin layer of the batter on the bottom. Set the pan on the rack and steam the batter with the wok cover on for about 2–3 minutes. Remove the cover. Sprinkle a few shrimp into the pan and steam another 2–3 minutes with the cover on.

3. Let the pan cool, then run a spatula along the edge, and carefully peel the noodle from the pan, rolling it over itself as you go. Repeat the process until you have as many long rolled noodles as you wish. You may want to have a number of cake pans on hand, so that you can steam additional noodles while the cooked ones are cooling.

4. Serve with Sweet Soy Sauce.

PER SERVING Calories: 108 | Fat: 2 grams | Protein: 6 grams | Sodium: 1,147 milligrams | Fiber: 0 grams | Carbohydrates: 16 grams | Sugar: 4 grams

Vegan Turnip Cake

Serve with Sweet Soy Sauce or Hot Chili Oil (see recipes in Chapter 2). Dried shrimp also makes a nice addition to the cake "batter" for those who eat meat.

INGREDIENTS | SERVES 8

1 tablespoon peanut oil
2 cups chopped daikon radish
½ cup chopped shiitake mushrooms
1 scallion, cut into ¼" lengths
1 cup water
2 cups rice flour
1 tablespoon salt
1 tablespoon white pepper
1 teaspoon sesame oil

1. Heat the peanut oil in a sauté pan or wok over medium heat. Sauté the radish, mushrooms, and scallions. When the radish starts to become translucent, about an hour, turn off the heat. Let the mixture cool.

2. In a large bowl, combine the remaining ingredients and add the radish mixture. Stir well. Pour into a loaf pan.

3. Bring several inches of water to a boil in a wok. Set a rack inside and place the loaf pan on top. Cover and steam for 30 minutes, checking occasionally to be sure there is enough water. Add more if necessary. The cake is done when a toothpick inserted in the middle comes out clean.

4. Let the turnip cake cool for 1–2 hours. Slice to serve. You may also sear the slices in a sauté pan with a little peanut oil to get a crunchy crust.

5. The loaf will keep in the refrigerator, covered with plastic wrap, for several days.

PER SERVING Calories: 174 | Fat: 3 grams | Protein: 2 grams | Sodium: 302 milligrams | Fiber: 1 gram | Carbohydrates: 34 grams | Sugar: 1 gram

CHAPTER 4

Soups and Salads

Watermelon and Watercress
Salad
90

Hot Spiced Cucumbers
91

Creamy Cucumber Salad
91

Bean Sprout and Carrot Salad
92

Cold Asparagus Salad
with Garlic
92

Hot Chicken Salad
93

Chicken Stock

This is a very "pure" stock, capturing the essence of the chicken only. It can be used in any sauce or soup, and other flavors can be added according to the recipe.

INGREDIENTS | MAKES 4 CUPS

1 chicken carcass

1 (3-pound) boiling chicken or chicken parts

6 cups water

1 knob ginger, cut into 1" lengths

Chinese Soup Stock

Unlike Western soup stocks, the Chinese version has very few seasonings, in order not to overpower recipe flavors. You will also notice that Chinese stock recipes call for parboiling the meat. This step helps reduce fats and the scum that rises when cooking.

1. In a large soup pot or Dutch oven, cover the chicken bones and parts with cold water and slowly bring to a boil over medium-high heat. Turn off the heat, remove the chicken, and rinse under cold water. Discard the water you have used for parboiling, and clean the pot.

2. Return the chicken and bones to the cleaned pot with the water. Add ginger, cover, and simmer over medium-low heat for 4 hours. Add more water if necessary. Strain.

PER SERVING (1 CUP) Calories: 5 | Fat: 0 grams | Protein: 0 grams | Sodium: 54 milligrams | Fiber: 0 grams | Carbohydrates: 0 grams | Sugar: 0 grams

Pork Stock

Only need a little stock at a time? Try freezing it in ice-cube trays and using individual cubes when you need them.

INGREDIENTS | MAKES 4 CUPS

2 pounds meaty pork bones

1 onion, cut into quarters

½ carrot

1 knob ginger, cut into 1" lengths

6 cups water

½ cup red or white wine

1. In a large soup pot or Dutch oven, cover the pork bones with cold water and slowly bring to a boil over medium-high heat. Turn off the heat, remove the pork bones, and rinse under cold water. Discard the water you have used for parboiling, and clean the pot.

2. Return the bones to the cleaned pot and add the remaining ingredients. Add the water, cover, and simmer over medium-low heat for 4 hours. Add more water if necessary, to yield 4 cups stock when done. Cool and strain. The stock can be used immediately, refrigerated, or frozen.

PER SERVING (1 CUP) Calories: 30 | Fat: 0 grams | Protein: 0 grams | Sodium: 70 milligrams | Fiber: 0 grams | Carbohydrates: 0 grams | Sugar: 0 grams

Beef Stock

Use as the base for stir-fry sauces or in Chinese Spice Beef Vegetable Soup (see recipe in this chapter).

INGREDIENTS | MAKES 4 CUPS

2 pounds meaty beef bones

1 onion, cut into quarters

1 knob ginger, cut into 1" lengths

½ cup red wine

6 cups water

1. In a large soup pot or Dutch oven, cover the beef bones with cold water and slowly bring to a boil over medium-high heat. Turn off the heat, remove the bones, and rinse under cold water. Discard the water you have used for parboiling, and clean the pot.

2. Return the bones to the cleaned pot and add the remaining ingredients. Cover, and simmer over medium-low heat for 4 hours, adding water as necessary to yield 4 cups of stock. Cool and strain. The stock may be used immediately, stored in the refrigerator, or frozen.

PER SERVING (1 CUP) Calories: 30 | Fat: 0 grams | Protein: 0 grams | Sodium: 70 milligrams | Fiber: 0 grams | Carbohydrates: 0 grams | Sugar: 0 grams

Vegetable Stock

Vegetable ends from cooking can be saved and frozen for making stock. The tops of onions and carrots, woody mushroom stems, and potato peelings are all good choices.

INGREDIENTS | MAKES 4 CUPS

3 carrots, cut into chunks

3 celery stalks, cut in 3" lengths

1 large onion, quartered

3" piece of ginger, cut into thick slices

6 cups water

1. Place all the ingredients in a large soup pot or Dutch oven and place over medium heat. Bring to a boil, reduce the heat, and simmer for 45 minutes, skimming the surface of any scum.

2. Let the stock cool slightly before straining. The liquid should have reduced to about 4 cups. Don't cook too long or the stock will start to lose flavor.

PER SERVING (1 CUP) Calories: 22 | Fat: 0 grams | Protein: 0 grams | Sodium: 28 milligrams | Fiber: 0 grams | Carbohydrates: 2 grams | Sugar: 0 grams

Wonton Soup

You can use homemade or store-bought wontons for this recipe. Making the soup is a snap, so give the wontons a whirl! (See Chapter 3 for how to make your own Wonton Wrappers.)

INGREDIENTS | SERVES 4

24 filled wonton dumplings
6 cups chicken broth or stock
½ cup shredded napa cabbage
1 teaspoon salt
½ teaspoon pepper
1 green onion, thinly sliced

1. Bring a large pot of water to a boil over high heat. Add the wonton dumplings, making sure there is enough room for them to move about freely. Boil for at least 5 minutes, until the wontons rise to the top and the filling is cooked through. Remove from the pot with a slotted spoon.

2. Bring the stock to a boil in a large saucepan over high heat. Add the cabbage and cook until tender, about 30 minutes. Add the cooked wontons, salt, and pepper, and bring the soup back to a boil. Remove the pot from the heat and add the green onion. When serving, allow 6 wontons per person.

PER SERVING (6 WONTONS) Calories: 709 | Fat: 39 grams | Protein: 28 grams | Sodium: 1,207 milligrams | Fiber: 2 grams | Carbohydrates: 58 grams | Sugar: 2 grams

Watercress Soup

This soup can be prepared with chicken stock or vegetarian style.

INGREDIENTS | SERVES 4

1 bunch watercress
4 cups chicken or vegetable stock
1 pinch salt
¼ teaspoon sugar
⅜ teaspoon white pepper

1. Wash the watercress and drain thoroughly. In a large saucepan, add the stock and bring to a boil over high heat.

2. Add the salt, sugar, and white pepper. Add the watercress, and cook for another 2–3 minutes. Serve hot.

PER SERVING Calories: 54 | Fat: 0 grams | Protein: 2 grams | Sodium: 137 milligrams | Fiber: 3 grams | Carbohydrates: 10 grams | Sugar: 5 grams

Egg Drop Soup

For contrast, serve Egg Drop Soup with a more strongly spiced main dish and a colorful stir-fried vegetable.

INGREDIENTS | SERVES 4

4 cups chicken or vegetable stock
⅛ teaspoon white pepper
¼ teaspoon salt
¼ teaspoon sugar
1 teaspoon Chinese rice wine or dry sherry
2 eggs, lightly beaten
2 green onions, minced
¼ teaspoon sesame oil

1. Bring the stock to a boil in a large saucepan over high heat.

2. When the broth is boiling, add the white pepper, salt, sugar, and rice wine. Cook for another minute.

3. Turn off the heat and pour the eggs into the soup in a steady stream, stirring rapidly in a clockwise direction until they form thin strands.

4. Add the green onions and sesame oil. Serve hot.

PER SERVING Calories: 76 | Fat: 4 grams | Protein: 7 grams | Sodium: 255 milligrams | Fiber: 0 grams | Carbohydrates: 4 grams | Sugar: 1 gram

Pork and Watercress Soup

The Chinese believe that soups have healing properties.
Watercress is said to be cooling, so this soup is good for fevers.

INGREDIENTS | SERVES 4

1 pound pork ribs
4 cups pork broth
2 cups water
1 bunch watercress (about 10 ounces)
1 teaspoon salt
½ teaspoon ground white pepper

1. Place the ribs in a large soup pot with cold water to cover and bring to a boil over high heat. Drain.

2. Rinse the ribs under cold water and return them to the pot with the pork broth and 2 cups of water. Bring to a boil over high heat, then reduce the heat to medium-low and simmer for about 1 hour, or until the rib meat has become tender and is ready to slide off the bones.

3. Meanwhile, wash and trim the watercress ends. Add the watercress to the soup and cook for another 15–30 minutes, depending on how soft you prefer it. Remove the ribs from the soup. Debone the meat, cut into bite-size pieces, and return to the soup. Season with salt and pepper before serving.

PER SERVING Calories: 371 | Fat: 26 grams | Protein: 20 grams | Sodium: 755 milligrams | Fiber: 3 grams | Carbohydrates: 12 grams | Sugar: 4 grams

Hot-and-Sour Soup

*This popular soup is reputed to be good for colds. Serve with Kung Pao Chicken
(see recipe in Chapter 9) or Restaurant-Style Mu Shu Pork (see recipe in Chapter 6).
Replace the chicken stock with vegetable stock and omit the pork to make a vegetarian version.*

INGREDIENTS | SERVES 6

6 dried mushrooms

¼ cup dried lily buds

6 cups chicken stock, or 5 cups stock and 1 cup mushroom soaking liquid

1 (12.3-ounce) block firm tofu, cut into cubes

¼ cup ground pork

1 teaspoon salt

2 tablespoons soy sauce

2 tablespoons rice vinegar

½ teaspoon white pepper, or to taste

1 tablespoon cornstarch

¼ cup water

1 egg white, lightly beaten

1 green onion, minced

¼ teaspoon sesame oil

Freezing Instructions

This dish can be prepared ahead of time and frozen. Prepare the soup, leaving out the tofu and egg. When ready to serve, thaw the soup, add the tofu, and bring to a boil. When the soup is boiling, add the beaten egg white.

1. Soak the dried mushrooms in hot water for 20 minutes to soften. Gently squeeze the mushrooms to remove excess water and cut into thin slices. Reserve the soaking liquid if desired and add to the stock. Soak the dried lily buds in hot water for 20 minutes. Drain.

2. In a large saucepan, bring the stock or stock/mushroom liquid mixture to a boil over high heat. When it is boiling, add the mushrooms, lily buds, tofu, and the ground pork.

3. Bring back to a boil and add the salt, soy sauce, rice vinegar, and white pepper.

4. In a small bowl, mix the cornstarch and water, and then slowly pour it into the soup, stirring constantly. When the soup thickens, turn off the heat.

5. Pour in the egg white and stir quickly to form thin shreds. Stir in the green onion. Drizzle with sesame oil before serving.

PER SERVING Calories: 146 | Fat: 5 grams | Protein: 10 grams | Sodium: 795 milligrams | Fiber: 3 grams | Carbohydrates: 15 grams | Sugar: 5 grams

Quick and Easy Hot-and-Sour Soup

This modified version of the famous Szechwan soup contains ingredients that are available at most local supermarkets. You can replace the meat with firm tofu if you like.

INGREDIENTS | SERVES 6

1 cup chicken or vegetable broth

6¼ cups water, divided

1 teaspoon salt

1 teaspoon sugar

2 tablespoons soy sauce

½ cup rinsed and drained canned bamboo shoots

2 shiitake mushrooms, sliced

½ cup cooked diced pork or chicken

3 tablespoons rice vinegar

¼ teaspoon white pepper

1 tablespoon cornstarch

1 egg, lightly beaten

1 green onion, minced

¼ teaspoon sesame oil

1. In a large saucepan, bring the chicken broth and 6 cups of water to a boil. When it is boiling, add the salt, sugar, soy sauce, bamboo shoots, mushrooms, and pork or chicken.

2. Bring back to a boil and add the rice vinegar and white pepper. Test the broth and adjust the taste if required.

3. In a small bowl, mix the cornstarch and ¼ cup of water and then slowly pour it into the soup, stirring. When the soup thickens, turn off the heat.

4. Pour in the beaten egg and stir quickly to form thin shreds. Stir in the green onion. Drizzle with the sesame oil. Serve hot.

PER SERVING Calories: 50 | Fat: 1 gram | Protein: 5 grams | Sodium: 757 milligrams | Fiber: 0 grams | Carbohydrates: 4 grams | Sugar: 1 gram

Walnut Soup

This soup is a nourishing hot broth, but it can also be chilled and served as a unique dessert soup.

INGREDIENTS | SERVES 4

6 whole walnuts

4 cups water

2 slices ginger

2 tablespoons plus 1 teaspoon sugar

1. In a medium saucepan over high heat, bring the walnuts and 4 cups of water to a boil. Reduce the heat to medium-low and simmer for 30 minutes.

2. Add the ginger slices. Simmer for at least another 30 minutes. Stir in the sugar. Remove the walnuts. Leave in the ginger or remove as desired. Serve hot or cold.

PER SERVING Calories: 78 | Fat: 5 grams | Protein: 1 gram | Sodium: 0 milligrams | Fiber: 0 grams | Carbohydrates: 8 grams | Sugar: 7 grams

Cucumber and Carrot Soup

This modified version of Winter Melon Soup (see recipe in this chapter) uses easy-to-find ingredients. Serve hot, or leave out the ham and chill.

INGREDIENTS | SERVES 4

1 cucumber

4 shiitake mushrooms, cut into thin slices

1 carrot, diced

½ cup cooked ham, diced

1 teaspoon Chinese rice wine or dry sherry

⅛ teaspoon salt

4 cups chicken broth

1 green onion, minced

¼ teaspoon sesame oil

1. Peel the cucumber, remove the seeds, and dice.

2. In a large saucepan, heat the cucumber, mushrooms, carrot, ham, rice wine, salt, and chicken broth over high heat. Bring the soup to a boil, then reduce the heat to low and simmer for about 20 minutes.

3. Turn off the heat and add the green onion. Drizzle with the sesame oil.

PER SERVING Calories: 116 | Fat: 4 grams | Protein: 10 grams | Sodium: 538 milligrams | Fiber: 1 gram | Carbohydrates: 9 grams | Sugar: 2 grams

Tomato Egg-Flower Soup

The Chinese traditionally eat little meat, except on special occasions or to honor a guest. This soup becomes a luxurious treat by adding thinly sliced flank steak at the end of the cooking process.

INGREDIENTS | SERVES 4

4 cups beef or vegetable stock

2 medium tomatoes

⅛ teaspoon white pepper

¼ teaspoon salt

½ teaspoon sugar

1 teaspoon Chinese rice wine or dry sherry

½ pound thinly sliced cooked flank steak

1 tablespoon cornstarch

4 tablespoons water

1 egg white, lightly beaten

2 green onions, minced

¼ teaspoon sesame oil

1. Bring the stock to a boil in a large saucepan over high heat.

2. In a medium saucepan, bring a large pot of water to a boil over high heat. Blanch the tomatoes briefly in the boiling water. (This will make it easier to remove the peel.) Peel the tomatoes and cut each into 6 equal pieces.

3. When the stock comes to a boil, add the white pepper, salt, sugar, rice wine, and tomatoes. Bring the broth back to boiling. Stir in the flank steak.

4. In a small bowl, mix the cornstarch and water, and then pour it into the soup, stirring to thicken. Turn off the heat.

5. Pour the egg white into the soup and quickly stir in a clockwise direction to form thin shreds.

6. Add the green onions and sesame oil. Serve hot.

PER SERVING Calories: 283 | Fat: 8 grams | Protein: 19 grams | Sodium: 350 milligrams | Fiber: 6 grams | Carbohydrates: 24 grams | Sugar: 6 grams

Winter Melon Soup

*For a more impressive presentation, purchase a whole winter melon
and steam the soup inside the melon.*

INGREDIENTS | SERVES 4

2 Chinese dried mushrooms

1 pound winter melon

3½ cups water

2½ cups chicken or vegetable stock

2 slices ginger

1 teaspoon Chinese rice wine or dry sherry

⅛ teaspoon salt

Drink Your Soup!

The Chinese believe that cold drinks and hot food don't mix, so soup normally takes the place of a beverage at meals. It's customary in Chinese-American restaurants for the waiter to bring a steaming pot of tea as soon as you're seated, but traditionally tea was looked upon as a digestive aid, to be consumed at the conclusion of a meal.

1. Cut the stems off the dried mushrooms and soak the mushrooms in hot water for 20 minutes. Gently squeeze the mushrooms to remove excess water and cut into thin slices.

2. Wash the winter melon and remove the green rind, seeds, and pulp. Cut into slices approximately 2" long and ½" thick.

3. In a large saucepan, add the winter melon to 3½ cups of water and bring to a boil over high heat. Reduce the heat to medium-low and simmer for 20 minutes or until the melon is tender.

4. Add the stock, dried mushrooms, and ginger.

5. Add the rice wine and salt. Simmer for another 15 minutes. Leave the ginger slices in or remove as desired. Serve hot.

PER SERVING Calories: 55 | Fat: 0 grams | Protein: 1 gram | Sodium: 257 milligrams | Fiber: 5 grams | Carbohydrates: 12 grams | Sugar: 3 grams

Emerald Soup

Made with spinach, ginger, and chicken broth, this soup is great for fighting colds. Blanching the spinach before stir-frying preserves its brilliant green color.

INGREDIENTS | SERVES 4

15 leaves of spinach

½ pound boneless, skinless chicken breast

1 slice ginger

1 tablespoon vegetable oil

¼ teaspoon salt

¼ teaspoon sugar

4½ cups chicken stock or broth

1 teaspoon soy sauce

1 teaspoon Chinese rice wine or dry sherry

1. Wash the spinach leaves and cut off the ends. Blanch the leaves briefly in boiling water, just until the leaves begin to wilt. Remove and sprinkle with cold water.

2. Cut the chicken into thin slices. Blanch briefly in boiling water with the ginger until it turns white. Remove from the water and set aside.

3. Heat a wok or frying pan over medium-high heat and add oil. When the oil is hot, stir-fry the spinach very briefly (under 1 minute), adding the salt and sugar.

4. Add the chicken broth to the spinach. Add the soy sauce and rice wine and bring to a boil.

5. Add the chicken and bring back to a boil. Serve hot.

PER SERVING Calories: 132 | Fat: 1 gram | Protein: 16 grams | Sodium: 367 milligrams | Fiber: 4 grams | Carbohydrates: 15 grams | Sugar: 6 grams

Sizzling Rice Soup

Success lies in keeping the soup hot while deep-frying the rice,
so that the rice crackles and pops when it meets the heated broth.

INGREDIENTS | SERVES 4

6 large dried black mushrooms

⅓ pound cooked shrimp

½ pound boneless, skinless chicken breast

6 cups chicken stock

½ (8-ounce) can water chestnuts, drained and sliced

½ cup frozen peas

1 teaspoon salt

1 tablespoon Chinese rice wine or dry sherry

¼ teaspoon white pepper

1 teaspoon sesame oil

4–6 cups oil for deep-frying

10 squares Rice Crisps (see recipe in Chapter 5)

1. Soak the mushrooms in hot water for 20 minutes to soften. Gently squeeze the mushrooms to remove any excess liquid and cut them into thin slices. Rinse the shrimp in warm water and pat dry.

2. Bring a large pan of water to a boil and poach the chicken very briefly (about 2–4 minutes) in the boiling water. Drain. Cut the chicken into thin slices.

3. In a large saucepan over high heat, bring the stock to a boil. Add the chicken, water chestnuts, mushrooms, shrimp, and peas. Bring the soup back to a boil.

4. Add the salt, rice wine, and white pepper to the soup. Drizzle with sesame oil. Pour the soup into a large tureen or serving bowl. Keep warm.

5. Heat the oil in a large, deep-sided pan. When the oil is hot, add the Rice Crisps. Deep-fry until the pieces puff up and turn brown. Remove from the wok and drain on paper towels.

6. At the table, slide the Rice Crisps into the soup. The rice will make crackling sounds.

PER SERVING Calories: 642 | Fat: 21 grams | Protein: 34 grams | Sodium: 865 milligrams | Fiber: 12 grams | Carbohydrates: 77 grams | Sugar: 12 grams

Chinese Spice Beef Vegetable Soup

This hearty home-style soup will quickly become a family favorite.

INGREDIENTS | SERVES 6

2 pounds beef short ribs

1 large onion, cut into eighths

3 carrots, cut into 1" chunks

3 tomatoes, cut into eighths

3 star anise pods

1 (4") strip orange zest, removed with a vegetable peeler

1" piece ginger, sliced thinly lengthwise

2 garlic cloves, lightly smashed and roughly minced

1 teaspoon salt, or to taste

1 teaspoon ground white pepper, or to taste

4 cups water

4 cups beef stock

1. Parboil the short ribs by placing them in a pot of cold water to cover and bringing to a boil. Turn off the heat, drain, and rinse the ribs under cold water.

2. Place the meat in a large soup pot and add the remaining ingredients. Bring to a boil over high heat, then reduce the heat to low and simmer at least 1 hour, until the meat is tender enough to fall off the bones.

3. Serve over rice or alone, taking care to remove the star anise pods and ginger.

PER SERVING Calories: 605 | Fat: 28 grams | Protein: 47 grams | Sodium: 1,076 milligrams | Fiber: 8 grams | Carbohydrates: 31 grams | Sugar: 7 grams

Bean Curd Soup

Use firm tofu for this soup so that it will hold its shape during cooking.

INGREDIENTS | SERVES 4

2 (12.3-ounce) blocks firm tofu

1 stalk green onion

1 tablespoon oil

1 teaspoon shredded ginger

5½ cups vegetable stock

¼ teaspoon salt

1 teaspoon Chinese rice wine or dry sherry

1 cup chopped bok choy

1. Place the tofu on a paper towel–lined plate. Top with more paper towels and a second plate. Top with a bowl or other weight to press down on the tofu. Set aside for 15 minutes, then drain. Cut the tofu into 1" cubes. Slice the green onion on the diagonal into 1" lengths.

2. In a large saucepan, heat the oil on medium-low heat. Add the ginger and cook briefly until aromatic.

3. Add the stock and bring to a boil. Add the salt, rice wine, tofu, and bok choy. Bring back up to a boil and simmer for about 10 minutes. Stir in the sliced green onion.

PER SERVING Calories: 215 | Fat: 11 grams | Protein: 17 grams | Sodium: 213 milligrams | Fiber: 3 grams | Carbohydrates: 12 grams | Sugar: 4 grams

West Lake Beef Soup

Pair this dish with Beef and Bean Sprouts in Black Bean Sauce (see recipe in Chapter 7) and steamed rice for a quick and easy dinner.

INGREDIENTS | SERVES 4

1 tablespoon soy sauce

1 teaspoon Chinese rice wine or dry sherry

½ teaspoon salt, divided

½ cup lean ground beef

1 tablespoon cornstarch

5 cups beef broth

1 teaspoon sugar

1½ tablespoons cornstarch mixed with ⅓ cup water

2 egg whites, lightly beaten

¼ teaspoon sesame oil

Thick or Thin?

In Chinese cooking, thin soups are soups in which the meat and vegetables are added to the heated broth during the final stages of cooking. With thick soups, the ingredients are all added together and the soup is slowly simmered, giving the flavors time to blend.

1. In a medium bowl, add the soy sauce, rice wine, and ¼ teaspoon of salt, to the ground beef. Stir in the cornstarch. Marinate for 15 minutes.

2. In a large saucepan over high heat, bring the broth to a boil. Stir in the marinated ground beef. Bring back to a boil and add the sugar and remaining salt.

3. Boil for 5 more minutes and add the cornstarch mixed with water, stirring to thicken. When the soup has thickened, turn off the heat.

4. Pour the egg whites into the soup in a steady stream, and quickly stir in a clockwise direction until they form thin shreds.

5. Drizzle with the sesame oil. Serve hot.

PER SERVING Calories: 362 | Fat: 13 grams | Protein: 18 grams | Sodium: 817 milligrams | Fiber: 7 grams | Carbohydrates: 31 grams | Sugar: 7 grams

Bird's Nest Soup

Be sure to take extra care when preparing this expensive delicacy. Combine bird's nest with rock sugar and water for a sweet dessert soup.

INGREDIENTS | SERVES 6

4 ounces bird's nest

6 cups chicken stock or broth

1½ teaspoons Chinese rice wine or dry sherry

½ teaspoon salt

½ teaspoon sugar

Basic Chicken Velvet (see recipe in Chapter 9)

⅛ teaspoon white pepper, or to taste

2 green onions, minced

Exotic Bird's Nest

Not keen to try a soup filled with twigs and branches? Actually, bird's nest isn't made from traditional nesting materials. Instead, the swiftlet—a type of swallow—makes a nest using its saliva, which hardens upon exposure to air. The swiftlet inhabits remote caves in China and Southeast Asia. Retrieving the nests can be hazardous; the men who perform this task often come from families that have been earning their living in this manner for generations.

1. To prepare the bird's nest, soak it overnight in water. Drain thoroughly. Spread out the bird's nest and use tweezers to carefully remove any foreign materials or dirt. Bring a large pot of water to a boil and simmer the bird's nest for 5 minutes. Drain thoroughly and check again for any foreign material.

2. In a large saucepan over high heat, bring stock to a boil. Add the bird's nest and simmer for 30 minutes. Add the rice wine, salt, and sugar.

3. Fold in the Basic Chicken Velvet and bring the soup back up to a boil. Add the white pepper. Stir in the green onions before serving.

PER SERVING Calories: 130 | Fat: 1 gram | Protein: 15 grams | Sodium: 329 milligrams | Fiber: 3 grams | Carbohydrates: 15 grams | Sugar: 6 grams

Pork and Spinach Soup

Ground pork is used more frequently than ground beef in Chinese cooking.
For a heartier soup, add a cup of Chinese noodles.

INGREDIENTS | SERVES 4

1 tablespoon soy sauce

1 teaspoon Chinese rice wine or dry sherry

1 tablespoon cornstarch

½ cup ground pork

¾ cup spinach leaves

5 cups pork or chicken stock

¼ teaspoon salt

1. In a medium bowl, add the soy sauce, rice wine, and cornstarch to the ground pork. Marinate the pork for 15 minutes.

2. Blanch the spinach in boiling water briefly, just until the leaves begin to wilt. Drain well.

3. In a large stockpot, bring the stock to a boil. Add the marinated pork and simmer for about 10 minutes. Add the salt and spinach. Heat through and serve hot.

PER SERVING Calories: 163 | Fat: 6 grams | Protein: 9 grams | Sodium: 500 milligrams | Fiber: 4 grams | Carbohydrates: 17 grams | Sugar: 6 grams

Steamed Beef Salad

This is an excellent dish to serve on summer days when you want something
more substantial than chicken wings or potato salad.

INGREDIENTS | SERVES 6

1 bunch romaine lettuce leaves

1 carrot, shredded

1 cup raw cherry tomatoes, halved

2 tablespoons red rice vinegar

2 teaspoons soy sauce

¼ teaspoon sesame oil

Spicy Steamed Beef (see recipe in Chapter 7), refrigerated overnight

1. Place the lettuce, carrot, and tomatoes in a medium-size bowl and toss with the red rice vinegar, soy sauce, and sesame oil.

2. Serve the steamed beef on a plate with the salad arranged around it.

PER SERVING Calories: 150 | Fat: 5 grams | Protein: 19 grams | Sodium: 779 milligrams | Fiber: 2 grams | Carbohydrates: 6 grams | Sugar: 3 grams

Chinese Potato Salad

For extra bite, add up to ½ teaspoon of curry paste to the potato salad before serving.

INGREDIENTS | SERVES 8

4 potatoes

3 tablespoons mayonnaise

1½ tablespoons soy sauce

1½ teaspoons chopped cilantro leaves

¾ teaspoon Hot Mustard Sauce (see recipe in Chapter 2)

¼ teaspoon plus a few drops sesame oil

2 hard-boiled eggs, peeled and sliced

1 cup shredded napa cabbage

⅓ cup chopped red onion

Main Dish Salad

The common Western tossed green salad is unknown in Chinese cuisine. A salad can be hot or cold, an appetizer or part of the main meal.

1. Place the potatoes in a large pot and cover with water. Bring to a boil over high heat. Reduce the heat to medium-low and simmer until tender, about 20 minutes. Drain and let the potatoes cool. Peel the potatoes and cut them into bite-size squares.

2. In a small bowl, mix the mayonnaise, soy sauce, cilantro leaves, and Hot Mustard Sauce. Stir in the sesame oil.

3. In a large bowl, combine the potatoes, eggs, shredded cabbage, and chopped red onion. Mix in the mayonnaise sauce. Keep in a sealed container in the refrigerator until ready to serve.

PER SERVING Calories: 112 | Fat: 3 grams | Protein: 3 grams | Sodium: 246 milligrams | Fiber: 1 gram | Carbohydrates: 16 grams | Sugar: 2 grams

Chinese-Style Gado Gado Salad

This Chinese take on the popular Indonesian salad features peanut sauce without the lime juice. Serve with scented rice for a light supper.

INGREDIENTS | SERVES 4

2 red potatoes
½ cup snow peas, strings removed
½ cup spinach leaves
½ cup carrots, chopped
½ cup mung bean sprouts
½ English cucumber, peeled and sliced
½ cup chopped cauliflower
2 hard-boiled eggs, peeled and sliced
Peanut Sauce (see recipe in Chapter 2)

1. In a medium saucepan, cover the potatoes with water and bring to a boil over high heat. Reduce the heat to medium-low and simmer until tender, about 20 minutes. Drain, cool, and slice potatoes.

2. Blanch the snow peas, spinach leaves, carrots, and bean sprouts.

3. Arrange the vegetables on a platter, working from the outside in. You can arrange the vegetables in any order, but the egg slices should be placed on top.

4. Pour the Peanut Sauce over the salad. Serve immediately.

PER SERVING Calories: 336 | Fat: 19 grams | Protein: 16 grams | Sodium: 1,270 milligrams | Fiber: 4 grams | Carbohydrates: 28 grams | Sugar: 9 grams

Watermelon and Watercress Salad

For extra flavor, you can add a few Spicy Roasted Peanuts (see recipe in Chapter 13)
to the dressing before processing.

INGREDIENTS | SERVES 2

¼ cup rice vinegar

½ teaspoon lemon juice

¼ teaspoon chili sauce

¼ teaspoon sesame oil

1 tablespoon sesame paste or peanut butter

2 tablespoons water

2 cups watercress

1 leaf romaine lettuce, shredded

1 small tomato, cut into thin slices

10 (1") cubes watermelon, green peel and seeds removed

1. For the dressing, place the rice vinegar, lemon juice, chili sauce, sesame oil, sesame paste, and water in a blender and process until smooth. Place in a bowl and set aside.

2. Wash the watercress. Drain thoroughly, and remove the stems.

3. Toss the watercress with the romaine lettuce and tomato. Place in a serving bowl and add the watermelon cubes. Drizzle the dressing over. Refrigerate leftover dressing in a sealed jar. It will keep for 3–4 days.

PER SERVING Calories: 99 | Fat: 5 grams | Protein: 5 grams | Sodium: 64 milligrams | Fiber: 2 grams | Carbohydrates: 11 grams | Sugar: 5 grams

Peanut Butter Is a Substitute

The more authentic version of this dish uses sesame paste. Made from toasted sesame seeds, sesame paste has a sweet flavor similar to peanut butter, which makes a convenient substitute. Although it is also made from ground sesame seeds, the Middle Eastern tahini is not a good substitute. Sesame paste is made with untoasted sesame seeds, giving it a very different flavor.

Hot Spiced Cucumbers

Rice vinegar and rice wine vinegar both mean the same thing.
Rice vinegar is simply rice wine that has been allowed to ferment.

INGREDIENTS | SERVES 2

½ English cucumber, peeled and thinly sliced
½ teaspoon salt
1 teaspoon grated ginger
1 garlic clove, finely minced
1 tablespoon plus 1 teaspoon red rice vinegar
1 tablespoon sugar
¼ teaspoon chili paste

1. Place cucumber slices in a bowl and toss with the salt. Set aside for 15 minutes.

2. In a small bowl combine the ginger, garlic, red rice vinegar, sugar, and chili paste.

3. Transfer the cucumbers to a clean bowl and pour the sauce mixture over. Serve immediately or chill.

PER SERVING Calories: 76 | Fat: 0 grams | Protein: 1 gram | Sodium: 1,165 milligrams | Fiber: 1 gram | Carbohydrates: 16 grams | Sugar: 15 grams

Creamy Cucumber Salad

This is a wonderful picnic dish with influences from different world cuisines.
For a less spicy version, leave out the chili paste.

INGREDIENTS | SERVES 2

1 English cucumber, peeled and sliced
¼ teaspoon salt
1 clove garlic, minced
½ cup plain yogurt
½ teaspoon cilantro leaves
1 teaspoon honey
1 teaspoon freshly squeezed lemon juice
¼ teaspoon chili paste
1 Asian pear, cored and sliced

1. Place the cucumber slices in a bowl and toss with salt. Set aside for 15 minutes.

2. In a blender, combine the garlic, yogurt, cilantro leaves, honey, lemon juice, and chili paste and process until smooth.

3. Serve the cucumber slices on a plate with the dressing on the side. Garnish with Asian pear slices.

PER SERVING Calories: 85 | Fat: 2 grams | Protein: 3 grams | Sodium: 320 milligrams | Fiber: 3 grams | Carbohydrates: 14 grams | Sugar: 11 grams

Bean Sprout and Carrot Salad

For an attractive presentation, trim the ends of the bean sprouts and serve on a plate of romaine lettuce leaves decorated with green onion brushes.

INGREDIENTS | SERVES 4

2 cups mung bean sprouts, rinsed and drained

½ carrot, shredded

1 tablespoon red rice vinegar

1 teaspoon sugar

1 tablespoon soy sauce

1 teaspoon chili with garlic sauce

¼ teaspoon sesame oil

1. Trim the ends of the bean sprouts if desired. Combine with the shredded carrot in a medium bowl.

2. In a small bowl, mix together the red rice vinegar, sugar, soy sauce, chili with garlic sauce, and sesame oil.

3. Drizzle the dressing over the bean sprouts and carrot. Refrigerate for at least 2 hours before serving.

PER SERVING Calories: 28 | Fat: 0 grams | Protein: 1 gram | Sodium: 265 milligrams | Fiber: 1 gram | Carbohydrates: 5 grams | Sugar: 3 grams

Cold Asparagus Salad with Garlic

This dish tastes excellent refrigerated and served the next day with a beef stir-fry and rice.

INGREDIENTS | SERVES 4

1 pound fresh asparagus, trimmed and sliced diagonally into 1½" pieces

1 clove garlic, chopped

2 tablespoons black rice vinegar

1 tablespoon soy sauce

⅛ teaspoon sesame oil

1. Bring a large pot of water to a boil. Parboil the asparagus for 5 minutes, then plunge it into cold water. Drain well.

2. In a medium bowl, mix together the garlic, vinegar, soy sauce, and sesame oil. Toss with the asparagus and serve.

PER SERVING Calories: 28 | Fat: 0 grams | Protein: 2 grams | Sodium: 252 milligrams | Fiber: 2 grams | Carbohydrates: 4 grams | Sugar: 2 grams

Hot Chicken Salad

For an interesting contrast in taste and texture, serve this dish with hard Chinese noodles such as chow mein or Deep-Fried Vermicelli (see recipe in Chapter 5).

INGREDIENTS | SERVES 4

4 boneless, skinless chicken breasts

½ cup soy sauce, divided

4 tablespoons red rice vinegar

3 teaspoons sesame oil

2 green onions, minced

½ teaspoon chili paste

1 head Romaine lettuce

1 red bell pepper, cored and thinly sliced

2 tablespoons toasted sesame seeds

How to Shred Meat

Hold a cleaver parallel to a cutting board and slice the meat horizontally into thin sections. Lay the cut pieces on top of each other, position the cleaver perpendicular to the board, and cut the meat lengthwise into thin slices, from ¼" to ⅛" thick. For easier shredding, partially freeze the meat ahead of time.

1. Marinate the chicken in ¼ cup soy sauce for 1 hour. Steam the chicken in a bamboo steamer in a wok until it is cooked through, about 20 minutes. Cool. Shred the cooked chicken meat.

2. In a small bowl, mix together ¼ cup of soy sauce, the red rice vinegar, sesame oil, green onions, and chili paste.

3. Arrange the lettuce and red bell pepper on a plate. Add the shredded cooked chicken. Drizzle with the red rice vinegar dressing and top with sesame seeds.

PER SERVING Calories: 238 | Fat: 7 grams | Protein: 32 grams | Sodium: 2,097 milligrams | Fiber: 5 grams | Carbohydrates: 10 grams | Sugar: 3 grams

CHAPTER 5

Rice and Noodles

Basic Cooked Rice

Most Chinese recipes call for long-grain rice, although medium-grain rice is also acceptable. Short-grain rice is reserved for desserts.

INGREDIENTS | SERVES 6

2 cups long-grain rice

3¼ cups water

Using a Rice Cooker

An electric rice cooker is indispensible to the Chinese household. As long as you measure the water properly, rice is prepared perfectly every time. One traditional measuring method that actually works is to stick your forefinger on top of the rice and add water up to the first knuckle.

1. If necessary, rinse the rice to remove any excess starch.

2. In a large saucepan, bring the rice and water to a boil over medium-high heat.

3. Once the rice is boiling, reduce the heat to medium-low. Put the lid at an angle on the pot, so that the pot is partially covered but some steam can escape.

4. When the water has evaporated to the point where you can see holes in the rice, put the lid on fully, about 15 minutes. Be sure to watch for the holes appearing in the rice as a measure of when to put the lid on.

5. Simmer the rice on low heat for 15 more minutes.

PER SERVING Calories: 205 | Fat: 0 grams | Protein: 4 grams | Sodium: 0 milligrams | Fiber: 0 grams | Carbohydrates: 45 grams | Sugar: 0 grams

Basic Scented Rice

The trick to making scented rice is to use less water, so that the rice is steamed rather than boiled.

INGREDIENTS | SERVES 6

2 cups jasmine or basmati scented rice
3 cups water

Rice = Food

Rice is central to the meal in China, and not just a side dish. There are two words for rice in Chinese, *mai*, which refers to the uncooked grain, and *fan*, for the cooked product. *Fan* is synonymous with "food" and "meal" for the Chinese.

1. Rinse the rice thoroughly to remove any excess starch. The water should be clear and not milky.

2. In a large saucepan, bring the rice and water to a boil over medium-high heat.

3. Reduce the heat to very low. Cover and simmer for about 20 minutes, or until the rice is cooked.

4. Remove the pot from heat. Let the rice cool for 15 minutes before removing from the pot. Fluff and serve.

PER SERVING Calories: 205 | Fat: 1 gram | Protein: 4 grams | Sodium: 2 milligrams | Fiber: 1 gram | Carbohydrates: 44 grams | Sugar: 0 grams

Basic Sticky Rice

Sticky rice is common in many Asian cuisines. You can serve it in place of regular rice or use for Pork-Filled Rice Balls (see recipe in this chapter).

INGREDIENTS | SERVES 4

1 cup short-grain sticky rice
2 cups water

What Is Sticky Rice?

Also known as glutinous rice, sticky rice is a short-grain varietal with a high starch content that makes it clump together when cooked. Despite the name, it does not actually contain gluten, so anyone with allergies need not worry.

1. Rinse rice well. Place in a bowl with enough water to cover and soak for at least 2 hours, preferably overnight. Drain well.

2. Place the rice and water in a medium saucepan over medium-high heat and bring to a boil, covered.

3. Reduce the heat to low. Do not remove the lid. Simmer for 20 minutes. Let cool for 15 minutes before serving.

PER SERVING Calories: 178 | Fat: 0 grams | Protein: 3 grams | Sodium: 5 grams | Fiber: 1 gram | Carbohydrates: 39 grams | Sugar: 0 grams

Basic Fried Rice

Creating your own favorite fried rice is easy. Just begin with leftover rice or cooled cooked rice and add ingredients of your choosing—tofu, your favorite vegetables, or any kind of cooked leftover meat. Stir-fry these additions in a hot wok before adding the rice.

INGREDIENTS | SERVES 4

6 tablespoons vegetable oil, divided

2 eggs, lightly beaten

1 tablespoon minced ginger

¼ cup scallions, cut into 1" lengths on the diagonal

4 cups cold cooked rice

4 teaspoons soy sauce

1 teaspoon ground white pepper

1. Heat a wok over medium heat. Swirl in 2 tablespoons of oil. Add the eggs and cook, stirring, until they are cooked through but not dry. Turn off heat. Gently transfer eggs to a bowl or plate.

2. Clean out the wok and add remaining oil. When the oil is hot, add the ginger and scallions and stir-fry about 30 seconds.

3. Add the rice and stir to coat. Add the soy sauce and pepper. Remove from the heat and stir in the eggs.

PER SERVING Calories: 416 | Fat: 23 grams | Protein: 8 grams | Sodium: 369 milligrams | Fiber: 1 gram | Carbohydrates: 42 grams | Sugar: 0 grams

Fried Glutinous Rice

Try this variation on regular fried rice.

INGREDIENTS | SERVES 4

2 tablespoons vegetable oil

2 cups glutinous rice

½ cup beef broth

2 tablespoons oyster sauce

1 teaspoon brown sugar

2 tablespoons water

1. Add the oil to a preheated heavy skillet or wok. When the oil is hot, add the rice and stir-fry for 2–3 minutes.

2. Add the remaining ingredients and mix thoroughly. Remove from the heat and serve.

PER SERVING Calories: 164 | Fat: 7 grams | Protein: 2 grams | Sodium: 349 milligrams | Fiber: 1 gram | Carbohydrates: 22 grams | Sugar: 1 gram

Beef Fried Rice

Concerned about cholesterol? Serve this fried rice without the strips of cooked egg on top.

INGREDIENTS | SERVES 6

2 large eggs

2½ tablespoons oyster sauce

⅛ teaspoon salt

⅛ teaspoon pepper

6 tablespoons vegetable oil, divided

2 garlic cloves, minced

½ onion, chopped

4 mushrooms, sliced

½ red bell pepper, seeded and cut into bite-size cubes

4 cups cold cooked rice

1 pound cooked beef, cut into bite-size cubes

1 tablespoon mushroom soy sauce

½ teaspoon sugar

1 green onion, cut into 1" pieces

1. Lightly beat the eggs. Stir in the oyster sauce, salt, and pepper.

2. Add 2 tablespoons of oil to a preheated wok or skillet. When the oil is hot, pour the egg mixture into the pan. Cook on medium to medium-high heat, using 2 spatulas to turn it over once. Don't scramble. Remove and cut into thin strips. Set aside.

3. Clean out the wok, if necessary. Add 2 tablespoons of oil. When the oil is hot, add the garlic and stir-fry until aromatic. Add the onion. Stir-fry for 1 minute, then add the mushrooms, and then the red pepper. Stir-fry the vegetables until they are tender. Remove from the wok and set aside.

4. Add 2 tablespoons of oil to the wok. When the oil is hot, add the rice, stirring to separate the grains. Stir-fry on medium heat for 2–3 minutes, then blend in the vegetables and beef. Stir in the mushroom soy sauce and sugar. Stir in the green onion. Serve hot, topped with the egg strips.

PER SERVING Calories: 440 | Fat: 22 grams | Protein: 26 grams | Sodium: 482 milligrams | Fiber: 1 gram | Carbohydrates: 32 grams | Sugar: 1 gram

Chicken Fried Rice

As with all hearty fried rice recipes, this can be a side dish or a complete meal in itself.

2 large eggs

2½ tablespoons oyster sauce, divided

¼ teaspoon salt, divided

¼ teaspoon pepper, divided

6 tablespoons vegetable oil, divided

2 stalks celery, diced

½ cup chopped onion

4 cups cold cooked rice

1½ cups cooked chicken, chopped

2 teaspoons thick soy sauce

2 green onions, minced

Flavorful Fried Rice

Instead of serving fried rice immediately, try storing it in the refrigerator in a sealed container to use another day. This gives the flavors more time to blend. Just be sure to allow the fried rice to cool completely before storing.

1. Lightly beat the eggs. Stir in 1 tablespoon of oyster sauce, ⅛ teaspoon of salt, and ⅛ teaspoon of pepper.

2. Add 2 tablespoons of oil to a preheated wok or skillet. When the oil is hot, pour the egg mixture into the pan. Cook on medium to medium-high heat, using 2 spatulas to turn it over once. Don't scramble. Remove and cut into thin strips. Set aside.

3. Clean out the wok if necessary. Add 2 tablespoons of oil. When the oil is hot, add the celery. Stir-fry for 1 minute, then add the onion. Stir-fry the vegetables until they are tender. Remove from the wok and set aside.

4. Add 2 tablespoons of oil to the wok. When the oil is hot, add the rice. Stir-fry on medium heat, stirring to separate the grains. Once the rice is fully coated with the oil, you may add the remaining ingredients. Add 1½ tablespoons of oyster sauce and the remaining salt and pepper. Blend in the chicken, onion, and celery. Stir in the thick soy sauce. Add extra salt and sugar if desired. To serve, garnish the chicken with the strips of egg and green onions.

PER SERVING Calories: 493 | Fat: 24 grams | Protein: 20 grams | Sodium: 704 milligrams | Fiber: 1 gram | Carbohydrates: 47 grams | Sugar: 1 gram

Fried Rice with Ham

Fried rice dishes can be prepared ahead of time and frozen. Thaw completely before reheating.

INGREDIENTS | SERVES 4

2 large eggs

⅛ teaspoon salt

⅛ teaspoon pepper

6 tablespoons vegetable oil, divided

½ cup chopped onion

½ cup frozen peas

4 cups cold cooked rice

1 tablespoon dark soy sauce

1 tablespoon oyster sauce

1 cup cooked ham

1 green onion, minced

Lumpy Leftovers

Fried rice tastes best when you use previously cooked rice instead of fresh, but leftover rice can get a bit lumpy. To remove any lumps, just sprinkle a bit of cold water on the rice and break them up with your fingers. Another trick is to add the lightly beaten egg to the cold rice before stir-frying, instead of cooking the egg separately. This makes the rice grains much easier to separate.

1. In a small bowl, lightly beat the eggs and add salt and pepper.

2. Add 2 tablespoons of oil to a preheated wok or heavy skillet and turn the heat on high. When the oil is hot, add the egg mixture. Scramble gently until the eggs are almost cooked but still moist. Remove from the heat and let sit for 1 minute before removing from the pan.

3. Clean out the wok and add 2 tablespoons of oil. When the oil is hot, add the onion. Stir-fry for 1 minute, then add the peas. Stir-fry until the peas are bright green and the onion tender. Remove.

4. Wipe the wok clean and add 2 tablespoons of oil. When the oil is hot, add the rice, stirring to separate the grains. Stir-fry for 2–3 minutes, then add the dark soy sauce and oyster sauce. Add the ham, green peas, and onion. Blend in the scrambled egg. Stir in the green onion and serve hot.

PER SERVING Calories: 520 | Fat: 25 grams | Protein: 19 grams | Sodium: 1,607 milligrams | Fiber: 2 grams | Carbohydrates: 53 grams | Sugar: 1 gram

Silken Tofu and Shiitake Fried Rice

Silken tofu can be used in place of scrambled eggs for many dishes.

INGREDIENTS | SERVES 4

¼ cup peanut oil

1 tablespoon minced ginger

2 scallions, cut into 1" lengths on the diagonal

2 cups sliced shiitake mushroom caps

½ (12-ounce) block silken tofu, cut into cubes

4 cups cooked rice, at room temperature

4 teaspoons soy sauce

1 teaspoon ground white pepper

1. Heat a wok on medium-high heat. Swirl in the oil. Add the ginger and scallions. Stir-fry about 30 seconds.

2. Add the mushrooms and stir-fry 3–4 minutes. Add the tofu, continuing to stir. It's okay if the cubes fall apart.

3. Once the tofu has heated through and absorbed the mushroom juices (about 1 minute), add the rice. Stir to coat, then add the soy sauce and pepper, and mix well. Serve when the rice has heated through.

PER SERVING Calories: 399 | Fat: 15 grams | Protein: 8 grams | Sodium: 341 milligrams | Fiber: 2 grams | Carbohydrates: 51 grams | Sugar: 3 grams

Ginger Fried Rice

This aromatic rice dish can be served as a side with vegetarian or meat-based entrées.

INGREDIENTS | SERVES 4

¼ cup peanut oil, divided

2 eggs, lightly beaten

2 tablespoons minced garlic

2 tablespoons minced ginger

2 cups thinly sliced leeks, white and light green parts only, rinsed and dried

4 cups cooked rice, at room temperature

4 teaspoons soy sauce

1 teaspoon ground white pepper

2 teaspoons sesame oil

1. Heat a wok over medium heat. Swirl in 2 tablespoons of peanut oil. Add the eggs and cook, stirring, until they are cooked through but not dry. Once the eggs hold solid, turn off the heat. Gently transfer the eggs to a bowl or plate.

2. Wipe the wok clean and return to the heat. Pour in the remaining oil. Add the ginger and garlic. Stir-fry about 30 seconds, until the aromas are released. Add the leeks and stir to coat. Turn heat to low and cook until the leeks are tender, about 10 minutes.

3. Raise the heat to medium and add rice. Stir to coat. Add the soy sauce and pepper, being sure to combine evenly. Return the eggs to the wok. Cook until heated through.

PER SERVING Calories: 420 | Fat: 19 grams | Protein: 8 grams | Sodium: 377 milligrams | Fiber: 1 gram | Carbohydrates: 53 grams | Sugar: 2 grams

Fried Rice with Eggs and Oyster Sauce

This recipe is very adaptable—enjoy as-is, or add your favorite meat and vegetable combinations.

INGREDIENTS | SERVES 4

3 large eggs
2½ tablespoons oyster sauce, divided
½ teaspoon salt, divided
¼ teaspoon pepper, divided
4 tablespoons vegetable oil, divided
4 cups cold cooked rice

Eggs and Rice

There are many ways to cook the beaten egg in fried rice. You can scramble it or fry it whole and cut it into strips to serve on top of the fried rice. For added variety, try scrambling half the beaten egg and frying the other half.

1. In a small bowl, lightly beat the eggs and add 1 tablespoon of oyster sauce, ⅛ teaspoon of salt, and ⅛ teaspoon of pepper.

2. Add 2 tablespoons of oil to a preheated wok or heavy skillet and turn the heat on high. When the oil is hot, add the egg mixture. Scramble gently until the eggs are almost cooked but still moist. Watch carefully to note the eggs' texture; cooking time varies. Remove from the heat and let sit for 1 minute before removing from the pan.

3. Wipe the wok clean and add 2 tablespoons of oil. When the oil is hot, add the rice, stirring to separate the grains. Stir-fry for 2–3 minutes, then blend in the scrambled egg. Add the remaining oyster sauce, salt, and pepper. Mix thoroughly and serve hot.

PER SERVING Calories: 387 | Fat: 18 grams | Protein: 9 grams | Sodium: 650 milligrams | Fiber: 0 grams | Carbohydrates: 45 grams | Sugar: 0 grams

Yangchow Fried Rice

This colorful dish flecked with yellow, orange, green, and pink is named for the city of Yangchow in Jiangsu province, famous for its rice dishes.

INGREDIENTS | SERVES 4

2 large eggs

2 tablespoons oyster sauce, divided

⅛ teaspoon salt

⅛ teaspoon pepper

4 cups cold cooked rice

6 tablespoons vegetable oil, divided

¼ pound fresh shrimp, peeled and deveined

½ cup baby carrots, halved

½ cup peas

½ teaspoon sugar

1 cup barbecued pork, cubed

1 green onion, sliced diagonally into 1" pieces

1. In a large bowl, lightly beat the eggs. Stir in 1 tablespoon of oyster sauce, salt, and pepper. Mix the egg mixture with the rice, stirring to separate the grains.

2. Add 2 tablespoons of oil to a preheated wok or heavy skillet. When the oil is hot, add the shrimp. Stir-fry about 2 minutes until they turn pink. Remove and drain on paper towels.

3. Clean out the wok and add 2 tablespoons of oil. When the oil is hot, add the carrots. Stir-fry for 1 minute, then add the peas. Stir-fry until the peas are bright green. Remove from the wok and set aside.

4. Wipe the wok clean and add 2 tablespoons of oil. When the oil is hot, add the rice and egg mixture. Stir-fry for 2–3 minutes, then add 1 tablespoon of oyster sauce and the sugar. Add the barbecued pork, shrimp, and reserved vegetables. Stir in the green onion and serve hot.

PER SERVING Calories: 605 | Fat: 29 grams | Protein: 25 grams | Sodium: 775 milligrams | Fiber: 1 gram | Carbohydrates: 58 grams | Sugar: 10 grams

Pork-Filled Rice Balls

Serve these rice balls as a fun side dish or as a party appetizer.

INGREDIENTS | SERVES 6

½ cup glutinous rice

2 dried mushrooms

1 green leaf from Stir-Fried Bok Choy (see recipe in Chapter 12) (optional)

¼ teaspoon salt

1 tablespoon soy sauce

1 tablespoon soaking liquid from the mushrooms

1 tablespoon Chinese rice wine or dry sherry

¼ teaspoon sugar

1 tablespoon cornstarch

1 cup ground pork

1 green onion, thinly sliced into small rounds

Fungus Fun

The Chinese believe dried mushrooms can lower blood pressure and they are also thought to be an aphrodisiac! Meanwhile, cloud ear, a strange-looking fungus that does vaguely resemble a human ear, is thought to improve blood circulation. Any kind of mushroom will add texture to a variety of dishes, from soups to stir-fries.

1. Rinse the rice several times, and soak for several hours or overnight if possible. Drain well.

2. Reconstitute the dried mushrooms by soaking them in hot water for at least 20 minutes. Reserve the soaking liquid. Cut the mushrooms into thin slices. Thinly slice the bok choy leaf, if using.

3. In a small bowl, combine the salt, soy sauce, mushroom liquid, rice wine, sugar, and cornstarch. Set aside.

4. In a medium bowl, mix the ground pork with the mushrooms, green onion, and bok choy leaf. Add the cornstarch mixture, 1 tablespoon at a time, and work it into the pork with your hands.

5. Place a piece of waxed paper on the counter and spread out the rice. Use your hands to shape the pork mixture into a ball roughly the size of a golf ball. Roll the ball over the rice, making sure it is covered with rice. Repeat with the remainder of the pork.

6. Steam the pork balls for about 30 minutes, or until they are firm and cooked through. Serve warm or cold.

PER SERVING Calories: 140 | Fat: 7 | Protein: 10 grams | Sodium: 315 milligrams | Fiber: 0 grams | Carbohydrates: 6 grams | Sugar: 1 gram

Rice and Chinese Sausage Stir-Fry

Dried shiitake mushrooms tend to have a more pungent flavor than the fresh variety. Use according to your taste.

INGREDIENTS | SERVES 4

1 cup baby carrots

4 dried shiitake mushrooms

2 green onions

¾ cup beef stock

2 teaspoons hoisin sauce

3 tablespoons vegetable oil, divided

4 Chinese sausages, cut into bite-size pieces

1 teaspoon minced shallot

3 cups cooked long-grain rice

Lap Cheong

Chinese sausage, or *lap cheong*, is sweet, salty, fatty, and dense. For some it may be an acquired taste, especially if you are expecting a Western-style sausage.

1. Blanch the carrots by plunging them briefly into boiling water. Cut the carrots in half. Soak the dried mushrooms in hot water for at least 20 minutes to soften. Cut into thin slices. Cut the green onions on the diagonal into ½" pieces.

2. In a small bowl, combine the beef stock and hoisin sauce; set aside.

3. Add 2 tablespoons of oil to a preheated wok or skillet. When the oil is hot, add the sausages. Stir-fry for 2–3 minutes, and remove from the wok.

4. Add 1 tablespoon of oil to the wok. When the oil is hot, add the shallot and stir-fry briefly until aromatic. Add the carrots, stir-fry for about 1 minute, and add the mushrooms.

5. Make a well in the middle of the wok. Add the beef/hoisin sauce in the middle and bring to a boil. Mix in the cooked rice. Add the sausages back to the wok. Stir in the green onions. Mix everything through and serve hot.

PER SERVING Calories: 489 | Fat: 23 grams | Protein: 16 grams | Sodium: 964 milligrams | Fiber: 3 grams | Carbohydrates: 51 grams | Sugar: 5 grams

Basic Hong Kong Jook

This may be eaten as a simple breakfast, snack, or late-night meal. For more flavor, replace the water with vegetable or meat stock. Serve jook with soy sauce to taste and sprinkled with chopped scallions and peanuts.

INGREDIENTS | SERVES 6

1 cup short-grain rice

2 cups water

2–4 cups additional water

1 tablespoon coarsely chopped ginger

Here's Jooking at You

Jook is the Cantonese word for rice porridge or rice congee. It is the ultimate comfort food. Served thin and plain, jook soothes an upset stomach. Cooked with leftover meats and vegetables from the refrigerator late at night, it's a homey end to a long day. Try jook many different ways—you can't go wrong!

1. Place the rice in a medium saucepan with the water. Set over high heat and bring to a boil. Turn heat to low and simmer, partially covered, for 1½ hours, until the rice grains are distinguishable but dissolving into the liquid. Check every 15 minutes or so to make sure that the rice mixture cooks without drying out. You want the finished jook to have the consistency of porridge. Stir and add water as necessary.

2. Add the ginger and simmer for another hour, continuing to stir and add water as necessary. The jook is done when it is creamy, like a thick soup.

PER SERVING Calories: 120 | Fat: 0 grams | Protein: 2 grams | Sodium: 4 milligrams | Fiber: 1 gram | Carbohydrates: 26 grams | Sugar: 0 grams

Chicken Jook

This is a hearty one-bowl meal, something between a soup and a stew. Serve with soy sauce to taste and sprinkle with chopped scallions and cilantro. Drizzle with sesame oil if you wish.

INGREDIENTS | SERVES 6

1 teaspoon peanut oil
½ (3-pound) chicken, cut up
1 tablespoon coarsely chopped ginger
1 tablespoon coarsely chopped garlic
½ onion, peeled and chopped
1 teaspoon salt
½ teaspoon pepper
4–6 cups water, divided
1 cup short-grain rice
2–4 cups additional water

1. Heat the oil in a large soup pot or Dutch oven over medium-high heat. Place the chicken, skin side down, in the hot oil. Brown about 3 minutes.

2. Stir in the ginger and garlic and cook about 30 seconds. Add onion and cook until translucent, about 3 minutes. Add salt, pepper, and 2 cups of water. Bring to a boil. Reduce the heat and simmer 15–20 minutes. Strain. Pour the liquid back into the pot. Reserve the chicken and vegetables.

3. Wash the rice and place it into pot with the cooking liquid. Add ½ cup of water. Set over high heat and bring to a boil. Turn the heat to low and simmer, partially covered, for 1½ hours, until the rice grains are distinguishable but dissolving into the liquid. Check every 15 minutes or so to make sure that the rice mixture cooks without drying out. Stir and add water as necessary.

4. Meanwhile, debone the chicken and discard the skin. Cut the meat into bite-size pieces. Return the chicken and reserved vegetables to the pot for the final 10 minutes of cooking. The jook is done once it is creamy and thick.

PER SERVING Calories: 400 | Fat: 15 grams | Protein: 34 grams | Sodium: 496 milligrams | Fiber: 1 gram | Carbohydrates: 27 grams | Sugar: 0 grams

Mushroom Jook

This is a flavorful, vegetarian variation of jook.

INGREDIENTS | SERVES 6

10 fresh or dried shiitake mushrooms
1 cup short-grain rice
2 cups vegetable stock
2–4 cups water
1 tablespoon coarsely chopped ginger
4 spring onions, cut into ¼" lengths
2 tablespoons soy sauce, to taste
¼ cup chopped scallions

1. If using dried shiitake mushrooms, soak for several hours to soften. Drain, keeping the liquid in reserve for use in cooking. Remove the mushroom stems and discard. Cut the mushroom caps into ¼"-thick slices.

2. Place the rice in a medium saucepan with the stock. Set over high heat and bring to a boil. Turn the heat to low and simmer, partially covered, for 1½ hours, until the rice grains are distinguishable but dissolving into the liquid. Check every 15 minutes or so to make sure that the rice mixture cooks without drying out. Stir and add water as necessary.

3. Add the ginger, mushrooms, and spring onions. Add the water from soaking the mushrooms. Simmer for another hour, stirring and adding water as necessary. The jook is done when the rice has completely dissolved and has a creamy consistency. Stir in soy sauce and scallions.

PER SERVING Calories: 146 | Fat: 0 grams | Protein: 3 grams | Sodium: 340 milligrams | Fiber: 2 grams | Carbohydrates: 32 grams | Sugar: 0 grams

Midnight Jook

Midnight Jook is the perfect meal after a long day. Garnish this dish with soy sauce, chopped scallions, and cilantro leaves.

INGREDIENTS | SERVES 4

2 pounds meaty pork bones
1 cup short-grain rice
2 cups pork stock
2–4 cups water
1 tablespoon minced ginger
1 cup roughly chopped bok choy
1 cup roughly chopped spinach

1. Place the pork bones in a medium saucepan. Cover with cold water and bring to a boil. Drain and rinse the bones under cold water. Set aside.

2. Wash the rice and place it in another medium saucepan with the stock. Set over high heat and bring to a boil. Turn the heat to low and simmer, partially covered, for 1½ hours, until the rice grains are distinguishable but dissolving into the liquid. Check every 15 minutes or so to make sure that the rice mixture cooks without drying out. Stir and add water as necessary.

3. Add the pork bones and the ginger. Simmer until thick and creamy, then add the bok choy and spinach and cook an additional 20 minutes.

PER SERVING Calories: 121 | Fat: 0 grams | Protein: 2 grams | Sodium: 14 milligrams | Fiber: 1 gram | Carbohydrates: 25 grams | Sugar: 0 grams

Hearty Family Ramen

Add fresh vegetables according to your taste!

INGREDIENTS | SERVES 4

1 tablespoon peanut oil

½ (3-pound) chicken, cut up

1 tablespoon minced ginger

1 tablespoon minced garlic

½ cup chopped onion

1 stalk celery, roughly diced

1 carrot, cut in coins

3 tablespoons soy sauce, divided

4 cups chicken stock

2 cups water

16 ounces fresh ramen noodles

¼ cup chopped scallions

¼ cup chopped cilantro

Modern Old-School Ramen

Does the word *ramen* make you think of convenience store–packages full of MSG? Ramen is in fact a traditional Chinese noodle, made fresh by trained artisans. Fresh ramen noodles are available in Asian markets, and well worth the effort to find.

1. Heat the oil in large soup pot or Dutch oven over medium-high heat. Place the chicken in the pot, skin side down, and brown for about 3 minutes. Add the ginger and garlic and cook about 30 seconds. Add the onion, celery, and carrots. Cook until the onions are translucent, about 3 minutes.

2. Add 1 tablespoon of soy sauce and stir to combine. Lower the heat to medium. Pour in the chicken stock and water. Bring to a boil, then reduce the heat to low and simmer 15–20 minutes. Turn off the heat.

3. Debone the chicken and discard the skin. Cut the meat into bite-size pieces. Skim the fat off the broth in the pot.

4. Return the chicken to the pot and bring to a boil again over high heat. Turn off the heat. Add the fresh ramen and stir to heat through. Divide the ramen into four bowls and top with scallions, cilantro, and the remaining soy sauce.

PER SERVING Calories: 532 | Fat: 7 grams | Protein: 42 grams | Sodium: 1,262 milligrams | Fiber: 15 grams | Carbohydrates: 80 grams | Sugar: 8 grams

Hearty Vegetarian Ramen

This basic recipe can be spiced up with ginger-garlic or chili sauce.
Serve with chopped scallions and additional soy sauce if you wish.

INGREDIENTS | SERVES 1

8 shiitake mushrooms, fresh or dried
1 tablespoon peanut oil
1 teaspoon minced ginger
1 teaspoon minced garlic
¼ cup finely chopped onion
½ carrot, cut into coins
½ cup roughly chopped bok choy
1 teaspoon soy sauce
¼ (12.3-ounce) block firm tofu, cut into 1" cubes
2 cups vegetable stock
6 ounces fresh ramen noodles

1. If using dried mushrooms, soak them in water to cover for several hours to rehydrate. Drain, reserving the water. Remove the stems, and save for soup stock if you wish. Cut the mushroom caps into strips. Set aside.

2. Heat a soup pot over high heat and pour in the peanut oil. Add the ginger and garlic, and cook, stirring, about 30 seconds. Add the onions and carrots. Cook until the onions become translucent, about 2–3 minutes.

3. Add the mushrooms. Reduce the heat to medium. Cook, stirring, until the mushrooms release their juices, 3–4 minutes. Add the bok choy and cook until bright green, another 3–4 minutes.

4. Add the soy sauce and tofu, stirring gently so that the tofu cubes don't fall apart. Pour in the vegetable stock and water used to hydrate the mushrooms and bring to a boil. Turn off the heat. Add ramen noodles and let them heat through.

PER SERVING Calories: 422 | Fat: 10 grams | Protein: 16 grams | Sodium: 613 milligrams | Fiber: 12 grams | Carbohydrates: 69 grams | Sugar: 4 grams

Hot, Sour, and Spicy Rice Noodles

Rice stick noodles come in many intriguing shapes and sizes.
They can be nearly as thin as strands of human hair.

INGREDIENTS | SERVES 6

¼ pound rice stick noodles

¼ cup dark soy sauce

1 teaspoon sugar

¼ teaspoon Hot Chili Oil (see Chapter 2)

¼ teaspoon Szechwan Salt and Pepper Mix (see Chapter 2)

¼ teaspoon chili paste

1 teaspoon black rice vinegar

½ cup water

1½ tablespoons vegetable oil

¼ cup chopped onion

1. Soak the rice stick noodles in hot water for 15 minutes or until they are softened. Drain thoroughly.

2. In a medium bowl, combine the dark soy sauce, sugar, Hot Chili Oil, Szechwan Salt and Pepper Mix, chili paste, vinegar, and water; set aside.

3. Add the oil to a preheated wok or skillet. When the oil is hot, add the chopped onion. Stir-fry until it is soft and translucent.

4. Add the rice noodles and stir-fry for 2–3 minutes. Add the prepared sauce in the middle of the wok. Mix in with the noodles and stir-fry until the noodles have absorbed all the sauce.

PER SERVING Calories: 122 | Fat: 4 grams | Protein: 3 grams | Sodium: 1,103 milligrams | Fiber: 0 grams | Carbohydrates: 16 grams | Sugar: 1 gram

Cellophane Noodles with Beef and Oyster Sauce

Not a fan of canned baby corn? Try substituting canned or fresh bamboo shoots instead.

INGREDIENTS | SERVES 4

½ pound flank steak, thinly sliced

2 tablespoons soy sauce

1½ teaspoons Chinese rice wine or dry sherry, divided

½ teaspoon sugar

½ teaspoon baking soda

2-ounce bag cellophane noodles

1 (15-ounce) can baby corn

½ cup beef broth

2 tablespoons oyster sauce

2 tablespoons dark soy sauce

1 tablespoon light soy sauce

4 tablespoons oil, for stir-frying

Mad about Mein!

Mein is the Chinese word for noodles. When it comes to important staple foods, noodles rank second only to rice in the Chinese diet. Noodles are steamed, stir-fried, added to soups, and used to make dumplings. Although noodles are enjoyed throughout China, they are particularly important in the north, where a harsher climate prohibits the cultivation of rice crops.

1. Place the steak in a small bowl. Add the soy sauce, 1 teaspoon of rice wine, sugar, and baking soda. Marinate the beef for 30 minutes.

2. Without removing the string wrapping, soak the cellophane noodles in hot water to soften. Cut the noodles along the string wrapping into thirds. Drain thoroughly. Rinse the baby corn in warm water and drain.

3. In a small bowl, combine the beef broth, oyster sauce, dark soy sauce, light soy sauce, and ½ teaspoon of rice wine, and set aside.

4. Add 2 tablespoons of oil to a preheated wok or skillet. When the oil is hot, add the beef. Stir-fry until it changes color and is nearly cooked through. Remove from the wok and set aside.

5. Add the remaining oil. Stir-fry the baby corn for 1–2 minutes. Add the sauce to the middle of the wok and bring to a boil. Add the noodles, stirring quickly to mix in with the sauce. Add the beef. Mix thoroughly and serve hot.

PER SERVING Calories: 445 | Fat: 22 grams | Protein: 21 grams | Sodium: 2,097 milligrams | Fiber: 3 grams | Carbohydrates: 40 grams | Sugar: 6 grams

Easy Family Ramen with Beef

Short on time? Try this quick and delicious recipe that the whole family will love.

INGREDIENTS | SERVES 4

1 teaspoon peanut oil

1 tablespoon ginger

1 tablespoon garlic

¼ cup finely chopped scallions

½ pound flank steak, sliced thinly across the grain

1 tablespoon soy sauce

4 cups beef stock

16 ounces fresh ramen noodles

1. Heat the oil in a soup pot over high heat. Add the ginger, garlic, and scallions. Cook, stirring rapidly, for 30 seconds–1 minute.

2. Add the flank steak and soy sauce. Cook, stirring, for 1 minute. Remove the steak. Reduce the heat to medium.

3. Add the beef stock and bring the mixture to a boil. Turn off the heat. Return the steak to the pot and add the ramen noodles. Let the hot broth heat the noodles thoroughly, about 5 minutes.

PER SERVING Calories: 577 | Fat: 10 grams | Protein: 31 grams | Sodium: 798 milligrams | Fiber: 17 grams | Carbohydrates: 84 grams | Sugar: 6 grams

Beef Chow Fun

This recipe also works well with other meats. Try substituting chicken, shrimp, or pork.

INGREDIENTS | SERVES 4

4 ounces wide rice noodles

1 cup mung bean sprouts

½ cup chicken stock or broth

1 teaspoon soy sauce

2 tablespoons vegetable oil

1 cup cooked beef, shredded

¼ teaspoon chili paste

1. Soak the noodles in hot water for at least 15 minutes to soften. Drain well. Blanch the bean sprouts by plunging them briefly into boiling water. Drain well.

2. In a small bowl, combine the chicken stock and soy sauce. Set aside.

3. Add the oil to a preheated wok or skillet. When the oil is hot, add the noodles. Stir-fry briefly, 1–2 minutes then add the sauce. Mix well and add the shredded beef. Stir in the chili paste. Add the mung bean sprouts. Serve hot.

PER SERVING Calories: 283 | Fat: 11 grams | Protein: 17 grams | Sodium: 177 milligrams | Fiber: 1 gram | Carbohydrates: 26 grams | Sugar: 1 gram

Noodle Pancake

Noodle Pancake makes a nice alternative to rice with stir-fries, and tastes great topped with any of the Egg Foo Yung sauces (see recipes in Chapter 6).

8 ounces steamed egg noodles

2 teaspoons sesame oil

5 tablespoons vegetable oil

1. Cook the noodles until they are tender. Drain thoroughly and toss with the sesame oil.

2. Add 3 tablespoons of vegetable oil to a preheated wok or skillet. When the oil is hot, add the noodles. Use a spatula to press down on the noodles and form them into a pancake shape. Cook until a thin brown crust forms on the bottom—this will take at least 5 minutes. Slide the pancake out of the pan onto a plate.

3. Add the remaining oil to the wok. Turn the noodle pancake over, put it back in the wok, and cook until the other side is browned. Remove from the wok. To serve, cut into quarters.

PER SERVING Calories: 251 | Fat: 20 grams | Protein: 2 grams | Sodium: 93 milligrams | Fiber: 0 grams | Carbohydrates: 14 grams | Sugar: 0 grams

Pork Chow Mein

The mushroom soaking liquid adds an earthy flavor to this dish. You can also use fresh mushrooms and ¼ cup water instead.

INGREDIENTS | SERVES 6

1 pound fresh egg noodles
¼ teaspoon sesame oil
1 pound pork tenderloin, cubed
1 tablespoon Chinese rice wine
½ teaspoon salt, divided
4 large dried mushrooms
⅓ cup chicken broth
⅛ cup water
4 teaspoons oyster sauce
6 tablespoons vegetable oil
2 garlic cloves, minced
1 carrot, diced
1 stalk celery, thinly sliced on the diagonal
½ green or red bell pepper, seeded and cut into cubes
2½ cups shredded napa cabbage
1 cup mung bean sprouts, rinsed and drained
1 teaspoon cornstarch mixed with 4 teaspoons water

1. Boil the noodles about 5 minutes. Drain and toss with the sesame oil.

2. Add the pork to a medium bowl along with the rice wine and ¼ teaspoon of salt and marinate for 30 minutes.

3. Soak the dried mushrooms for at least 20 minutes to soften. Drain, reserving soaking liquid, and thinly slice mushrooms.

4. In a small bowl, combine the chicken broth, water, ⅛ cup of mushroom soaking liquid, oyster sauce, and remaining salt. Set aside.

5. Add 2 tablespoons of oil to a preheated wok or skillet. Add the pork and stir-fry until it is nearly cooked, about 5 minutes. Remove and drain on paper towels.

6. Add 2 tablespoons of oil. When the oil is hot, add the noodles and stir-fry until light brown. Remove from the wok and keep warm. Clean out the wok.

7. Add 2 tablespoons of oil. When the oil is hot, add the garlic and stir-fry briefly until aromatic. Stir-fry the carrot, celery, bell pepper, dried mushrooms, cabbage, and bean sprouts, adding each new ingredient after 2–3 minutes.

8. Add the prepared sauce to the middle of the wok and bring to a boil. Add the cornstarch-and-water mixture, stirring quickly to thicken. Add the pork and heat through. Serve hot over the noodles.

PER SERVING Calories: 345 | Fat: 17 grams | Protein: 20 grams | Sodium: 393 milligrams | Fiber: 2 grams | Carbohydrates: 26 grams | Sugar: 3 grams

Chicken Chow Mein

*Like chop suey, this is a great one-dish meal to make when it's time
to clean out the vegetable section of the refrigerator.*

INGREDIENTS | SERVES 6

1 pound fresh egg noodles

¼ teaspoon sesame oil

1 pound boneless, skinless chicken breasts

10 teaspoons oyster sauce, divided

½ teaspoon salt, divided

1 bunch (about 2½ cups after cutting) bok choy

⅓ cup chicken broth

¼ cup water

6 tablespoons vegetable oil, divided

2 garlic cloves, minced

8 large mushrooms, thinly sliced

2 stalks celery, thinly sliced on the diagonal

½ red bell pepper, seeded and cut into thin slices

1 cup mung bean sprouts, rinsed and drained

1 teaspoon cornstarch mixed with 4 teaspoons water

1. Boil the noodles about 5 minutes. Drain thoroughly and toss with the sesame oil.

2. Cut the chicken breasts into thin strips and place in a medium bowl. Marinate in 6 teaspoons of oyster sauce and ¼ teaspoon of salt for 30 minutes.

3. Cut the bok choy leaves across and thinly slice the stalks on the diagonal.

4. In a small bowl, combine the chicken broth, water, remaining oyster sauce, and remaining salt. Set aside.

5. Add 2 tablespoons of oil to a preheated wok or skillet. Add the chicken and stir-fry until it is nearly cooked, 3–4 minutes. Drain on paper towels.

6. Add 2 tablespoons of oil. Add the noodles and stir-fry until they turn light brown. Remove and keep warm. Clean out the wok.

7. Add 2 tablespoons of oil. Add the garlic and stir-fry briefly until aromatic. Stir-fry the mushrooms, bok choy stalks, celery, bell pepper, bok choy leaves, and bean sprouts, adding one vegetable at a time, adding each new ingredient after 2–3 minutes.

8. Add the prepared sauce to the middle of the wok and bring to a boil. Add the cornstarch/water mixture, stirring quickly to thicken. Add the sugar. Add the chicken and heat through. Serve hot over the noodles.

PER SERVING Calories: 371 | Fat: 17 grams | Protein: 24 grams | Sodium: 1,089 milligrams | Fiber: 3 grams | Carbohydrates: 30 grams | Sugar: 3 grams

Beef Chow Mein

Feel free to add seasonal vegetables such as tomatoes and green beans in this recipe.

INGREDIENTS | SERVES 6

1 pound fresh egg noodles

1 pound beef flank steak

1 tablespoon soy sauce

½ teaspoon baking soda

⅓ cup beef broth

¼ cup water

1 tablespoon oyster sauce

1 teaspoon sugar

⅛ teaspoon salt

6 tablespoons vegetable oil

2 garlic cloves, minced

½ cup carrots, thinly sliced

½ cup snow peas, trimmed

½ red bell pepper, seeded and cut into thin slices

1 cup mung bean sprouts, rinsed and drained

1 teaspoon cornstarch mixed with 4 teaspoons water

½ teaspoon sesame oil

1. Boil the noodles until they are soft, about 5 minutes. Drain thoroughly.

2. Cut the beef into thin strips and place in a medium bowl. Add the soy sauce and baking soda, and marinate the beef for 30 minutes.

3. In a small bowl, combine the beef broth, water, oyster sauce, sugar, and salt. Set aside.

4. Add 2 tablespoons of oil to the wok. When the oil is hot, add the beef. Stir-fry until it changes color and is nearly cooked, 3–4 minutes. Remove and drain on paper towels.

5. Add 2 tablespoons of oil. When the oil is hot, add the noodles. Stir-fry until they are golden but still soft. Remove.

6. Add 2 tablespoons of oil to the wok. When the oil is hot, add the garlic. Stir-fry until aromatic. Add the carrots. Stir-fry for 1 minute, then add the snow peas, red pepper, and bean sprouts. Stir-fry until the vegetables are colorful and tender.

7. Make a well in the middle of the wok. Add the prepared sauce and bring to a boil. Add the cornstarch-and-water mixture, stirring to thicken. Add the beef. Drizzle with sesame oil. Mix everything through and serve over the noodles.

PER SERVING Calories: 374 | Fat: 20 grams | Protein: 21 grams | Sodium: 465 milligrams | Fiber: 2 grams | Carbohydrates: 25 grams | Sugar: 3 grams

Post-Thanksgiving Turkey Chow Mein

This is an unusual way to make use of leftover Thanksgiving turkey. Serve with Egg Drop Soup (see recipe in Chapter 4) for a nourishing fall meal.

INGREDIENTS | SERVES 4

4 cups dry chow mein noodles

1 cup bean sprouts

2 stalks celery, sliced diagonally

4½ tablespoons vegetable oil, divided

4 mushrooms, sliced

1 tablespoon soy sauce

2 cups snow peas, trimmed

½ cup cashews

2 cups cooked turkey

2 tablespoons oyster sauce

1 tablespoon cornstarch mixed with 4 tablespoons water

1. Boil the chow mein noodles according to the directions on the package. Drain well. Keep warm.

2. Blanch the bean sprouts and celery separately by briefly plunging them into boiling water; drain thoroughly.

3. Add 2 tablespoons of oil to a preheated wok or skillet. Stir-fry the celery on medium-high heat. Add the mushrooms, bean sprouts, and soy sauce. Stir-fry 3–4 minutes, remove, and set aside. Add the snow peas and stir-fry 4–5 minutes. Remove and set aside.

4. Add 1½ tablespoons of oil to the wok or frying pan. Add the cashews and stir-fry on medium heat very briefly (no more than 1 minute). Remove and set aside.

5. Add 1 tablespoon of oil to the wok. Add the turkey and the oyster sauce. Add the vegetables and mix thoroughly.

6. Make a well in the middle of the pan and add the cornstarch-and-water mixture, stirring to thicken. Stir in the cashews. Serve over the chow mein noodles.

PER SERVING Calories: 655 | Fat: 41 grams | Protein: 30 grams | Sodium: 765 milligrams | Fiber: 5 grams | Carbohydrates: 42 grams | Sugar: 5 grams

Beefy Fried Rice Noodles

For a different flavor, replace the oyster sauce in the
chicken broth mixture with 1 tablespoon of hoisin sauce.

INGREDIENTS | SERVES 6

½ pound beef flank or sirloin steak

2½ teaspoons oyster sauce, divided

⅛ teaspoon salt

¼ teaspoon baking soda

4 ounces medium-width rice stick noodles

2 tablespoons dark soy sauce

½ cup chicken stock or broth

4 cups vegetable oil

¼ cup cornstarch

1 teaspoon finely chopped ginger

2 garlic cloves, finely chopped

1 red bell pepper, seeded and cut into thin slices

1 cup mung bean sprouts, rinsed and drained

1. Cut the beef across the grain into thin strips about 2" long and place in a medium bowl. Add 1½ teaspoons of oyster sauce, salt, and baking soda. Marinate the beef for 30 minutes.

2. Soak the rice noodles in hot water for 20 minutes or until they are softened.

3. In a small bowl, combine the remaining oyster sauce, dark soy sauce, and chicken stock. Set aside.

4. Heat 4 cups of oil in the wok to 375°F. Lightly dust the marinated beef with the cornstarch. Deep-fry the beef in the hot oil for a few minutes, until it turns light brown (about 3–4 minutes). Drain on paper towels.

5. Remove all but 3 tablespoons of oil from the wok or heat 3 tablespoons of oil in a second wok or heavy skillet. When the oil is hot, add the ginger and garlic and stir-fry until aromatic. Add the red pepper and stir-fry until it is tender and has a bright color, 4–5 minutes (stir-fry in 2 batches, if necessary). Add the bean sprouts; stir-fry about 2 minutes. Push the vegetables up to the side, add the sauce, and bring to a boil.

6. Turn down the heat slightly and add the noodles. Stir-fry briefly and add the beef. If necessary, add a bit of water. Mix everything through and serve hot.

PER SERVING Calories: 365 | Fat: 13 grams | Protein: 10 grams | Sodium: 564 milligrams | Fiber: 1 gram | Carbohydrates: 25 grams | Sugar: 2 grams

Cold Szechwan Sesame Noodles

Italian pasta can be substituted for Chinese egg noodles in this recipe.
For added flair, garnish with cilantro leaves.

INGREDIENTS | SERVES 4

8 ounces egg noodles
1 cucumber
½ teaspoon salt
1 tablespoon toasted sesame seeds
Spicy Szechwan Peanut Sauce (see recipe in Chapter 2)

1. Prepare the egg noodles according to the instructions on the package.

2. Peel the cucumber, slice and toss with salt, and leave for 15 minutes.

3. Allow the noodles to cool. When cold, toss with the peanut sauce and sprinkle with sesame seeds. Serve over the cucumber slices.

PER SERVING Calories: 430 | Fat: 20 grams | Protein: 13 grams | Sodium: 1,113 milligrams | Fiber: 3 grams | Carbohydrates: 50 grams | Sugar: 7 grams

Deep-Fried Vermicelli

Top these noodles with dishes that have a lot of sauce, such as
Mongolian Beef with Vegetables (see recipe in Chapter 7).

INGREDIENTS | SERVES 8

4 cups vegetable oil
4 ounces vermicelli noodles

1. Heat the oil in a preheated wok or heavy saucepan to 375°F. If the noodles come with string wrappings, cut them off. Do not soak the noodles.

2. Drop one 2-ounce package of noodles into the wok. It should puff up immediately. Remove and drain on paper towels. Repeat with the other package. Cut the noodles into serving portions or serve as-is.

PER SERVING Calories: 128 | Fat: 8 grams | Protein: 0 grams | Sodium: 25 milligrams | Fiber: 0 grams | Carbohydrates: 11 grams | Sugar: 0 grams

Singapore Fried Rice Noodles

For a different taste and texture, try substituting chicken for the pork and experimenting with rice noodles of different thicknesses.

INGREDIENTS | SERVES 4

4 ounces rice vermicelli

2 teaspoons mild curry powder

¼ teaspoon turmeric

½ teaspoon grated ginger

½ cup chicken stock or broth

2 tablespoons plus 1 teaspoon soy sauce

½ teaspoon sugar

4 tablespoons vegetable oil

2 ounces shrimp, peeled and deveined

½ red bell pepper, seeded and chopped

1 cup mung bean sprouts, rinsed and drained

4 ounces barbecued pork, cut into very thin slices

⅛ teaspoon freshly ground pepper

1. Soak the rice noodles in hot water for 20 minutes or until softened. Drain thoroughly.

2. In a small bowl, combine the curry powder, turmeric, and ginger. Set aside. In a separate small bowl, combine the chicken stock, soy sauce, and sugar. Set aside.

3. Add 2 tablespoons of oil to a preheated wok or skillet. When the oil is hot, add the shrimp and stir-fry briefly until they turn pink. Remove and set aside.

4. Add 2 tablespoons of oil. When the oil is hot, add the curry powder mixture and stir-fry until aromatic; you will know how long by the smell. Add the red pepper and bean sprouts, stir-frying until you see the pepper change color to a bright red, about 3–4 minutes. Add the noodles and stir-fry for 2–3 minutes, adding water if necessary.

5. Add the chicken-stock sauce in the middle of the wok. Bring to a boil. Add the barbecued pork and mix through. Add the stir-fried shrimp. Sprinkle with the freshly ground pepper and serve hot.

PER SERVING Calories: 314 | Fat: 16 grams | Protein: 10 grams | Sodium: 798 milligrams | Fiber: 1 gram | Carbohydrates: 31 grams | Sugar: 5 grams

Dan Dan Noodles

A mild, sweetened rice vinegar works very well in this recipe.
If you want to add a vegetable, try 1 cup of blanched bean sprouts.

INGREDIENTS | SERVES 4

8 ounces fresh egg noodles

2 teaspoons plus 1 tablespoon sesame oil, divided

3 tablespoons peanut butter

2 tablespoons dark soy sauce

1 tablespoon light soy sauce

3 tablespoons rice vinegar

1 teaspoon sugar

1 tablespoon Hot Chili Oil (see recipe in Chapter 2)

1½ tablespoons toasted sesame seeds

3 green onions, cut into 1" pieces

1. Bring a pot of water to boil, and cook the noodles al dente, no longer than 5 minutes. Drain thoroughly and toss with 2 teaspoons of sesame oil. Cool.

2. In a blender or food processor, combine the peanut butter, dark soy sauce, light soy sauce, rice vinegar, sugar, 1 tablespoon of sesame oil, and Hot Chili Oil. Process until smooth.

3. Mix the sauce in with the noodles. Sprinkle the toasted sesame seeds over. Garnish with the green onion.

PER SERVING Calories: 233 | Fat: 15 grams | Protein: 7 grams | Sodium: 766 milligrams | Fiber: 2 grams | Carbohydrates: 18 grams | Sugar: 2 grams

Rice Crisps

Crispy rice is used to make Sizzling Rice Soup (see recipe in Chapter 4), a popular restaurant dish with seafood and vegetables swimming in a rich broth.

INGREDIENTS | MAKES 10 SQUARES

1 cup short-grain rice

1 cup water

1. In a medium saucepan over high heat, bring the rice and water to boil, uncovered.

2. Cover and reduce the heat to low. Simmer for 30 minutes. Remove from the burner and allow to cool.

3. Spread the rice out on a baking sheet, making sure it is no more than ¼ -nch thick.

4. Bake at 300°F for 50 minutes or until dry. When cooled, cut into 2" squares and store in a canister to use as needed.

PER SERVING (2 SQUARES) Calories: 142 | Fat: 0 grams | Protein: 0 grams | Sodium: 2 milligrams | Fiber: 1 gram | Carbohydrates: 31 grams | Sugar: 0 grams

Beef Lo Mein

To cook noodles al dente, boil until they are tender, but still firm and not mushy.

INGREDIENTS | SERVES 4

1 pound flank steak

2 teaspoons oyster sauce

1½ teaspoons sugar, divided

½ teaspoon baking soda

6 dried mushrooms, cut into thin slices

8 ounces fresh egg noodles

2 tablespoons dark soy sauce

1 tablespoon light soy sauce

1 teaspoon Chinese rice wine or dry sherry

¼ cup water

3 tablespoons vegetable oil, divided

6 cabbage leaves, shredded

¼ teaspoon salt

Chow Mein or Lo Mein?

People are often surprised to learn that the difference between these popular dishes has more to do with cooking styles than specific ingredients. Chow Mein are fried noodles cooked separately from the meat and vegetables. Lo Mein dishes feature boiled noodles that are combined with the other ingredients during the final stages of cooking.

1. Cut the steak into thin slices, about 2" in length and place in a medium bowl. Add the oyster sauce, ½ teaspoon of sugar, and baking soda. Marinate the steak for 30 minutes.

2. Soak the dried mushrooms in hot water for at least 20 minutes to soften.

3. In a large pot of water, boil the noodles until the flour is removed but they are still firm, no longer than 5 minutes. Drain thoroughly.

4. In a small bowl, combine the dark soy sauce, light soy sauce, 1 teaspoon of sugar, rice wine, and water, and set aside.

5. Add 2 tablespoons of oil to a preheated wok or skillet. When the oil is hot, add the steak. Stir-fry until it changes color and is nearly cooked through, 4–5 minutes. Remove and drain on paper towels.

6. Add 1 tablespoon of oil to the wok. When the oil is hot, add the cabbage leaves. Stir-fry until they are bright green and tender. Add the mushrooms and salt. Stir-fry briefly.

7. Add the prepared sauce in the middle of the wok and bring to a boil. Turn down the heat slightly and add the beef. Add the noodles. Mix everything through and serve hot.

PER SERVING Calories: 381 | Fat: 17 grams | Protein: 29 grams | Sodium: 1,249 milligrams | Fiber: 2 grams | Carbohydrates: 25 grams | Sugar: 4 grams

Chicken Lo Mein

Leftover Tea-Smoked Chicken (see recipe in Chapter 9)
works very well in this recipe, imparting a lovely smoky flavor.

INGREDIENTS | SERVES 4

8 ounces fresh egg noodles

½ cup mushrooms, fresh or dried

2 tablespoons oyster sauce

1 tablespoon soy sauce

1 teaspoon sugar

1 teaspoon Chinese rice wine or dry sherry

½ cup water

3 tablespoons vegetable oil, divided

4 cabbage leaves, shredded

¼ teaspoon salt

½ cup mung bean sprouts, rinsed and drained

1 cup cooked chicken, thinly sliced

1. In a large pot of water, boil the noodles until the flour is removed and they are tender, about 5 minutes. Drain thoroughly.

2. If using dried mushrooms, soak them in hot water for at least 20 minutes to soften. Slice the mushrooms.

3. In a small bowl, combine the oyster sauce, soy sauce, sugar, rice wine, and water, and set aside.

4. Add 2 tablespoons of oil to a preheated wok or skillet. When the oil is hot, add the cabbage leaves. Stir-fry until they turn bright green and are tender. Season with salt. Add 1 tablespoon of oil.

5. Add the mushrooms. Stir-fry briefly, then add the bean sprouts.

6. Add the prepared sauce in the middle of the wok. Bring to a boil. Turn down the heat slightly and add the chicken. Add the noodles. Mix everything through and serve hot.

PER SERVING Calories: 239 | Fat: 12 grams | Protein: 12 grams | Sodium: 709 milligrams | Fiber: 1 gram | Carbohydrates: 21 grams | Sugar: 4 grams

Savory Shanghai Noodles

Frying the shrimp briefly in 1 cup of hot oil gives it a soft, velvety texture.

INGREDIENTS | SERVES 4

½ pound medium shrimp, tails and vein removed

½ teaspoon sugar

½ teaspoon cornstarch

¾ cup chicken broth

¼ cup water

2 tablespoons plus 2 teaspoons oyster sauce

1 teaspoon Chinese rice wine or dry sherry

1 cup vegetable oil

1 bunch spinach, washed and drained

1 garlic clove, finely chopped

2 slices ginger, finely chopped

½ pound fresh Shanghai noodles

½ teaspoon sesame oil

Noodle Lore

The Chinese have been enjoying noodles since ancient times. Symbolizing a long life in Chinese culture, noodles occupy an important place in festive celebrations such as Chinese New Year. And birthday celebrations wouldn't be complete without a heaping bowl of longevity noodles.

1. Rinse the shrimp in warm water and pat dry. Place the shrimp in a medium bowl with the sugar and cornstarch and marinate for 15 minutes.

2. In a small bowl, mix together the chicken broth, water, oyster sauce, and rice wine, and set aside.

3. Add the vegetable oil to a preheated wok or skillet. When the oil is hot, add the shrimp and fry briefly for 2 minutes, until the shrimp turn pink and firm up around the edges. Remove the shrimp from the wok with a slotted spoon and drain on paper towels.

4. Remove all but 2 tablespoons of oil from the wok. Add the spinach and fry until it changes color, 2–3 minutes. Remove from the wok and set aside.

5. Add the garlic and ginger, and stir-fry briefly until aromatic. Add the noodles. Stir-fry and toss with the sesame oil.

6. Make a well in the middle of the wok and add the prepared sauce. Bring to a boil. Add the spinach and the shrimp back into the wok. Mix everything through and serve hot.

PER SERVING Calories: 382 | Fat: 16 grams | Protein: 20 grams | Sodium: 699 milligrams | Fiber: 7 grams | Carbohydrates: 41 grams | Sugar: 3 grams

Oyster Sauce Pork with Cellophane Noodles

Because it resembles a bird's nest, a packet of deep-fried cellophane noodles is sometimes used to replace authentic bird's nest in mock bird's nest soup.

INGREDIENTS | SERVES 4

1 pound boneless pork, cut into bite-size cubes

3 tablespoons soy sauce, divided

1 green onion, cut in thirds

2 stalks celery

2 tablespoons oyster sauce

1 teaspoon sugar

¼ teaspoon Chinese rice wine or dry sherry

½ cup chicken broth

4 cups vegetable oil

1 (2-ounce) package cellophane noodles

Cellophane Noodles

Made from mung bean starch, cellophane noodles are also called bean thread or glass noodles. After soaking they become very absorbent, picking up the flavors of the foods they are cooked with. Deep-frying without soaking first causes them to puff up immediately. Use cellophane noodles in dishes with lots of flavorful sauce.

1. In a large bowl, marinate the pork in 1 tablespoon of soy sauce and the green onion for 30 minutes.

2. Blanch the celery by plunging it briefly into boiling water. Drain well. Cut into thin slices along the diagonal.

3. In a small bowl, combine the oyster sauce, 2 tablespoons soy sauce, sugar, rice wine, and chicken broth. Set aside.

4. Add 4 cups of oil to a preheated wok and heat to at least 350°F. While the oil is heating, remove the string wrappings from the cellophane noodles. When the oil is hot, add the noodles. Deep-fry briefly until it puffs up and forms a "nest." Remove and drain on paper towels. Leave as-is or cut into individual servings.

5. Drain all but 2 tablespoons of oil from the wok. Add the pork and stir-fry until it changes color and is almost cooked through, 4–5 minutes. Remove and drain on paper towels.

6. Add the celery and stir-fry until it turns shiny and is tender, 3–4 minutes. Add the prepared sauce to the middle of the wok and bring to a boil. Add the pork. Mix everything through. Serve over the noodles.

PER SERVING Calories: 514 | Fat: 35 grams | Protein: 26 grams | Sodium: 1,198 milligrams | Fiber: 0 grams | Carbohydrates: 22 grams | Sugar: 5 grams

Crab Rangoon (Chapter 3)

Clams in Black Bean Sauce (Chapter 10)

Wonton Soup (Chapter 4)

Pork Pot Stickers with Rice Wine (Chapter 3)

Quick and Easy Orange Chicken (Chapter 9)

Peanut Sauce (Chapter 2)

Deep-Fried Tofu with Garlic and Chilies
(Chapter 11)

Basic Hong Kong Jook (Chapter 5)

Cold Szechwan Sesame Noodles (Chapter 5)

Chinese Sausage and Cabbage Stir-Fry (Chapter 8)

Spicy Eggplant Stir-Fry (Chapter 12)

Beef with Broccoli (Chapter 7)

Watercress Soup (Chapter 4)

Shumai (Chapter 3)

Almond Jelly (Chapter 13)

Pork Riblets in Black Bean Sauce (Chapter 3)

Spring Rolls (Chapter 3)

Hearty Vegetarian Ramen (Chapter 5)

Har Gow Dumplings (Chapter 3)

Quick and Easy Salt and Pepper Squid
(Chapter 10)

Chicken Fried Rice (Chapter 5)

Char Siu Bao (Chapter 3)

Stir-Fried Bok Choy (Chapter 12)

Char Siu (Chinese Barbecue Pork) (Chapter 8)

CHAPTER 6

Comfort Classics

Mu Shu Pancakes

Add water slowly until you are sure how much is needed. Everything from altitude to the age of the flour can affect the amount required.

INGREDIENTS | MAKES 9 PANCAKES

2 cups all-purpose flour
¾–1 cup boiling water
¼ cup sesame oil

Pancakes for Dinner

Besides making a tasty snack, these pancakes are served with the northern dishes mu shu pork and Peking duck. In the case of mu shu pork, the pork is wrapped in the pancakes, which are brushed with hoisin sauce.

1. Place the flour in a large bowl. Add the boiling water and quickly stir with a wooden spoon.

2. As soon as you can withstand the heat, knead the warm dough on a lightly floured surface until it is smooth. Cover with a damp cloth and let stand for 30 minutes.

3. Cut the dough in half. Roll each half into a 9" cylinder. Using a tape measure, lightly score and cut the dough into 1" pieces. You will have 18 pieces at this point.

4. Shape each piece into a ball and then flatten it into a circle between the palms of your hands. Brush the top of each piece with sesame oil, and then place two pieces on top of each other, oiled sides together.

5. Using a lightly floured rolling pin, roll the pieces into a 5½"–6" circle. (Don't worry if the edges overlap.) Continue with the rest of the dough.

6. Heat a dry pan on low-medium heat. When the pan is hot, add one of the paired pancakes and cook on each side for 2 minutes or until brown bubbles appear (the second side will cook more quickly). Remove from the pan and pull the pancakes apart while they are still hot. Place on a plate and cover with a damp cloth while cooking the remainder.

PER SERVING (1 PANCAKE) Calories: 154 | Fat: 6 grams | Protein: 2 grams | Sodium: 2 milligrams | Fiber: 0 grams | Carbohydrates: 21 grams | Sugar: 0 grams

Restaurant-Style Mu Shu Pork

Softened dried mushrooms absorb the hoisin sauce and other seasonings in this simplified version of a traditional Beijing dish.

INGREDIENTS | SERVES 4

½ pound boneless pork chops

3 green onions

1 tablespoon soy sauce

2½ teaspoons sugar, divided

2 teaspoons cornstarch

½ teaspoon baking soda

4 dried mushrooms

1 tablespoon dark soy sauce

1 tablespoon hoisin sauce

¼ teaspoon sesame oil

2 eggs

¼ teaspoon salt

4 tablespoons vegetable oil, divided

1 slice ginger

1 cup canned bamboo shoots, rinsed and drained

1 cup canned water chestnuts, rinsed and drained

1. Trim any fat from the pork, cut into thin strips, and place in a medium bowl. Chop 1 green onion and add to the bowl along with soy sauce, ½ teaspoon of sugar, cornstarch, and baking soda. Marinate the pork for 30 minutes.

2. Soak the dried mushrooms in hot water for at least 20 minutes to soften. Drain and reserve the soaking liquid. Gently squeeze the mushrooms to remove any excess water and thinly slice. Cut the remaining 2 green onions into 1" pieces.

3. In a small bowl, combine ½ cup of reserved mushroom liquid, dark soy sauce, 2 teaspoons of sugar, hoisin sauce, and sesame oil, and set aside.

4. Lightly beat the eggs and stir in the salt. Add 1 tablespoon of oil to a preheated wok or skillet. When the oil is hot, turn down the heat and add the eggs. Scramble quickly and remove from the wok. Wipe the wok clean if necessary.

5. Add 2 more tablespoons of oil. When the oil is hot, add the pork strips and stir-fry until they turn white and are nearly cooked through, 3–4 minutes. Remove from the wok and set aside.

6. Add 1 tablespoon of oil to the wok. Add the ginger and green onion and stir-fry briefly. Add the mushrooms, bamboo shoots, and water chestnuts. Add the prepared sauce and bring to a boil. Stir in the pork and the scrambled egg. Serve hot.

PER SERVING Calories: 286 | Fat: 18 grams | Protein: 17 grams | Sodium: 1,048 milligrams | Fiber: 2 grams | Carbohydrates: 14 grams | Sugar: 5 grams

Traditional Mu Shu Pork

For an authentic touch, use green onion brushes to brush the hoisin sauce onto the Mu Shu Pancakes (see recipe in this chapter).

INGREDIENTS | SERVES 4

½ pound boneless pork chops

3 green onions

1 tablespoon soy sauce

½ teaspoon sesame oil

2 teaspoons cornstarch

½ teaspoon baking soda

4 dried mushrooms

15 dried lily buds

4 tablespoons wood fungus

2 tablespoons dark soy sauce

2 teaspoons sugar

¼ teaspoon sesame oil

2 eggs

¼ teaspoon salt

3 tablespoons vegetable oil, divided

1 slice ginger

½ cup canned bamboo shoots, rinsed and drained

10 fresh water chestnuts, peeled and cut in half

Mu Shu Pancakes (see recipe in this chapter)

½ cup hoisin sauce

Green Onion Brushes

This attractive garnish is easy to make. Simply slice a green onion into 3" pieces, then, starting in the middle and going left, cut several slits with a pin. Repeat in the other direction. (Leave a small section in the middle untouched so that the green onion doesn't fall apart.)

1. Trim any fat from the pork, cut into thin strips, and place in a medium bowl. Chop 1 green onion and add to the bowl along with the soy sauce, sesame oil, cornstarch, and baking soda. Marinate the pork for 30 minutes.

2. Soak the dried mushrooms, dried lily buds, and wood fungus in hot water for at least 20 minutes to soften. Drain and reserve the mushroom soaking liquid. Gently squeeze the mushrooms to remove any excess water and thinly slice. Cut the remaining 2 green onions into 1" pieces.

3. In a small bowl, combine ½ cup of reserved mushroom liquid, the dark soy sauce, sugar, and sesame oil and set aside.

4. Lightly beat the eggs and stir in the salt. Add 1 tablespoon of oil to a preheated wok or skillet. When the oil is hot, scramble the eggs. Remove from the wok and set aside.

5. Add 2 more tablespoons of oil. When the oil is hot, add the pork strips and stir-fry until they turn white and are nearly cooked through, 4–5 minutes. Add the ginger and green onions and stir-fry briefly. Add the mushrooms, lily buds, wood fungus, bamboo shoots, and water chestnuts.

6. Add the prepared sauce and bring to a boil. Stir in the pork and the scrambled egg.

7. To serve, brush a pancake with the hoisin sauce, add a generous helping of Mu Shu Pork, and roll up the pancake.

PER SERVING (FOR 8 MU SHU PANCAKES) Calories: 630 | Fat: 28 grams | Protein: 24 grams | Sodium: 1,740 milligrams | Fiber: 4 grams | Carbohydrates: 69 grams | Sugar: 12 grams

Mu Shu Chicken

While Mu Shu Pork is a popular restaurant dish, the basic recipe can be adjusted to use with chicken, beef, and even vegetables.

INGREDIENTS | SERVES 4

½ pound boneless, skinless chicken legs or thighs

1 tablespoon soy sauce

2½ teaspoons sugar, divided

2 teaspoons cornstarch

½ cup water

1 tablespoon dark soy sauce

1 tablespoon hoisin sauce

¼ teaspoon sesame oil

2 eggs

¼ teaspoon salt

4 tablespoons vegetable oil, divided

1 slice ginger, minced

2 green onions, cut into 1" pieces on the diagonal

4 fresh water chestnuts, peeled and cut in half

1. Cut the chicken into thin slices and add to a medium bowl. Add the soy sauce and 2 teaspoons of sugar. Stir in the cornstarch. Marinate the chicken for 30 minutes.

2. In a small bowl, combine the water, dark soy sauce, hoisin sauce, ½ teaspoon of sugar, and sesame oil, and set aside.

3. Lightly beat the eggs and stir in the salt. Add 1 tablespoon of oil to a preheated wok or skillet. When the oil is hot, turn up the heat and scramble the eggs. Scramble quickly and remove from the wok.

4. Add 2 more tablespoons of oil to the wok. When the oil is hot, add the chicken and stir-fry until it changes color and is nearly cooked through, about 4–5 minutes. Remove from the wok and set aside.

5. Add 1 tablespoon of oil to the wok. Add the ginger and green onions and stir-fry until aromatic. Add the water chestnuts.

6. Make a well in the middle of the wok, add the prepared sauce and bring to a boil. Stir in the chicken and scrambled egg. Serve hot.

PER SERVING Calories: 264 | Fat: 18 grams | Protein: 15 grams | Sodium: 788 milligrams | Fiber: 0 grams | Carbohydrates: 8 grams | Sugar: 4 grams

Mu Shu Beef

For a more flavorful dish, try marinating the beef in oyster sauce,
sugar, and cornstarch, adding the cornstarch last.

INGREDIENTS | SERVES 4

½ cup water

1 tablespoon dark soy sauce

1 tablespoon plus 1 teaspoon hoisin sauce

1 teaspoon sugar

1 teaspoon oyster sauce

¼ teaspoon sesame oil

2 eggs, lightly beaten

¼ teaspoon salt

4 tablespoons vegetable oil, divided

½ pound lean beef, thinly sliced

1 slice ginger, minced

½ cup mung bean sprouts, rinsed and drained

1. In a small bowl, combine the water, dark soy sauce, hoisin sauce, sugar, oyster sauce, and sesame oil, and set aside.

2. Mix the eggs with the salt. Add 1 tablespoon of oil to a preheated wok or skillet. When the oil is hot, scramble the eggs and remove from the wok.

3. Add 2 more tablespoons of oil to the wok. When the oil is hot, add the beef and stir-fry until it changes color and is nearly cooked through, about 4 minutes. Remove from the wok and set aside.

4. Add 1 tablespoon of oil to the wok. Add the ginger and stir-fry briefly until aromatic. Add the bean sprouts. Add the prepared sauce and bring to a boil. Add the beef and the scrambled egg. Mix everything together and serve hot.

PER SERVING Calories: 265 | Fat: 20 grams | Protein: 15 grams | Sodium: 587 milligrams | Fiber: 0 grams | Carbohydrates: 4 grams | Sugar: 3 grams

Mu Shu Vegetables

The combination of eggs and vegetables makes this a nutritious, quick, and easy meal for busy weekdays.

INGREDIENTS | SERVES 4

2 bok choy stalks

¼ cup water

¼ cup chicken broth

1 tablespoon dark soy sauce

1 teaspoon sugar

¼ teaspoon salt

2 eggs, lightly beaten

3 tablespoons vegetable oil, divided

4 fresh mushrooms, sliced

½ red bell pepper, seeded and cut into thin strips

½ teaspoon sesame oil

Wrap It Up!

Meat and vegetables cooked in the mu shu style make a great filling for tortilla wraps. To make, adjust the recipe by draining some of the sauce so that the filling isn't too wet. Lay the wrap in front of you and add ½ cup of filling to the bottom. Fold over the right side of the wrap. Fold the bottom of the wrap over the food, and continue rolling up the wrap. For added variety, try the flavored wraps, such as spinach, pesto, or garlic.

1. Separate the bok choy stalks and leaves. Cut the stalks diagonally into 1" pieces. Cut the leaves crosswise into 1" pieces.

2. In a small bowl, combine the water, chicken broth, dark soy sauce, and sugar. Set aside.

3. Stir ¼ teaspoon of salt into the eggs. Add 1 tablespoon of oil to a preheated wok or skillet. When the oil is hot, scramble the eggs. Remove from the wok and set aside.

4. Clean out the wok and add 2 tablespoons of oil. When the oil is hot, add the bok choy stalks. Stir-fry for about 1 minute, then add the mushrooms and red pepper. Stir-fry briefly and add the bok choy leaves.

5. Add the prepared sauce in the middle of the wok. Bring to a boil. Stir in the scrambled egg. Drizzle the sesame oil over the vegetables. Serve hot.

PER SERVING Calories: 160 | Fat: 13 grams | Protein: 5 grams | Sodium: 498 milligrams | Fiber: 1 gram | Carbohydrates: 6 grams | Sugar: 3 grams

Basic Sweet-and-Sour Pork

For extra flavor, use 2 tablespoons of black rice vinegar and ¼ cup of white rice vinegar when making the sauce.

INGREDIENTS | SERVES 4

1 pound pork loin, center cut, bone-in

1 tablespoon soy sauce

1 tablespoon cornstarch

1 teaspoon baking soda

1 (20-ounce) can pineapple chunks in juice

½ red bell pepper

½ green bell pepper

¼ pound baby carrots

⅓ cup rice vinegar

½ cup brown sugar

1 tablespoon Worcestershire sauce

¼ cup ketchup

¼ cup water

3 tablespoons vegetable oil, divided

2 teaspoons cornstarch mixed with 4 teaspoons water

1. Cut away the bone from the pork and remove any fat. Cut the pork into cubes and add to a medium bowl. Add the soy sauce, cornstarch, and baking soda to the pork. Marinate the pork in the refrigerator for 1½ hours.

2. Open the can of pineapple chunks and remove ⅔ cup of pineapple and ½ cup of juice. Set aside. Blanch the peppers and carrots by plunging them briefly into boiling water. Remove the seeds from the green and red peppers, and cut into cubes. Cut the carrots in half.

3. In a small saucepan over medium-high heat, bring the rice vinegar, brown sugar, Worcestershire sauce, ketchup, reserved pineapple juice, and water to a boil. Reduce the heat to low and keep warm.

4. Add 2 tablespoons of oil to a preheated wok or skillet. When the oil is hot, add the pork. Stir-fry until it changes color and is nearly cooked through, about 5 minutes. Remove from the wok and drain on paper towels.

5. Add 1 tablespoon of oil. When the oil is hot, add the carrots. Stir-fry for 1 minute and add the red and green peppers.

6. Bring the sauce back up to a boil over medium-high heat. Add the cornstarch-and-water mixture, stirring vigorously to thicken.

7. Mix the pineapple chunks in with the sauce in the saucepan. Push the vegetables up to the sides of the wok and add the prepared sauce in the middle. Add the pork back into the wok. Mix thoroughly and serve hot.

PER SERVING Calories: 462 | Fat: 20 grams | Protein: 23 grams | Sodium: 881 milligrams | Fiber: 1 gram | Carbohydrates: 47 grams | Sugar: 39 grams

Deep-Fried Sweet-and-Sour Pork

This is one of the most popular dishes served at Chinese restaurants.
The sweet-and-sour sauce works well with pork, spareribs, and chicken.

INGREDIENTS | SERVES 4

1 pound pork loin, center cut, deboned and cubed
1 tablespoon soy sauce
3 tablespoons cornstarch, divided
1 teaspoon baking soda
½ red bell pepper
½ green bell pepper
¼ pound baby carrots
3 tablespoons flour
2 medium eggs
4 cups vegetable oil
⅓ cup rice vinegar
½ cup brown sugar
1 tablespoon Worcestershire sauce
¼ cup ketchup
½ cup juice from canned pineapple
¼ cup water
2 teaspoons cornstarch mixed with
4 teaspoons water
⅔ cup canned pineapple chunks

1. In a medium bowl, mix the pork cubes, soy sauce, 1 tablespoon of cornstarch, and baking soda. Marinate in the refrigerator for 1½ hours.

2. Blanch the peppers and carrots in boiling water. Deseed and cube the green and red peppers. Cut the carrots in half.

3. In a shallow bowl, combine the flour, remaining cornstarch, and eggs. Mix until a batter forms. Coat the pork in the batter.

4. Add 4 cups of oil to the wok and heat to at least 350°F. Deep-fry the pork cubes in batches, turning occasionally, until golden, 5–7 minutes. Remove and drain on paper towels.

5. Increase the oil temperature to 400°F.

6. While waiting for the oil to heat, bring the rice vinegar, brown sugar, Worcestershire sauce, ketchup, pineapple juice, and water to boil in a small saucepan over medium-high heat. Reduce the heat to low.

7. When the oil is ready, add the pork cubes. Deep-fry a second time until they turn brown and crispy, about 5 minutes. Remove and drain on paper towels.

8. Remove all but 2 tablespoons of oil from the wok. When the oil is hot, add the carrots. Stir-fry for 1 minute and add the red and green peppers.

9. Bring the brown sugar sauce back up to a boil over medium-high heat. Add the cornstarch-and-water mixture, stirring vigorously to thicken. Add the canned pineapple.

10. Push the vegetables up to the sides of the wok and add the brown sugar sauce in the middle. Add the pork back into the wok. Mix thoroughly and serve hot.

PER SERVING Calories: 720 | Fat: 39 grams | Protein: 26 grams | Sodium: 914 milligrams | Fiber: 2 grams | Carbohydrates: 63 grams | Sugar: 40 grams

Sweet-and-Sour Chicken

This is a variation on another popular restaurant dish, Chinese pineapple chicken, where the chicken is deep-fried in batter before mixing with the sauce.

INGREDIENTS | SERVES 4

¾ cup pineapple juice

2 tablespoons rice vinegar

1 teaspoon black rice vinegar

1 tablespoon soy sauce

2 tablespoons vegetable oil

1½ cups chopped boneless, skinless chicken thighs

2 tablespoons plus 1 teaspoon sugar

½ green bell pepper, seeded and cut into bite-size cubes

½ red bell pepper, seeded and cut into bite-size cubes

¼ cup pineapple chunks

1 tablespoon cornstarch mixed with 4 tablespoons water

Or Make It Pineapple-Orange Chicken

To transform the sweet-and-sour sauce into a pineapple-orange sauce, just decrease the amount of pineapple juice to ½ cup and add 1 tablespoon plus 1 teaspoon of orange juice. Include or leave out the peppers and pineapple chunks as desired.

1. In a small bowl, mix together the pineapple juice, rice vinegar, black rice vinegar, and soy sauce, and set aside.

2. Add the oil to a preheated wok or skillet. When the oil is hot, add the chicken. Stir-fry until it changes color and is nearly cooked through, 4–5 minutes.

3. In a medium saucepan, bring the pineapple juice mixture to a boil over medium-high heat. Add the sugar, stirring to dissolve. Add the green and red peppers and the pineapple chunks. Bring back to a boil and add the cornstarch-and-water mixture, stirring quickly to thicken.

4. Pour the sauce over the stir-fried chicken and heat through.

PER SERVING Calories: 302 | Fat: 10 grams | Protein: 28 grams | Sodium: 516 milligrams | Fiber: 1 gram | Carbohydrates: 24 grams | Sugar: 15 grams

Sweet-and-Sour Chicken Wings

Unused wing tips are perfect for making soup stock. Serve the sweet-and-sour wings with watercress soup for an interesting combination of flavors.

INGREDIENTS | SERVES 5

5 chicken wings

Sweet-and-Sour Sauce with Ketchup (see recipe in Chapter 2)

1. Cut the wing tip off the wings. Discard tips or reserve for another use. Blanch the wings in boiling water for 2 minutes and drain.

2. Brush the chicken wings with the sauce, making sure both sides are covered. Reserve any leftover sauce. Marinate the chicken wings for 1 hour.

3. Preheat the oven to 400°F. Place the wings on a baking sheet. Brush the chicken with half the leftover sauce and bake the chicken wings for 30 minutes. Turn the wings over and brush with the remainder of the leftover sauce and bake for another 30 minutes. Remove from the stove and cool.

PER SERVING Calories: 126 | Fat: 4 grams | Protein: 5 grams | Sodium: 300 milligrams | Fiber: 0 grams | Carbohydrates: 14 grams | Sugar: 12 grams

Sweet-and-Sour Shrimp

The delicate sweet flavor of pineapple goes well with shrimp.
Serve with Basic Scented Rice (see recipe in Chapter 5).

INGREDIENTS | SERVES 4

⅓ cup rice vinegar

¼ cup brown sugar

2 tablespoons ketchup

1 tablespoon soy sauce

½ cup water

2 teaspoons cornstarch mixed with 4 teaspoons water

½ cup pineapple chunks

½ green bell pepper, seeded and cut into bite-size cubes

½ red bell pepper, seeded and cut into bite-size cubes

2 tablespoons vegetable oil

20 large fresh shrimp, peeled and deveined

1. In a small saucepan, combine the rice vinegar, brown sugar, ketchup, soy sauce, and water, and bring to a boil over medium-high heat.

2. Stir in the cornstarch-and-water mixture, stirring vigorously to thicken. Add the pineapple and peppers. Turn the heat to low and keep the sauce warm while stir-frying the shrimp.

3. Add the oil to a preheated wok or skillet. When the oil is hot, add the shrimp. Stir-fry briefly until they are cooked, 4–5 minutes. Remove from the wok.

4. Pour the sauce over the shrimp and serve hot.

PER SERVING Calories: 192 | Fat: 7 grams | Protein: 8 grams | Sodium: 392 milligrams | Fiber: 1 gram | Carbohydrates: 22 grams | Sugar: 19 grams

Sweet-and-Sour Fish

Ginger makes a frequent appearance in seafood dishes because it helps to mask fishy odors.

INGREDIENTS | SERVES 6

1 pound fish fillets

2 teaspoons Chinese rice wine or dry sherry

2 tablespoons soy sauce

½ cup rice vinegar

½ cup brown sugar

½ cup water

3 tablespoons tomato paste

3 tablespoons oil, divided

2 slices ginger, minced

1 cup mushrooms, thinly sliced

1 stalk celery, thinly sliced on the diagonal

⅓ cup canned bamboo shoots, shredded

1 teaspoon cornstarch

4 teaspoons water

1 green onion, thinly sliced on the diagonal

1. Wash the fish fillets and pat dry. Cut them into pieces approximately 2" × ½" and place in a medium bowl. Marinate the fish in the rice wine and soy sauce for 30 minutes.

2. In a small bowl, combine the rice vinegar, brown sugar, water, and tomato paste. Set aside.

3. Add 2 tablespoons of oil to a preheated wok or skillet. When the oil is hot, add the fish and stir-fry until it is nicely browned all over, about 5 minutes. Remove and drain on paper towels.

4. Add 1 tablespoon of oil to the wok. Add the ginger and stir-fry briefly until aromatic. Add the mushrooms. Stir-fry for 1 minute, then add the celery and the bamboo shoots. Stir-fry until tender.

5. Push the vegetables up to the side of the wok and add the prepared sauce in the middle. Bring to a boil. Mix the cornstarch and water, and add to the wok, stirring quickly to thicken. Add the fish and stir in the green onion. Cook for 2–3 more minutes and serve hot.

PER SERVING Calories: 258 | Fat: 11 grams | Protein: 16 grams | Sodium: 487 milligrams | Fiber: 1 gram | Carbohydrates: 22 grams | Sugar: 19 grams

Sweet-and-Sour Spareribs

This recipe can easily be doubled to serve as a main dish for 6–8 people.

INGREDIENTS | SERVES 4

1½ pounds spareribs

4 teaspoons sugar, divided

2 tablespoons plus 1 teaspoon rice vinegar, divided

2 tablespoons ketchup

2 tablespoons Worcestershire sauce

4 tablespoons soy sauce

2 tablespoons vegetable oil

1. Separate ribs into serving-size pieces. Marinate in 1 teaspoon of sugar and 1 teaspoon of rice vinegar for 30 minutes.

2. In a small bowl, mix together 3 teaspoons of sugar, 2 tablespoons of rice vinegar, the ketchup, Worcestershire sauce, and soy sauce, and set aside.

3. Add the oil to a preheated wok or skillet. When the oil is hot, add the ribs and stir-fry for about 5 minutes, until brown.

4. Add the prepared sauce, turn down the heat, cover, and simmer the ribs for 45 minutes to 1 hour.

PER SERVING Calories: 259 | Fat: 20 grams | Protein: 10 grams | Sodium: 1,211 milligrams | Fiber: 0 grams | Carbohydrates: 8 grams | Sugar: 7 grams

Egg Foo Yung Hoisin Sauce

This savory combination of oyster and hoisin sauce makes a nice accompaniment to Egg Foo Yung with Shrimp (see recipe in this chapter).

INGREDIENTS | MAKES ⅓ CUP

1 tablespoon oyster sauce

2 teaspoons hoisin sauce

1 teaspoon Chinese rice wine or dry sherry

2 tablespoons water

1 teaspoon cornstarch mixed with 4 teaspoons water

1. In a small saucepan, bring the oyster sauce, hoisin sauce, rice wine, and water to a boil.

2. Add the cornstarch-and-water mixture and stir vigorously to thicken. Serve with egg foo yung.

PER SERVING (2 TABLESPOONS) Calories: 19 | Fat: 0 grams | Protein: 0 grams | Sodium: 280 milligrams | Fiber: 0 grams | Carbohydrates: 4 grams | Sugar: 1 gram

Egg Foo Yung Sauce with Beef Broth

*This robust sauce goes well with omelet dishes containing meat,
such as Egg Foo Yung with Pork (see recipe in this chapter).*

INGREDIENTS | MAKES ½ CUP

½ cup beef broth

1 teaspoon sugar

¼ teaspoon sesame oil

1 tablespoon cornstarch mixed with
4 tablespoons water

1. In a small saucepan over medium-high heat, bring the beef broth, sugar, and sesame oil to a boil.

2. Add the cornstarch-and-water mixture, stirring vigorously. Serve with egg foo yung.

PER SERVING (2 TABLESPOONS) Calories: 37 | Fat: 1 gram | Protein: 0 grams | Sodium: 195 milligrams | Fiber: 0 grams | Carbohydrates: 5 grams | Sugar: 2 grams

Egg Foo Yung Chicken Sauce

*For a thicker sauce, add 1 teaspoon of cornstarch mixed with 4 teaspoons of water.
Pour the sauce over the egg foo yung or serve separately.*

INGREDIENTS | MAKES ½ CUP

½ cup chicken broth or stock

1 tablespoon soy sauce

1 tablespoon Chinese rice wine or dry sherry

¼ teaspoon sesame oil

Pinch freshly ground black pepper

Combine all the ingredients in a small saucepan over medium-high heat and bring to a boil. Serve with egg foo yung.

PER SERVING (2 TABLESPOONS) Calories: 36 | Fat: 0 grams | Protein: 1 gram | Sodium: 581 milligrams | Fiber: 0 grams | Carbohydrates: 7 grams | Sugar: 3 grams

Vegetable Egg Foo Yung

*In this Chinese version of an omelet, the fillings are mixed with
the egg prior to cooking, not added in the pan.*

INGREDIENTS | SERVES 4

1 cup mung bean sprouts

6 eggs

¼ teaspoon salt

⅛ teaspoon pepper

1 teaspoon Chinese rice wine or dry
sherry

½ teaspoon sugar

½ red bell pepper, seeded and cut into
bite-size pieces

4 mushrooms, thinly sliced

1 green onion, thinly sliced

1 cube fermented bean curd, mashed

2 tablespoons vegetable oil

Raw or Cooked?

Lightly cooking vegetables by blanching or
sautéing prior to combining with the egg
mixture helps coax out their natural flavors.
However, if you prefer a crisper texture and
higher nutrient content, feel free to skip
this step. Another option is to top the egg
foo yung with an assortment of raw veg-
gies such as bean sprouts and red and
green bell peppers.

1. Blanch the bean sprouts by plunging them briefly into
   boiling water, and drain.

2. In a large bowl, lightly beat the eggs. Stir in the salt,
   pepper, rice wine, and sugar. Add the bean sprouts,
   red pepper, mushrooms, green onion, and mashed
   bean curd. Mix well.

3. Add 2 tablespoons of oil to a preheated wok or skillet.
   When the oil is hot, add a quarter of the egg mixture.
   Cook until the bottom is cooked, then turn the omelet
   over and cook the other side, about 5 minutes per side,
   watching carefully that the egg fu yung is browned but
   not burned. Continue with the remainder of the
   mixture, making 4 omelets. Serve with an egg foo yung
   sauce, Vegetarian Brown Sauce (see recipe in Chapter
   2), or soy sauce.

PER SERVING Calories: 262 | Fat: 19 grams | Protein:
15 grams | Sodium: 1,187 milligrams | Fiber: 2 grams |
Carbohydrates: 6 grams | Sugar: 3 grams

Egg Foo Yung with Shrimp

This is a great dish for a weekend brunch or days when you want to make something special. Enjoy as is, or serve with Egg Foo Yung Hoisin Sauce (see recipe in this chapter).

INGREDIENTS | SERVES 4

½ cup mung bean sprouts

4 snow peas

3½ tablespoons vegetable oil

1 oyster mushroom cap, thinly sliced

2 button mushrooms, thinly sliced

6 eggs

¼ teaspoon salt

⅛ teaspoon pepper

1 tablespoon oyster sauce

½ teaspoon sugar

¼ red bell pepper, seeded and sliced into thin slices

1 green onion, cut into 1" pieces

6 ounces cooked shrimp, peeled, deveined, and chopped

Egg Foo Yung Without the Sauce

Although they taste fine on their own, egg foo yung dishes are normally meant to be accompanied by a savory sauce. If not serving a sauce, consider adding small amounts of powerful seasonings such as chili paste or hoisin sauce to the egg mixture.

1. Blanch the bean sprouts and snow peas by plunging them briefly into boiling water and quickly removing. Drain well. Chop the snow peas.

2. Add ½ tablespoon of oil to a preheated wok or skillet. When the oil is hot, sauté the oyster mushroom slices briefly, just until they collapse. (You can sauté the button mushrooms as well or leave them raw.) Remove from the wok and set aside.

3. In a large bowl, lightly beat the eggs. Stir in the salt, pepper, oyster sauce, and sugar. Mix in the vegetables and the cooked shrimp.

4. Add 2 tablespoons of oil to a preheated wok or skillet. When the oil is hot, add a quarter of the egg mixture. Cook until the bottom is cooked, then turn over and cook the other side, about 5 minutes per side, watching to make sure the egg fu yung is browned but not burned. Continue with the remainder of the egg mixture, adding more oil if necessary, making 4 omelets.

PER SERVING Calories: 323 | Fat: 23 grams | Protein: 20 grams | Sodium: 578 milligrams | Fiber: 1 gram | Carbohydrates: 6 grams | Sugar: 2 grams

Egg Foo Yung with Pork

Barbecued or roast pork works well in this recipe. Be sure to remove any bones before adding the pork to the egg mixture. Serve with an egg foo yung sauce or soy sauce.

INGREDIENTS | SERVES 6

⅔ cup mung bean sprouts

1 stalk celery

5 tablespoons vegetable oil

½ teaspoon salt, divided

6 eggs

⅛ teaspoon pepper

1 teaspoon Chinese rice wine or dry sherry

1 cup cooked pork, cut into small pieces

¼ red bell pepper, seeded and sliced into thin slices

4 button mushroom caps, thinly sliced

1. Blanch the bean sprouts by plunging them briefly into boiling water. Blanch the celery by plunging it into the boiling water and boiling for 2–3 minutes. Drain the blanched vegetables thoroughly. Cut the celery into thin slices on the diagonal.

2. Add 2 teaspoons of oil to a preheated wok or skillet. When the oil is hot, add the celery and stir-fry on medium-high heat. Add ¼ teaspoon of salt. Remove the cooked celery from the wok.

3. Lightly beat the eggs. Stir in the pepper, ¼ teaspoon of salt, and the rice wine. Add the pork and vegetables, mixing well.

4. Add 2 tablespoons of oil to a preheated wok or skillet. When the oil is hot, add one-sixth of the egg mixture. Cook until the bottom is cooked, then turn over and cook the other side, about 5 minutes per side, watching to ensure that the egg fu yung is browned but not burned. Continue with the remainder of the egg mixture, making 6 omelets. Add more oil while cooking as necessary.

PER SERVING Calories: 256 | Fat: 20 grams | Protein: 16 grams | Sodium: 395 milligrams | Fiber: 0 grams | Carbohydrates: 2 grams | Sugar: 1 gram

Pork Chop Suey

Vegetables take center stage in this dish; the meat is there only to add a bit of flavor.

INGREDIENTS | SERVES 4

½ pound pork tenderloin

2 teaspoons Chinese rice wine or dry sherry

2 teaspoons soy sauce

2 teaspoons baking soda

2 tablespoons oyster sauce

2 tablespoons chicken broth or stock

1 teaspoon sugar

4 tablespoons vegetable oil, divided

6 fresh mushrooms, thinly sliced

1 stalk celery, thinly sliced on the diagonal

2 stalks bok choy including leaves, thinly sliced on the diagonal

1 (8-ounce) can bamboo shoots, drained

2 green onions, thinly sliced on the diagonal

1. Cut the pork into thin slices and place in a medium bowl. Marinate the pork with the rice wine, soy sauce, and baking soda for 30 minutes.

2. In a small bowl combine the oyster sauce, chicken broth, and sugar. Set aside.

3. Add 2 tablespoons of oil to a preheated wok or skillet. When the oil is hot, add the pork. Stir-fry until it changes color and is nearly cooked through, about 5 minutes. Remove from the wok.

4. Add 1 tablespoon of oil to the wok. When the oil is hot, add the mushrooms and stir-fry for about 1 minute. Add the celery and the bok choy stalks, then the bamboo shoots, stir-frying each for about 1 minute in the middle of the wok before adding the next vegetable. (If the wok is too crowded, stir-fry each vegetable separately.)

5. Add 1 more tablespoon of oil, pushing the vegetables up to the side of the wok until the oil is heated. Add the bok choy leaves and the green onion.

6. Add the prepared sauce to the middle of the wok and bring to a boil. Add the pork. Mix thoroughly and serve hot.

PER SERVING Calories: 221 | Fat: 15 grams | Protein: 14 grams | Sodium: 1,253 milligrams | Fiber: 1 gram | Carbohydrates: 7 grams | Sugar: 3 grams

Vegetable Chop Suey

This is a dish with a lot of flexibility. Adapt it to your personal taste. Don't have any bok choy on hand? You can use broccoli instead of bok choy and green beans instead of snow peas.

INGREDIENTS | SERVES 4

1 bunch bok choy

4 tablespoons vegetable oil, divided

¼ teaspoon salt

1½ tablespoons water

½ teaspoon minced ginger

½ teaspoon minced garlic

½ red onion, chopped

1 green bell pepper, seeded and cut into thin strips

1 red bell pepper, seeded and cut into thin strips

½ pound snow peas, trimmed

1 cup sliced fresh mushrooms

1 teaspoon sugar

½ cup water chestnuts, peeled and sliced

1 carrot, thinly sliced on the diagonal

½ cup mung bean sprouts, rinsed and drained

1 tablespoon cornstarch mixed with 4 tablespoons water

2 tablespoons oyster sauce

1. Separate the bok choy stalks and leaves. Cut the stalks diagonally and cut the leaves across.

2. Add 2 tablespoons of oil to a preheated wok or frying pan. When the oil is ready, add the bok choy stalks. Cook for about 1 minute, then add the leaves. Add the salt, and sprinkle with water. Cover and cook on medium heat until the bok choy is tender but still firm, 3–4 minutes. Remove and set aside.

3. Wipe out the wok with a paper towel and add 2 tablespoons of oil. When the oil is hot, add the ginger and garlic and stir-fry until aromatic. Add the red onion and stir-fry. Remove from the wok and set aside.

4. Add the green and red peppers and the snow peas to the wok. Stir-fry for about 1 minute, then add the mushrooms and sugar and continue stir-frying. Remove from the wok and set aside.

5. Add the water chestnuts and carrot to the wok. Stir-fry for 1 minute, then add the bean sprouts.

6. Return all vegetables to the wok and mix well.

7. In a small bowl, combine cornstarch mixture with oyster sauce. Make a well in the center and gradually add the cornstarch/oyster sauce mixture, stirring to thicken. Bring to a boil, remove from heat, and serve hot.

PER SERVING Calories: 260 | Fat: 15 grams | Protein: 8 grams | Sodium: 549 milligrams | Fiber: 7 grams | Carbohydrates: 27 grams | Sugar: 11 grams

CHAPTER 7

Beef Dishes

Basic Beef Stir-Fry

This is a good basic recipe for marinating and stir-frying beef that you can adapt according to your tastes and the ingredients you have on hand.

INGREDIENTS | SERVES 2

½ pound lean beef

2 teaspoons soy sauce

1 teaspoon cornstarch

¼ teaspoon baking soda

3 tablespoons vegetable oil, divided

1 clove garlic, smashed

1 tablespoon Chinese rice wine or dry sherry

½ teaspoon sugar

Searing Meat

While stir-frying is normally a hands-on process, when cooking meat it's best to give the spatula a brief rest. Lay the meat out flat in the wok and brown for about 30 seconds before stir-frying.

1. Cut the beef across the grain into thin strips and place in a medium bowl. Add the soy sauce, cornstarch, and baking soda to the meat, in that order. Use your hands to mix in the cornstarch and baking soda. Marinate the meat for 30 minutes, add 1 tablespoon of oil, and marinate for another 30 minutes.

2. Add the remaining oil to a preheated wok or skillet. When the oil is hot, add the garlic and stir-fry about 30 seconds until aromatic. Add the beef, laying it flat on the wok. Let the meat cook for 1 minute. Turn it over to brown on the other side and then begin stir-frying. When it is nearly cooked through, another 2–3 minutes, add the rice wine and sugar. When the meat is cooked, remove from the wok and drain on paper towels.

PER SERVING Calories: 374 | Fat: 27 grams | Protein: 24 grams | Sodium: 620 milligrams | Fiber: 0 grams | Carbohydrates: 6 grams | Sugar: 3 grams

Mongolian Beef with Vegetables

This northern Chinese favorite makes a complete meal when served with rice.
For a more authentic dish, use bamboo shoots instead of baby corn.

INGREDIENTS | SERVES 4

1 pound sirloin or flank steak

1 egg white

⅛ teaspoon salt

1½ teaspoons sesame oil, divided

1 tablespoon cornstarch

1 cup plus 1½ tablespoons vegetable oil, divided

2 garlic cloves, minced

½ teaspoon chili sauce

1 (15-ounce) can baby corn, rinsed and drained

1 tablespoon Chinese rice wine or dry sherry

2 tablespoons hoisin sauce

1 tablespoon dark soy sauce

½ teaspoon sugar

1½ teaspoons cornstarch

2 tablespoons water

2 green onions, diagonally sliced into thirds

1. Slice the beef across the grain into thin strips and place in a medium bowl. Add the egg white, salt, 1 teaspoon of sesame oil, and cornstarch to the beef, adding the cornstarch last. Marinate the beef for 30 minutes. Add 1½ tablespoons of oil and marinate for another 30 minutes.

2. Add 1 cup of oil to a preheated wok or skillet. When the oil is hot, carefully slide the beef into the wok, a few pieces at a time. Fry the beef until it changes color, 3–4 minutes. Remove from the wok with a slotted spoon and drain on paper towels.

3. Remove all but 2 tablespoons of oil. When the oil is hot, add the garlic and chili sauce. Stir-fry briefly until the garlic is aromatic, about 30 seconds. Add the baby corn.

4. Add the beef back into the wok. Add the rice wine, hoisin sauce, dark soy sauce, and sugar.

5. In a small bowl, mix the cornstarch and water, and add to the middle of the wok, stirring vigorously to thicken.

6. Mix all the ingredients together thoroughly. Stir in the green onion. Drizzle with ½ teaspoon of sesame oil and serve hot.

PER SERVING Calories: 442 | Fat: 27 grams | Protein: 27 grams | Sodium: 680 milligrams | Fiber: 1 gram | Carbohydrates: 22 grams | Sugar: 4 grams

Mongolian Beef with Rice Noodles

Leeks are a popular vegetable in northern China, where cooks rely on hardy vegetables that can survive cold winters and a short growing season.

INGREDIENTS | SERVES 6

1 pound sirloin or flank steak

3 tablespoons dark soy sauce, divided

1 tablespoon Chinese rice wine or dry sherry

1 teaspoon sesame oil

1 tablespoon cornstarch

8 ounces rice vermicelli noodles

1 bunch leeks

2 tablespoons hoisin sauce

½ teaspoon sugar

½ teaspoon chili sauce

1½ cups vegetable oil

2 garlic cloves, minced

1½ teaspoons cornstarch

2 tablespoons water

1. Slice the beef across the grain into thin slices and place in a medium bowl. Add 2 tablespoons of dark soy sauce, the rice wine, sesame oil, and cornstarch, adding the cornstarch last. Marinate the beef for 30 minutes.

2. Soak the rice vermicelli in hot water for 15–20 minutes to soften. Drain thoroughly.

3. Wash the leek bunch, and cut into slices about 1½" long.

4. In a small bowl, mix together the hoisin sauce, sugar, chili sauce, and 1 tablespoon of dark soy sauce. Set aside.

5. Heat the oil to 350°F in a preheated wok. When the oil is hot, add the rice vermicelli. Deep-fry until they puff up and turn crispy. Remove and drain on paper towels.

6. Remove all but 2 tablespoons of oil. When the oil is hot, add the garlic and stir-fry briefly until aromatic. Add the beef and stir-fry until it changes color and is nearly cooked through, 3–4 minutes. Remove and drain on paper towels.

7. Add more oil, if necessary. Add the leeks to the wok. Stir-fry for about 1 minute. Add the prepared sauce to the middle of the wok.

8. In a small bowl, mix the cornstarch and water and add to the sauce in the wok, stirring to thicken. Bring to a boil.

9. Add the beef back into the wok and mix all the ingredients together. Serve over the rice noodles.

PER SERVING Calories: 408 | Fat: 18 grams | Protein: 18 grams | Sodium: 722 milligrams | Fiber: 1 gram | Carbohydrates: 39 grams | Sugar: 3 grams

Steak Kew

This Cantonese dish is popular at many restaurants. The filet mignon makes it especially luxurious. For everyday eating, a different cut of meat may be substituted.

INGREDIENTS | SERVES 4

1 tablespoon oyster sauce

1 tablespoon soy sauce

½ teaspoon sugar

2 teaspoons cornstarch

¾ pound filet mignon, cut into 1" cubes

2 tablespoons peanut oil

1 clove garlic, chopped

3 slices ginger, minced

1 scallion, chopped

1 cup snow pea pods

½ carrot, cut into coins

1 cup chopped bok choy

1 cup sliced mushrooms, shiitake or variety of your choice

2 tablespoons Xiaoshing rice wine

1. In a medium bowl, combine the oyster and soy sauces, sugar, and cornstarch and add the cubed beef. Mix well and marinate 15–30 minutes.

2. Heat the wok over a medium-high flame and swirl in the peanut oil. Add the garlic, ginger, scallion, pea pods, carrots, bok choy, and mushrooms, stir-frying until the pea pods turn bright green and the bok choy leaves just begin to wilt, 5–7 minutes total. Sprinkle in the cooking wine, and cover to allow the vegetables to steam for 1 minute.

3. Add the marinated beef to the wok and stir-fry 2–3 minutes, turning the meat to ensure that it cooks through evenly. Add water, a tablespoon at a time, if the sauce becomes too thick.

PER SERVING Calories: 367 | Fat: 25 grams | Protein: 19 grams | Sodium: 496 milligrams | Fiber: 2 grams | Carbohydrates: 14 grams | Sugar: 5 grams

Beef with Peppers

Eye of round is another good cut to use in this dish—it is one of the leanest cuts of beef and is also very tender.

INGREDIENTS | SERVES 6

1½ pounds flank steak

2 tablespoons dark soy sauce

2 tablespoons Chinese rice wine or dry sherry, divided

1 teaspoon sesame oil

1 tablespoon cornstarch

¼ cup water

2 tablespoons soy sauce

1 teaspoon sugar

4½ tablespoons vegetable oil, divided

2 garlic cloves, chopped

2 slices ginger, chopped

½ red bell pepper, seeded and cut into thin strips

½ green bell pepper, seeded and cut into thin strips

½ cup canned bamboo shoots, rinsed and drained

Why Cut Meat Across the Grain?

The "grains" running across a piece of flank steak are muscle fibers. Since the muscle is the part of the body that does all the work, these fibers are tough. Cutting the meat across—instead of along with—the grain shortens the muscle fibers, giving the meat a more tender texture. This technique is not as important with pork and chicken, as the meat is more tender to begin with.

1. Cut the beef in thin slices across the grain and place the slices in a medium bowl. Mix in the dark soy sauce, 1 tablespoon of rice wine, sesame oil, and cornstarch, adding the cornstarch last. Marinate the beef for 30 minutes.

2. In a small bowl, mix together the water, 1 tablespoon of rice wine, soy sauce, and sugar. Set aside.

3. Add 3 tablespoons of oil to a preheated wok or skillet. Add the garlic and ginger and stir-fry briefly until aromatic. Add the beef and stir-fry in batches until it changes color, 3–4 minutes. Remove and set aside.

4. Wipe the wok with a paper towel. Add 1½ tablespoons of oil to the wok. When the oil is hot, add the red and green peppers. Stir-fry briefly and add the bamboo shoots. Add the prepared sauce and bring to a boil.

5. Add the beef. Mix everything through and serve hot.

PER SERVING Calories: 295 | Fat: 18 grams | Protein: 26 grams | Sodium: 778 milligrams | Fiber: 1 gram | Carbohydrates: 5 grams | Sugar: 2 grams

Beef with Tomatoes

Blanching tomatoes makes the skin easy to peel off.

INGREDIENTS | SERVES 4

1 pound round or flank steak

2 tablespoons dark soy sauce

½ teaspoon salt

⅛ teaspoon pepper, or to taste

2 teaspoons cornstarch

½ teaspoon baking soda

4 large tomatoes

4 tablespoons vegetable oil, divided

3 slices ginger, minced

½ cup beef broth

1 tablespoon oyster sauce

1 teaspoon sugar

1 tablespoon cornstarch

4 tablespoons water

¼ teaspoon sesame oil

Baking Soda—The Secret Tenderizer

As a general rule of thumb, you can use ½ teaspoon of baking soda per pound of meat in a marinade. When cooking with a very tough cut of meat, add the baking soda alone first. Use your fingers to rub it over the meat. Wait 20 minutes and then rinse thoroughly to remove any baking-soda flavor before adding the other marinade ingredients.

1. Cut the beef across the grain into slices that are approximately 1½"–2" long and place in a medium bowl. Add the dark soy sauce, salt, pepper, cornstarch, and baking soda to the beef. Marinate the beef for 20 minutes.

2. Bring a large pot of water to a boil. Blanch the tomatoes: drop them into the boiling water for 15 seconds, then remove and cool quickly in a bowl of ice water. Peel off the skin and cut each into 6 equal pieces.

3. Add 2 tablespoons of oil to a preheated wok or skillet. Add the beef. Fry until it changes color and it is nearly cooked through, turning it over once, about 2 minutes a side. Fry in batches if necessary. Remove the beef from the wok.

4. Wipe the wok if necessary and add 2 tablespoons of oil to the wok. When the oil is hot, add the ginger and stir-fry briefly until aromatic, about 1 minute. Add the tomatoes and stir-fry briefly, making sure they don't soften too much, no more than 1–2 minutes.

5. Add the beef broth, oyster sauce, and sugar, and bring to a boil. Add the cornstarch mixed with the water to the middle of the wok, stirring to thicken.

6. Add the beef back into the wok. Cover and simmer until everything is cooked through, 2–3 minutes. Drizzle with the sesame oil.

PER SERVING Calories: 352 | Fat: 21 grams | Protein: 26 grams | Sodium: 1,162 milligrams | Fiber: 2 grams | Carbohydrates: 12 grams | Sugar: 5 grams

Beef with Broccoli

Serve this restaurant favorite on a bed of white rice or cooked noodles.

INGREDIENTS | SERVES 4

¾ pound top round steak

3 teaspoons Chinese rice wine or dry sherry

1½ teaspoons cornstarch

½ teaspoon baking soda

6–8 broccoli stalks with flowerets

1½ cups vegetable oil

2 garlic cloves, minced

¼ red onion, chopped

Brown Sauce (see recipe in Chapter 2)

1. Cut the beef across the grain into thin strips about 2" long and place in a medium bowl. Add the rice wine, cornstarch, and baking soda. Marinate the beef for 1 hour.

2. Blanch the broccoli by plunging it into boiling water for about 3 minutes. Drain thoroughly. Separate the flowers and the stalks, and cut the stalks into spears along the diagonal.

3. Add the oil to a preheated wok or skillet. When the oil is hot, velvet the beef by adding it to the hot oil just until it changes color, then quickly removing it from the wok. Drain the velveted beef on paper towels.

4. Remove all but 2 tablespoons of oil from the wok. Add the garlic and stir-fry briefly until aromatic. Add the broccoli. Stir-fry for 1 minute and then add the red onion. Stir-fry the broccoli until it turns bright green and the red onion until it is soft and translucent, 3–4 minutes.

5. Push the vegetables up to the sides and add the Brown Sauce into the middle of the wok. Turn up the heat and bring the sauce to a boil, stirring vigorously to thicken. Add the beef back into the wok. Mix everything through and serve hot.

PER SERVING Calories: 389 | Fat: 18 grams | Protein: 28 grams | Sodium: 741 milligrams | Fiber: 8 grams | Carbohydrates: 31 grams | Sugar: 9 grams

Beef with Snow Peas

The crunch of the snow peas is a refreshing contrast to the hearty beef flavor.

INGREDIENTS | SERVES 4

¾ pound flank steak

2 teaspoons soy sauce

1 teaspoon cornstarch

¼ teaspoon baking soda

½ cup snow peas, trimmed

1 cup mung bean sprouts

1 tablespoon dark soy sauce

1 tablespoon oyster sauce

1 tablespoon Chinese rice wine or dry sherry

1 teaspoon sugar

¼ teaspoon sesame oil

2 tablespoons water

3 tablespoons vegetable oil, divided

2 garlic cloves, minced

1. Cut the beef across the grain into thin strips about 2" long and place in a medium bowl. Add the soy sauce, cornstarch, and baking soda. Marinate the beef for 30 minutes.

2. Blanch the bean sprouts and snow peas by plunging them briefly into boiling water. Drain well.

3. In a small bowl, combine the dark soy sauce, oyster sauce, rice wine, sugar, sesame oil, and water and set aside.

4. Add 2 tablespoons of vegetable oil to a preheated wok or skillet. When the oil is hot, add the beef and stir-fry until it changes color, about 3–4 minutes. Remove from the wok and drain on paper towels.

5. Add another tablespoon of oil to the wok. When the oil is hot, add the garlic and stir-fry briefly until aromatic. Add the snow peas and bean sprouts and stir-fry briefly. Add the sauce in the middle of the wok and bring to a boil. Mix with the vegetables.

6. Add the beef back to the wok. Add 1–2 more tablespoons of water if desired. Mix everything together and serve hot.

PER SERVING Calories: 245 | Fat: 14 grams | Protein: 20 grams | Sodium: 702 milligrams | Fiber: 1 gram | Carbohydrates: 7 grams | Sugar: 4 grams

Beef and Bean Sprouts in Black Bean Sauce

*This dish can also be made with green jalapeño peppers—seed and
chop 3 jalapeño peppers and stir-fry with the chili paste.*

INGREDIENTS | SERVES 4

½ pound flank or round steak

2 teaspoons soy sauce

¼ teaspoon salt

½ teaspoon sugar

1 teaspoon cornstarch

¼ teaspoon baking soda

1 cup mung bean sprouts

1 teaspoon fermented black beans

¼ teaspoon chili paste

½ cup chicken stock or broth

1 tablespoon dark soy sauce

1 teaspoon sugar

3 tablespoons vegetable oil, divided

1 garlic clove, minced

1 teaspoon red rice vinegar

Do You Need to Buy a Chinese Cleaver?

Strictly speaking, no. Successful stir-frying demands food that is evenly cut, but many types of knives will do the job. Still, a Chinese cleaver has many advantages. The cleaver's wide rectangular shape makes it handy for cutting beef, pounding chicken, smashing garlic, and using its thicker-side blade to separate individual garlic cloves.

1. Cut the beef across the grain into thin strips about 2" long and place in a medium bowl. Add the soy sauce, salt, sugar, cornstarch, and baking soda. Marinate the beef for 30 minutes.

2. Blanch the bean sprouts by plunging them very briefly into boiling water. Drain thoroughly. Soak the black beans for about 30 minutes, mash, and mix with the chili paste.

3. In a small bowl, mix together the chicken broth, dark soy sauce, and sugar. Set aside.

4. Add 2 tablespoons of oil to a preheated wok or skillet. When the oil is hot, add the beef and stir-fry until it changes color and is nearly cooked through, 3–4 minutes. Remove from the wok and drain on paper towels.

5. Add 1 tablespoon of oil to the wok. When the oil is hot, add the garlic and chili paste mixture. Stir-fry briefly until aromatic. Add the bean sprouts. Stir-fry briefly, and then add the red rice vinegar.

6. Add the prepared sauce in the middle of the wok and bring to a boil. Add the beef. Simmer until everything is cooked through.

PER SERVING Calories: 195 | Fat: 13 grams | Protein: 14 grams | Sodium: 747 milligrams | Fiber: 0 grams | Carbohydrates: 4 grams | Sugar: 2 grams

Dry Fried Beef

This dish tastes great combined with mustard in a sandwich or smoked in tea leaves and spices, a process described in the Tea-Smoked Chicken recipe (see recipe in Chapter 9).

INGREDIENTS | SERVES 4

2 tablespoons soy sauce

1 teaspoon Chinese rice wine or dry sherry

½ teaspoon sugar

½ teaspoon baking soda

1 pound flank steak, shredded

6 tablespoons vegetable oil

1. In a medium bowl, add the soy sauce, rice wine, sugar, baking soda, and beef. Marinate the beef for 30 minutes.

2. Add 3 tablespoons of oil to a preheated wok or skillet. When the oil is hot, add half the beef. Lay flat and fry for 2 minutes, then turn over and fry for another 2 minutes. Stir-fry the beef until it turns a dark brown (this will take about 8 minutes). Remove from the wok and drain on paper towels. Repeat with the remainder of the oil and beef.

PER SERVING Calories: 350 | Fat: 26 grams | Protein: 25 grams | Sodium: 735 milligrams | Fiber: 0 grams | Carbohydrates: 2 grams | Sugar: 1 gram

Beef Satay

This recipe draws on Indonesian culture, and adds a Chinese twist. Serve with Hoisin Satay Sauce (see recipe in Chapter 2).

INGREDIENTS | SERVES 4

½ pound sirloin steak

¼ cup dark soy sauce

¼ teaspoon chili paste

1 tablespoon hoisin sauce

1 teaspoon sugar

1 teaspoon orange marmalade

1 clove garlic, minced

1 slice ginger, minced

1. Cut the beef into thin strips, about 1" long and place in a medium bowl. Stir in the remaining ingredients. Marinate the beef in the refrigerator for at least 2 hours. Drain the beef, reserving the marinade.

2. Thread 2 slices of the marinated beef onto a skewer, weaving them in and out like an accordion. Brush with the reserved marinade. Repeat with remaining beef.

3. Grill the beef on both sides, no more than 2–3 minutes to ensure it remains tender.

PER SERVING Calories: 100 | Fat: 2 grams | Protein: 14 grams | Sodium: 1,101 milligrams | Fiber: 0 grams | Carbohydrates: 5 grams | Sugar: 3 grams

Braised Beef with Daikon Radish

Daikon radish is a root vegetable similar to a turnip, but with a milder taste. The Chinese word for it is the same as for carrot. One is called a white carrot, and the other, red.

INGREDIENTS | SERVES 8

2 pounds cubed boneless stewing beef

1 tablespoon cornstarch

3 tablespoons soy sauce

3 tablespoons peanut oil, divided

3 tablespoons coarsely minced ginger

2 scallions, coarsely minced

¼ cup Xiaoshing rice wine

3 star anise pods

2 cups beef stock

2 cups water

2 pounds daikon radish, peeled and cut into 2" chunks

1. In a medium bowl, combine the beef, cornstarch, 1 tablespoon of soy sauce, and 1 tablespoon of peanut oil. Mix thoroughly to coat the beef. Let stand 15–30 minutes.

2. Heat 2 tablespoons of peanut oil in a heavy-bottomed stew pot over medium-high heat and add the beef. Brown on all sides. Add the ginger and scallions. Cook, stirring, until their aromas are released, about 1 minute. Pour in the Xiaoshing wine and mix well.

3. Add the star anise pods and remaining soy sauce. Pour in the stock and water. Lower the heat to medium and cook until the mixture boils, then lower again to keep the liquid at a bare simmer. Cook 45 minutes, or until the beef is tender.

4. Add the daikon radish, making sure there is enough liquid to cover. Add water if necessary. Simmer for 30 minutes, stirring occasionally, until the daikon is tender but not mushy.

PER SERVING Calories: 285 | Fat: 12 grams | Protein: 26 grams | Sodium: 564 milligrams | Fiber: 3 grams | Carbohydrates: 14 grams | Sugar: 6 grams

Star Anise Beef

This rich dish pairs well with bitter greens, such as Chinese broccoli (gai lan).

INGREDIENTS | SERVES 8

5 cups water

⅓ cup whiskey

½ cup soy sauce

⅓ cup crushed Chinese rock sugar

5 star anise pods

1 teaspoon whole cloves

2 (4") strips orange zest

1½" piece ginger, sliced thinly lengthwise

3 scallions, sliced at a diagonal into 2" lengths

4 pounds meaty beef shanks

1 pound carrots, peeled and cut into 2" chunks

1 pound daikon radish, peeled and cut into 2" chunks

1. Place the water, whiskey, soy sauce, rock sugar, star anise, cloves, orange zest, ginger, and scallions in a heavy-bottomed stockpot and bring to a boil. Reduce the heat and simmer 10 minutes.

2. Add the beef shanks, cover in the liquid, and keep at a simmer 1½–2 hours, until the beef is starting to fall off the bones.

3. Add the carrots and daikon radish, add more water if necessary. Cook another 30 minutes or until the vegetables are tender. The liquid should be reduced and the consistency of gravy, not soup. .

PER SERVING Calories: 399 | Fat: 12 grams | Protein: 48 grams | Sodium: 155 milligrams | Fiber: 1 gram | Carbohydrates: 13 grams | Sugar: 11 grams

Beef Curry

Curries are often associated with Indian cuisine, but they are common in Chinese cooking, too.

INGREDIENTS | SERVES 4

½ pound flank steak, sliced thinly across the grain

1 tablespoon soy sauce

1 teaspoon cornstarch

1 teaspoon plus 3 tablespoons peanut oil, divided

2 garlic cloves, minced

1 tablespoon minced ginger

1 teaspoon curry powder, such as Madras

1 teaspoon turmeric

2 star anise

1 medium onion, finely chopped

1 medium carrot, diced

1 cup fresh or frozen peas

1 cup beef stock

1. Combine the beef with soy sauce, cornstarch, and 1 teaspoon of oil in a medium bowl.

2. Heat a wok or stockpot over high heat. Swirl in the remaining oil. Add the garlic, ginger, curry powder, turmeric, and star anise. Stir-fry about 30 seconds to release the aromas of the spices.

3. Reduce the heat to medium and add the onion, carrots, and peas. Stir-fry 3–4 minutes, until the onions are translucent. Add the beef. Stir-fry 2–3 minutes. Add the stock and cook until most of the liquid has reduced and the sauce is thick, about 20 minutes.

PER SERVING Calories: 261 | Fat: 15 grams | Protein: 15 grams | Sodium: 331 milligrams | Fiber: 4 grams | Carbohydrates: 13 grams | Sugar: 4 grams

Basic Red-Cooked Beef

*Don't have any stewing beef? Red cooking is a nice way to add flavor
to less popular cuts of meat, such as liver.*

INGREDIENTS | SERVES 6

6 dried mushrooms

1 cup light soy sauce

4 tablespoons dark soy sauce

4 tablespoons Chinese rice wine or dry sherry

4 teaspoons sugar

4 tablespoons plus 2 teaspoons brown sugar

½ teaspoon five-spice powder

2 tablespoons vegetable oil

2 slices ginger

2 garlic cloves, minced

1½ pounds boneless stewing beef, cut into chunks

2 cups water

1 large daikon, peeled and cut into ½" slices

Make Your Own Sauce for Red Cooking

In red cooking, previously browned meat is stewed in a combination of soy sauce and other ingredients. To make your own red cooking sauce, experiment with different combinations of light and dark soy sauce, rice wine, and other liquid ingredients until you find one you like. For extra flavor, add stronger seasonings such as star anise and dried tangerine peel.

1. Soak the dried mushrooms in hot water for at least 20 minutes to soften. Gently squeeze them to remove any excess water, and slice.

2. In a small bowl, combine the light soy sauce, dark soy sauce, rice wine, white sugar, brown sugar, and five-spice powder; set aside.

3. Add the oil to a preheated wok or skillet. When the oil is hot, add the ginger and garlic and stir-fry briefly until aromatic. Add the beef and cook until browned. The time will vary according to the size of the beef cubes. Make sure to watch for the meat to change color from red to brown. The center will not be cooked through, but will cook in the stewing process.

4. Add the prepared sauce and water to the wok. Bring to a boil, then turn down the heat and simmer. After 1 hour, add the daikon and dried mushrooms. Simmer for 30 minutes, or until the liquid is reduced and thickened.

PER SERVING Calories: 321 | Fat: 10 grams | Protein: 31 grams | Sodium: 3,515 milligrams | Fiber: 1 gram | Carbohydrates: 26 grams | Sugar: 18 grams

Spicy Red-Cooked Beef

Star anise is a star-shaped seed pod with a strong flavor reminiscent of licorice, used to flavor meat dishes.

INGREDIENTS | SERVES 8

6 dried mushrooms

2 tablespoons vegetable oil

2 slices ginger

3 small garlic cloves, minced

2 pounds boneless stewing beef, cut into chunks

3 cups water

½ cup dark soy sauce, divided

¼ cup light soy sauce, divided

1 piece dried tangerine peel, 2–3" wide

1 star anise

1 (1-ounce) piece yellow rock sugar

1 large daikon, peeled and cut into ½" slices

Shopping for a Chinese Cleaver

When choosing a Chinese cleaver, look for one made of stainless steel or a combination of stainless and carbon steel, with a handle that attaches firmly to the blade. Try out several to find one that you're comfortable holding.

1. Soak the dried mushrooms in hot water for at least 20 minutes to soften. Gently squeeze them to remove any excess water and slice.

2. Add the oil to a preheated wok or skillet. When the oil is hot, add the ginger and garlic and stir-fry briefly until aromatic. Add the beef and cook until browned. The time for browning will vary according to the size of the chunks. Watch for the beef to turn from red to a deep brown. The beef will not be cooked all the way through. The rest of the cooking will take place in the stewing process.

3. Add the water, ¼ cup of dark soy sauce, 2 tablespoons of light soy sauce, the tangerine peel, and star anise, and bring to a boil. Reduce the heat and simmer for 45 minutes.

4. Add the remaining dark and light soy sauce, the rock sugar, the daikon, and the dried mushrooms. Simmer for another 45 minutes, or until liquid is reduced.

PER SERVING Calories: 235 | Fat: 9 grams | Protein: 27 grams | Sodium: 1,576 milligrams | Fiber: 1 gram | Carbohydrates: 8 grams | Sugar: 5 grams

Beef with Red Onions

Red onions add a distinctive flavor to this simple dish. Serve on a bed of steamed rice.

INGREDIENTS | SERVES 4

1 pound flank or sirloin steak, shredded

1 tablespoon soy sauce

½ teaspoon baking soda

4 tablespoons vegetable or peanut oil, divided

1 clove garlic, minced

1 teaspoon minced ginger

1 large red onion, peeled and chopped

2 tablespoons dark soy sauce

1 tablespoon Chinese rice wine or dry sherry

¼ teaspoon chili paste with garlic

2 green onions, diagonally cut into 1½" slices

1. In a medium bowl, mix the beef, soy sauce, and baking soda, using your fingers to mix in the baking soda. Marinate the beef for 30 minutes. Add 1 tablespoon of oil and marinate the beef for another 30 minutes.

2. Add 2 tablespoons of oil to a preheated wok or skillet. When the oil is hot, add the beef. Stir-fry until it changes color and is nearly cooked through, 3–4 minutes. Remove from the wok and drain on paper towels.

3. Add 1 tablespoon of oil to the wok. When the oil is hot, add the garlic and ginger, and stir-fry briefly until aromatic. Add the red onion, and stir-fry until soft and translucent.

4. Stir in the dark soy sauce, rice wine, and chili paste. Add the beef. Stir in the green onions. Mix everything together and cook for a few more minutes on medium heat, making sure the beef is cooked through. Serve hot.

PER SERVING Calories: 296 | Fat: 19 grams | Protein: 25 grams | Sodium: 1,004 milligrams | Fiber: 0 grams | Carbohydrates: 3 grams | Sugar: 1 gram

Peppery Beef

For a less biting dish, forgo the chili paste and substitute black pepper for the Szechwan peppercorn.

INGREDIENTS | SERVES 4

1 tablespoon soy sauce

½ teaspoon Chinese rice wine or dry sherry

1¼ teaspoons sugar, divided

¼ teaspoon baking soda

½ pound flank steak, shredded

½ cup chicken stock

2 tablespoons dark soy sauce

3 tablespoons vegetable oil, divided

1 clove garlic, minced

1 teaspoon minced ginger

¼ teaspoon chili paste

½ green bell pepper, seeded and cut into thin slices

½ red bell pepper, seeded and cut into thin slices

¼ teaspoon sesame oil

⅛ teaspoon Szechwan peppercorns, roasted and ground

1. In a medium bowl, combine the soy sauce, rice wine, ¼ teaspoon of sugar, baking soda, and beef. Marinate the beef for 30 minutes.

2. In a small bowl, combine the chicken stock, dark soy sauce, and 1 teaspoon of sugar in a small bowl and set aside.

3. Add 2 tablespoons of oil to a preheated wok or skillet. When the oil is hot, add the beef and stir-fry until it changes color and is nearly cooked through, 3–4 minutes. Remove from the wok and drain on paper towels.

4. Add 1 tablespoon of oil to the wok. Add the garlic, ginger, and chili paste. Stir-fry briefly until aromatic. Add the bell peppers and stir-fry briefly, until they have a bright color and are tender.

5. Add the prepared sauce to the middle of the wok and bring to a boil. Stir in the sesame oil. Add the beef and Szechwan peppercorns. Mix everything through and serve hot.

PER SERVING Calories: 205 | Fat: 13 grams | Protein: 14 grams | Sodium: 888 milligrams | Fiber: 1 gram | Carbohydrates: 6 grams | Sugar: 4 grams

Stir-Fried Orange Beef

This sweet and tangy dish is a pleasant treat for picky young eaters.

INGREDIENTS | SERVES 4

1 pound sirloin or flank steak, shredded

2 teaspoons Chinese rice wine or dry sherry, divided

½ teaspoon baking soda

2 tablespoons soy sauce

1 teaspoon sugar

¼ teaspoon chili paste

3 tablespoons vegetable oil, divided

2 slices ginger, minced

1 clove garlic, minced

1 green onion, diagonally cut into 1½" slices

⅓ cup thinly sliced dried orange peel

Orange Peel Cold Cure

Have a cold? Why not try an orange peel cure? For centuries, Chinese medical practitioners have recommended dried orange peel to treat everything from colds to insomnia. Whatever their medicinal value, there is no doubt that the peel contains more vitamin C than any other part of the orange.

1. Place the beef in a medium bowl and add 1 teaspoon of rice wine and the baking soda to it, mixing with your fingers. Marinate the beef for 30 minutes.

2. In a small bowl, combine the soy sauce, sugar, chili paste, and 1 teaspoon of rice wine. Set aside.

3. Add 2 tablespoons of oil to a preheated wok or skillet. When the oil is hot, add the beef. Stir-fry until it is nearly cooked through, about 3–4 minutes. Remove from the wok and drain on paper towels.

4. Add 1 tablespoon of oil to the wok. Add the ginger, garlic, green onion, and dried orange peel. Stir-fry until the orange peel is aromatic, about 1 minute.

5. Add the prepared sauce in the middle and bring to a boil. Add the beef back in. Mix well and stir-fry until the beef is cooked through. Serve hot.

PER SERVING Calories: 266 | Fat: 16 grams | Protein: 25 grams | Sodium: 763 milligrams | Fiber: 0 grams | Carbohydrates: 4 grams | Sugar: 2 grams

Spicy Steamed Beef

This dish can be served hot or cold. For a tasty appetizer, deep-fry the steamed beef twice in a flour, cornstarch, and egg batter.

INGREDIENTS | SERVES 4

1 tablespoon Szechwan peppercorns

1 pound sirloin or flank steak

1 tablespoon soy sauce

½ teaspoon baking soda

2 tablespoons dark soy sauce

½ teaspoon sugar

¼ teaspoon dried crushed chili flakes

1 tablespoon dried orange peel

Make Your Own Orange Peel

To make dried orange peel, remove the skin from an orange. Use a paring knife to remove the white pith inside. Leave the peel to dry in the sun or dry quickly by placing in a previously warmed oven. Remove the peel before it hardens.

1. Toast the peppercorns on low heat in a heavy pan, shaking occasionally, until the peppercorns turn fragrant and begin to smoke. Remove and cool. Grind the peppercorns in a pepper mill or with a mortar and pestle. Set aside.

2. Cut the beef across the grain into thin slices about 1½" long and place in a medium bowl. Add the soy sauce and baking soda, using your fingers to mix in the baking soda. Marinate the beef for 30 minutes.

3. In a small bowl, combine the dark soy sauce, sugar, and crushed chili flakes.

4. Cut the dried orange peel into thin slices.

5. Prepare the wok for steaming. Place the beef on a heatproof plate on a bamboo steamer. Rub the toasted peppercorns over the beef. Brush on half of the sauce. Place the orange peel around the beef.

6. Steam the beef for 20 minutes or until it is cooked through. Brush on the remainder of the sauce during steaming.

PER SERVING Calories: 179 | Fat: 7 grams | Protein: 26 grams | Sodium: 976 milligrams | Fiber: 0 grams | Carbohydrates: 1 gram | Sugar: 0 grams

Beef with String Beans

When choosing string beans, look for younger ones with a firm texture and bright color.

INGREDIENTS | SERVES 4

1 pound flank or sirloin steak

1 tablespoon soy sauce

1 green onion, cut into 1" pieces

1 tablespoon cornstarch

1 cup string beans

¼ cup chicken stock or broth

1 tablespoon Chinese rice wine or dry sherry

1 teaspoon sugar

¼ teaspoon salt

3 tablespoons vegetable oil, divided

1 clove garlic, minced

¼ teaspoon chili paste with garlic

1 teaspoon cornstarch mixed with 4 teaspoons water

1. Cut the beef across the grain into thin slices, about 1½" long and place in a medium bowl. Add the soy sauce, green onion, and cornstarch, using your fingers to mix in the cornstarch. Marinate the beef for 30 minutes.

2. Trim the string beans and parboil them by plunging them briefly into boiling water. Drain thoroughly and cut lengthwise into thin slices.

3. In a small bowl, combine the chicken broth, rice wine, sugar, and salt. Set aside.

4. Add 2 tablespoons of oil to a preheated wok or skillet. When the oil is hot, add the beef. Stir-fry until it changes color and is nearly cooked, 3–4 minutes. Remove and set aside.

5. Add 1 tablespoon of oil to the wok. When the oil is hot, add the garlic and the chili paste with garlic. Stir-fry briefly until aromatic. Add the string beans. Stir-fry for 3–4 minutes. Push the string beans up to the side of the wok and add the prepared sauce in the middle. Bring to a boil.

6. Stir in the cornstarch and water mixture, stirring quickly to thicken. Add the beef. Mix thoroughly and cook over medium heat for a few more minutes until the beef is cooked. Serve hot.

PER SERVING Calories: 282 | Fat: 16 grams | Protein: 25 grams | Sodium: 493 milligrams | Fiber: 1 gram | Carbohydrates: 8 grams | Sugar: 2 grams

Spicy Orange Beef

This recipe shows fiery Szechwan cuisine at its finest—for a less spicy dish, leave out the dried chili.

INGREDIENTS | SERVES 4

1 pound flank steak

4 tablespoons soy sauce

2 teaspoons Chinese rice wine or dry sherry

2 teaspoons sugar

½ teaspoon chili paste

2 medium eggs

3 tablespoons flour

2 tablespoons cornstarch

4 cups vegetable oil

2 garlic cloves, minced

3 slices ginger, minced

1 dried chili, seeded and chopped

1 teaspoon dried orange peel or 1 small piece dried tangerine peel

1. Cut the beef across the grain into thin slices about 2" in length.

2. In a small bowl, combine the soy sauce, rice wine, sugar, and chili paste, and set aside.

3. In a shallow bowl, beat the eggs and mix with the flour and cornstarch into a batter. Coat the beef slices with the batter, using your fingers.

4. Heat the oil to 350°F. When the oil is hot, add a few pieces of beef into the hot oil and deep-fry until they turn light brown, about 5 minutes. Remove with a slotted spoon and drain on paper towels. Continue with the rest of the beef.

5. Raise the oil temperature to 400°F. Deep-fry the beef pieces a second time, until they turn brown and crispy, another 5 minutes. Remove and drain.

6. Remove all but 2 tablespoons of oil from the wok. Add the garlic, ginger, chili, and orange peel. Stir-fry until aromatic.

7. Add the prepared sauce and bring to a boil. Stir in the beef and serve hot.

PER SERVING Calories: 496 | Fat: 35 grams | Protein: 29 grams | Sodium: 1,129 milligrams | Fiber: 0 grams | Carbohydrates: 13 grams | Sugar: 3 grams

Ginger Beef

Ginger juice is easy to make—just grate the ginger and squeeze out the fresh juice.

INGREDIENTS | SERVES 4

¾ pound flank or sirloin steak

8 tablespoons soy sauce, divided

4 teaspoons Chinese rice wine or dry sherry, divided

2½ teaspoons sugar, divided

2 teaspoons freshly squeezed ginger juice, divided

2 teaspoons sesame oil

¼ teaspoon chili flakes

½ cup water

2 medium eggs

3 tablespoons flour

2 tablespoons cornstarch

4 cups vegetable oil

1 clove garlic, minced

1 slice ginger, minced

1 teaspoon cornstarch mixed with 4 teaspoons water

1. Cut the beef along the grain into matchstick strips and place in a medium bowl. Add 2 tablespoons of soy sauce, 1 teaspoon of rice wine, ½ teaspoon of sugar, and 1 teaspoon of ginger juice to the beef. Marinate for 30 minutes.

2. In a small bowl, combine 6 tablespoons of soy sauce, 3 teaspoons of rice wine, 2 teaspoons of sugar, 1 teaspoon of ginger juice, the sesame oil, chili flakes, and water. Set aside.

3. In a shallow bowl, beat the eggs and mix with the flour and cornstarch into a batter. Coat the beef in the batter, using your fingers to spread it.

4. Add the oil to the wok and heat to 350°F. When the oil is ready, deep-fry the beef in batches, turning occasionally, until they turn golden, about 5 minutes. Remove and drain on paper towels.

5. Raise the oil temperature to 400°F. Deep-fry the beef a second time, until it turns brown and crispy, another 5 minutes. Drain on paper towels.

6. Remove all but 2 tablespoons of oil from the wok. When the oil is hot, add the garlic and ginger and stir-fry briefly until aromatic.

7. Add the prepared sauce and bring it to a boil. Add the cornstarch-and-water mixture, stirring quickly to thicken. Return beef to the wok. Mix well and serve hot.

PER SERVING Calories: 464 | Fat: 35 grams | Protein: 22 grams | Sodium: 2,105 milligrams | Fiber: 0 grams | Carbohydrates: 16 grams | Sugar: 4 grams

Dry Ginger Beef

For added ginger flavor, top with a few slices of preserved red ginger before serving.

INGREDIENTS | SERVES 2

1 tablespoon soy sauce

½ teaspoon Chinese rice wine or dry sherry

¼ teaspoon sugar

¼ teaspoon baking soda

½ pound flank steak, shredded

2 tablespoons dark soy sauce

1 tablespoon plus 1 teaspoon oyster sauce

1½ teaspoons sugar

½ cup water

4 tablespoons vegetable oil, divided

2 slices ginger, minced

½ cup mushrooms, sliced

½ red bell pepper, seeded and thinly sliced

Ginger Beef Origins

According to rumor, ginger beef originated in Alberta, the beef capital of Canada. However, it is based on an authentic Chinese dish. Authentic ginger beef is much dryer, and lacks the sweet sauce found in the Alberta version. It is frequently made with preserved red ginger.

1. In a medium bowl, add the soy sauce, rice wine, sugar, and baking soda to the beef. Marinate the beef for 30 minutes.

2. In a small bowl, combine the dark soy sauce, oyster sauce, sugar, and water and set aside.

3. Add 3 tablespoons of oil to a preheated wok or skillet. When the oil is hot, add the beef. Lay flat and fry for 2 minutes, then turn over and fry for another 2 minutes. Stir-fry the beef until it turns a dark brown (this will take about 8 minutes). Remove from the wok and drain on paper towels.

4. Add 1 tablespoon of oil to the wok. When the oil is hot, add the ginger and stir-fry briefly until aromatic. Add the mushrooms and red pepper and stir-fry until tender.

5. Add the prepared sauce to the middle of the wok and bring to a boil. Return the beef to the wok and mix thoroughly. Serve hot.

PER SERVING Calories: 454 | Fat: 33 grams | Protein: 28 grams | Sodium: 2,066 milligrams | Fiber: 1 gram | Carbohydrates: 9 grams | Sugar: 6 grams

Beef and Lotus Root with Oyster Sauce

In the Buddhist religion, the beautiful white lotus flower is a symbol of purity. Lotus root can be boiled, stir-fried, or deep-fried. Always peel it before using.

INGREDIENTS | SERVES 2

1 piece lotus root (about 2"–3")
½ pound round or flank steak
6 teaspoons oyster sauce, divided
2 teaspoons cornstarch
¼ cup chicken broth
1 teaspoon sugar
½ teaspoon sesame oil
3 tablespoons vegetable oil, divided
1 slice ginger

1. Peel the lotus root. Cut into 6 thin rounds, about ¼" wide. Blanch the lotus-root rounds briefly in boiling water.

2. Cut the beef in thin slices and place in a medium bowl with 2 teaspoons of oyster sauce and the cornstarch. Marinate the beef for 30 minutes.

3. In a small bowl, combine 4 teaspoons of oyster sauce, chicken broth, sugar, and sesame oil. Set aside.

4. Add 2 tablespoons of oil to a preheated wok or skillet. When the oil is hot, add the beef. Stir-fry until it changes color and is nearly cooked through, 3–4 minutes. Remove and drain on paper towels.

5. Add 1 tablespoon of oil to the wok. When the oil is hot, add the ginger. Stir-fry briefly until aromatic. Add the lotus root. Stir-fry for 1–2 minutes.

6. Add the prepared sauce in the middle of the wok and bring to a boil. Add the beef and cook for 1–2 more minutes. Serve hot.

PER SERVING Calories: 427 | Fat: 27 grams | Protein: 26 grams | Sodium: 582 milligrams | Fiber: 3 grams | Carbohydrates: 17 grams | Sugar: 2 grams

CHAPTER 8

Pork Entrées

Ants Climbing a Tree

For easier handling of the noodles, don't remove the string wrapping until the noodles have been soaked and drained.

INGREDIENTS | SERVES 4

4 ounces rice vermicelli noodles

4 shiitake mushrooms, dried or fresh

1 bunch spinach leaves

3 tablespoons vegetable oil, divided

2 slices ginger, finely chopped

½ pound ground pork

1 tablespoon soy sauce

1 tablespoon Chinese rice wine or dry sherry

½ teaspoon sesame oil, divided

¼ teaspoon sugar

¼ teaspoon salt

1 tablespoon chili sauce

¼ cup chicken broth

2 green onions, chopped

Intriguing Recipe Names

Like most cooking styles, Chinese cuisine has its share of intriguing recipe names. In Ants Climbing a Tree, the tiny flecks of marinated pork are meant to resemble ants, while the fried noodles are the bark of the tree. This dish is also known as Ants Creeping Up a Tree and Ants Climbing a Log.

1. Soak the noodles in hot water for 5 minutes or until they are softened. If using dried mushrooms, soak them in hot water for at least 20 minutes to soften. Drain the mushrooms, remove the stems, and cut the cap into thin slices.

2. Blanch the spinach in boiling water briefly, just until the leaves begin to wilt. Drain well and chop finely.

3. Add 2 tablespoons of oil to a preheated wok or skillet. When the oil is hot, add the ginger and stir-fry briefly until aromatic. Add the ground pork. Mix in the soy sauce, rice wine, and ¼ teaspoon of sesame oil. Stir-fry the ground pork until it loses its pink color, 2–3 minutes. Remove from the wok and set aside.

4. Wipe the wok clean with a paper towel and add 1 tablespoon of oil. When the oil is hot, add the spinach. Add the sugar and salt and stir-fry briefly, for less than 1 minute. Add the mushrooms.

5. Push the spinach up to the sides of the wok and add the pork. Stir in the chili sauce, and then the noodles. Add the chicken broth and continue to cook until most of the liquid is absorbed. Stir in the green onions. Drizzle with ¼ teaspoon of sesame oil and serve.

PER SERVING Calories: 421 | Fat: 26 grams | Protein: 14 grams | Sodium: 585 milligrams | Fiber: 3 grams | Carbohydrates: 32 grams | Sugar: 2 grams

Lion's Head Meatball Stew

Lion's Head Meatballs can be made in advance and frozen.
Bring the meatballs back to room temperature before reheating.

INGREDIENTS | SERVES 4

1 pound ground pork
1 tablespoon soy sauce
1 teaspoon sugar
½ teaspoon sesame oil
2 tablespoons Chinese rice wine or dry sherry, divided
2 bunches spinach leaves
3 tablespoons vegetable oil
1 cup chicken broth or stock
¼ teaspoon salt
White pepper, to taste

1. Place the pork in a medium-size bowl. Mix in the soy sauce, sugar, sesame oil, and 1 tablespoon of rice wine. Marinate the pork for 20 minutes.

2. Blanch the spinach in boiling water briefly, just until the leaves begin to wilt. Drain thoroughly.

3. Form the marinated pork into 4 large meatballs, each roughly the size of a tennis ball. (Alternatively, you can make the meatballs the size of golf balls, which will give you more meatballs.)

4. Add the oil to a preheated wok or skillet. Pan-fry the meatballs on medium heat for 4–5 minutes on each side until they brown. (The meatballs will not be cooked through.) Remove and drain on paper towels.

5. While the meatballs are frying, preheat the oven to 375°F.

6. In a small saucepan over high heat, bring the chicken broth or stock to a boil. Stir in the salt, white pepper, and 1 tablespoon of rice wine. Remove from the heat.

7. Line the bottom of a casserole dish with the spinach leaves. Add the meatballs and pour the chicken stock mixture over. Bake at 375°F for 30 minutes, or until the meatballs are cooked through.

PER SERVING Calories: 467 | Fat: 35 grams | Protein: 24 grams | Sodium: 673 milligrams | Fiber: 4 grams | Carbohydrates: 14 grams | Sugar: 5 grams

Honey Roasted Pork

The marinade can also be used on a pork butt, and the meat used for sandwiches.

INGREDIENTS | SERVES 4

1½ pounds spareribs

2 tablespoons honey

4 tablespoons hoisin sauce

4 tablespoons dark soy sauce

2 tablespoons Chinese rice wine or dry sherry

PER SERVING Calories: 560 | Fat: 40 grams | Protein: 28 grams | Sodium: 1,463 milligrams | Fiber: 0 grams | Carbohydrates: 20 grams | Sugar: 15 grams

1. Separate the pork into pieces about 2" × 6" and place in a medium bowl. Combine the honey, hoisin sauce, dark soy sauce, and rice wine. Add to the pork ribs and marinate in the refrigerator for at least 2 hours, preferably overnight.

2. Preheat oven to 375°F.

3. Drain the pork, reserving the marinade. Fill a shallow pan with boiling water and place at the bottom of the oven. Place the pork on a roasting rack in the pan, cover with half the reserved marinade and roast the pork for 15 minutes. Brush the pork with the remaining marinade and roast for another 15 minutes, or until the pork turns golden brown and is cooked. Cool.

Curry Spareribs

Commonly associated with Southeast Asian cooking, spicy curry is also featured in southern Chinese dishes.

INGREDIENTS | SERVES 4

1 pound pork ribs

4 tablespoons soy sauce

2 tablespoons Chinese rice wine or dry sherry

2 teaspoons sugar

2 teaspoons curry paste

1 teaspoon turmeric

1 large clove garlic, chopped

PER SERVING Calories: 290 | Fat: 21 grams | Protein: 16 grams | Sodium: 1,084 milligrams | Fiber: 0 grams | Carbohydrates: 6 grams | Sugar: 3 grams

1. Cut the ribs into bite-size pieces and place in a medium bowl. Add the soy sauce, rice wine, sugar, curry paste, turmeric, and chopped garlic. Marinate the ribs for 30 minutes.

2. Bring several inches of water to boil in a wok. Decrease the heat to keep the water at a simmer. Set a rack in the wok and place the ribs on a dish or plate inside a bamboo steamer.

3. Cover the wok and steam for about 25 minutes, until the ribs are cooked through. Alternatively, you may deep-fry the ribs in 2–4 cups of oil until the ribs turn a deep brown and rise to the surface, about 5 minutes.

Braised Spareribs in Black Bean Sauce

Savory fermented black beans nicely complement the delicate sweet flavor of pork in this recipe.

INGREDIENTS | SERVES 4

1½ pounds spareribs
1 tablespoon fermented black beans
1 garlic clove, minced
3 tablespoons hoisin sauce
3 tablespoons soy sauce
1½ teaspoons sugar
½ cup water
2 tablespoons vegetable oil
2 green onions, cut into 1" pieces

Fermented Black Beans

These are not the dried black beans that enliven many Mexican dishes. Instead, fermented black beans (also called salted black beans) are made with black soybeans that have been fermented in salt, garlic, and a number of spices. Fermented black beans are sold in cans and plastic bags in Asian markets. In a pinch, black bean sauce can be used as a substitute, but the dish won't have the same flavor.

1. Wash the spareribs, pat dry, and separate.

2. Mash the black beans with the back edge of a knife or cleaver. Mix with the garlic and a bit of water.

3. In a small bowl, combine the hoisin sauce, soy sauce, sugar, and water. Set aside.

4. Add the oil to a preheated wok or skillet. Stir-fry the pork for 2–3 minutes. Add the fermented bean-and-garlic mixture and stir-fry until aromatic.

5. Add the prepared sauce and bring to a boil. Turn down the heat, cover, and simmer for 20–25 minutes, until the spareribs are cooked. Stir in the green onions.

PER SERVING Calories: 584 | Fat: 47 grams | Protein: 29 grams | Sodium: 1,303 milligrams | Fiber: 1 gram | Carbohydrates: 8 grams | Sugar: 5 grams

Stir-Fried Pork and Green Beans

Like many Chinese stir-fries, this makes a complete meal served with rice.

INGREDIENTS | SERVES 4

1 pound boneless pork loin
1 tablespoon soy sauce
1 tablespoon cornstarch
3 tablespoons peanut oil
1 garlic clove, minced
1 teaspoon minced ginger
2 scallions, coarsely chopped
1 cup green beans, cut into 1"–2" lengths
½ cup water

1. Slice the pork thinly, across the grain. Place in a dish with the soy sauce and cornstarch and combine, using your fingers to ensure that the pork is thoroughly coated.

2. Preheat the wok over medium-high heat and swirl in the peanut oil. Add the garlic, ginger, and scallions. Stir-fry about 30 seconds. Add the pork, turning quickly with chopsticks or wooden spoon so that it cooks evenly.

3. Once the pork has changed color, about 2 minutes, add the green beans. Stir-fry until the beans are a bright green, another 2–3 minutes.

4. Pour in the water, stirring constantly. When the liquid has reached a boil and the sauce is thickened, turn off the heat and serve.

PER SERVING Calories: 236 | Fat: 13 grams | Protein: 25 grams | Sodium: 516 milligrams | Fiber: 1 gram | Carbohydrates: 4 grams | Sugar: 0 grams

Five-Spice Spareribs

*These spicy ribs nicely complement a less highly seasoned dish
such as Three-Vegetable Stir-Fry (see recipe in Chapter 12).*

INGREDIENTS | SERVES 4

2 garlic cloves, smashed and peeled

3 tablespoons soy sauce

1 teaspoon sesame oil

1 tablespoon Chinese rice wine or dry sherry

2 teaspoons brown sugar

1 teaspoon Hot Chili Oil (see recipe in Chapter 2)

½ teaspoon Szechwan Salt and Pepper Mix (see recipe in Chapter 2)

½ teaspoon five-spice powder

2 tablespoons water

1½ pounds spareribs

1. Mix together all the ingredients except for the spareribs. Pour the resulting mixture over the spareribs in a shallow dish. Marinate the spareribs for 30 minutes.

2. Preheat oven to 350°F. Remove spareribs from the marinade, reserving liquid.

3. Brush half of the reserved marinade on the spareribs and roast for 15 minutes. Brush on the rest of the marinade and roast the spareribs for another 15 minutes or until they are cooked.

PER SERVING Calories: 527 | Fat: 42 grams | Protein: 28 grams | Sodium: 1,080 milligrams | Fiber: 0 grams | Carbohydrates: 5 grams | Sugar: 3 grams

Garlicky Stir-Fry Pork

Serve this dish with steamed rice.

INGREDIENTS | SERVES 4

1 pound boneless pork, cut into thin strips

4 cloves garlic, minced

1 teaspoon cornstarch

1 teaspoon plus 1 tablespoon peanut oil

1 teaspoon minced ginger

1 teaspoon red chili flakes

½ cup water

1 teaspoon salt

½ cup celery, sliced thinly on the diagonal

2 tablespoons minced cilantro

1. In a medium bowl, combine the pork with the garlic, cornstarch, and 1 teaspoon of oil. Let marinate, covered, for 2–4 hours.

2. Heat a wok over medium heat. Swirl in the remaining oil. Add the ginger and chili flakes. Stir-fry 30 seconds, then add pork. Stir-fry about 2 minutes.

3. Add salt and celery. Stir-fry another 2–3 minutes. The celery should be bright green.

4. Add water and mix well. Once the liquid has come to a boil, the sauce will thicken. Turn off the heat. Garnish with cilantro.

PER SERVING Calories: 187 | Fat: 8 grams | Protein: 25 grams | Sodium: 643 milligrams | Fiber: 0 grams | Carbohydrates: 1 gram | Sugar: 0 grams

Pork with Young Bamboo Shoots

Due to their strong flavor, young bamboo shoots are considered to be a great delicacy in China. If you live near an Asian grocery, ask about fresh bamboo shoots instead of canned. You will notice the difference in flavor.

INGREDIENTS | SERVES 2

½ pound pork tenderloin

3 teaspoons Chinese rice wine or dry sherry, divided

½ teaspoon sugar

1½ teaspoons cornstarch

8 ounces canned or fresh peeled young bamboo shoots

½ cup chicken stock or broth

1 teaspoon rice vinegar

3 tablespoons vegetable oil, divided

Why Waste a Wok?

Don't hide your wok in the cupboard when you're not cooking Chinese food. It is the perfect combination between a pot and saucepan, great for all-purpose use. In addition, a well-seasoned wok, washed with hot water but no soap and dried over a flame, will develop a nonstick surface. Experiment with cooking other cuisines in your wok!

1. Cut the pork into thin slices and place in a medium bowl. Add 2 teaspoons of rice wine, the sugar, and cornstarch. Marinate the pork for 30 minutes.

2. If using fresh bamboo shoots, soften in boiling water for at least 5 minutes. The canned variety are often soft already. Drain thoroughly and chop.

3. In a small bowl, combine chicken stock, 1 teaspoon of rice wine, and rice vinegar. Set aside.

4. Add 2 tablespoons of oil to a preheated wok or skillet. When the oil is hot, add the pork and stir-fry until it changes color and is nearly cooked, 4–5 minutes. Remove and drain on paper towels.

5. Add 1 tablespoon of oil to the wok. Add the bamboo shoots and stir-fry. Add the prepared sauce in the middle of the wok and bring to a boil. Add the pork. Turn down the heat and simmer for 5 minutes.

PER SERVING Calories: 417 | Fat: 28 grams | Protein: 27 grams | Sodium: 212 milligrams | Fiber: 2 grams | Carbohydrates: 15 grams | Sugar: 6 grams

Twice-Cooked Pork

Pork is cooked twice in this simple but popular Szechwan dish.
Serve on a bed of steamed rice or noodles.

INGREDIENTS | SERVES 2

½ pound boneless pork

½ red bell pepper, seeded

½ green bell pepper, seeded

3 tablespoons vegetable oil

2 slices ginger, chopped

1 clove garlic, chopped

1 teaspoon hot bean paste with garlic

2 tablespoons dark soy sauce

1 teaspoon sugar

Meat in Traditional Chinese Cuisine

Because China is a country with limited means, traditional Chinese eat little meat relative to developed Western nations. Cows and oxen are valued more as work animals rather than food. Pigs are cheaper to feed, and require less grazing space, thus pork is more commonly served than beef.

1. Place the pork in a medium saucepan and cover with water. Boil the pork over medium-high heat for 20–25 minutes. Remove from water and cool. Cut into thin strips.

2. Blanch the red and green peppers by plunging them briefly into boiling water. Cut into thin slices.

3. Add the oil to a preheated wok or skillet. When the oil is hot, add the ginger, garlic, and hot bean paste. Stir-fry briefly until the garlic and ginger are aromatic. Add the pepper slices and stir-fry.

4. Mix in the dark soy sauce and sugar. Add the pork. Combine all the ingredients thoroughly and stir-fry for about 1 more minute. Serve hot.

PER SERVING Calories: 366 | Fat: 25 grams | Protein: 27 grams | Sodium: 1,061 milligrams | Fiber: 1 gram | Carbohydrates: 6 grams | Sugar: 4 grams

Pork in Plum Sauce

For best results, make the Plum Sauce ahead of time so that the flavors have a chance to blend. Serve with steamed rice.

INGREDIENTS | SERVES 4

1 pound boneless pork loin chops

1 tablespoon soy sauce

1 tablespoon cornstarch

1 teaspoon baking soda

2 carrots, peeled and cut into ½" slices

3 tablespoons vegetable oil, divided

2 slices ginger

½ cup Plum Sauce (see recipe in Chapter 2)

2 green onions, thinly sliced on the diagonal

Eastern and Northern China

The cuisine of eastern China features red-cooked dishes—stews that have been slowly cooked in soy sauce and seasonings. And northern China is famous for noodle-based dishes and festive specialties such as Mu Shu Pork and Peking Duck with pancakes. The influence of the Mongol warriors can be seen in dishes such as Mongolian Beef.

1. Cut the pork into cubes and place in a medium bowl. Add the soy sauce, cornstarch, and baking soda. Marinate the pork in the refrigerator for 90 minutes.

2. Blanch the carrots by plunging them into boiling water and draining.

3. Add 2 tablespoons of oil to a preheated wok or skillet. When the oil is hot, add the pork. Stir-fry until it changes color and is nearly cooked through, about 5 minutes. Remove from the wok and drain on paper towels.

4. Add 1 tablespoon of oil to the wok. When the oil is hot, add the ginger slices and stir-fry briefly until aromatic. Add the carrots and stir-fry for about 1 minute. Add the Plum Sauce and bring to a boil.

5. Add the pork. Stir in the green onions. Mix everything through and serve hot.

PER SERVING Calories: 288 | Fat: 14 grams | Protein: 26 grams | Sodium: 643 milligrams | Fiber: 1 gram | Carbohydrates: 12 grams | Sugar: 8 grams

Pork in Bean Sauce

*Serve with any crunchy vegetable recipe for a nutritious meal
with an interesting combination of textures.*

INGREDIENTS | SERVES 4

1 pound boneless pork tenderloin chops

1 tablespoon oyster sauce

½ teaspoon sugar

1½ teaspoons cornstarch

2 tablespoons black bean sauce

2 tablespoons dark soy sauce

2 teaspoons Chinese rice wine or dry sherry

2 teaspoons sugar

¼ teaspoon salt

¼ cup water

¼ teaspoon sesame oil

2 tablespoons vegetable oil

¼ teaspoon chili paste

Szechwan and Cantonese Cooking

Fiery Szechwan cuisine is famous for its "mouth burners"—dishes like Kung Pao Chicken (see recipe in Chapter 9) and Ma Po Tofu (see recipe in Chapter 11) made with hot chilies and toasted Szechwan peppercorns. Cantonese cuisine may be more familiar to the Western palate, in part because it has been adapted according to "new world" standards. Think about your favorite Chinese take-out dishes, such as Sweet-and-Sour Pork and Lobster Cantonese. Traditionally, Cantonese cuisine features fresh ingredients whose flavors are not masked with heavy seasoning or overcooking. The quick method of stir-frying is one such example of Cantonese-style cuisine.

1. Cut the pork into thin strips and place in a medium bowl. Add the oyster sauce, sugar, and cornstarch, adding the cornstarch last. Marinate the pork for 30 minutes.

2. In a small bowl, combine the black bean sauce, dark soy sauce, rice wine, sugar, salt, water, and sesame oil. Set aside.

3. Add the oil to a preheated wok or skillet. When the oil is hot, add the chili paste and stir-fry briefly until aromatic. Add the pork. Stir-fry until it changes color and is nearly cooked through, 4–5 minutes.

4. Push the pork up to the side of the wok and add the prepared sauce in the middle. Bring to a boil. Mix the sauce with the pork. Cover and simmer for 2–3 more minutes until the pork is cooked through.

PER SERVING Calories: 226 | Fat: 10 grams | Protein: 24 grams | Sodium: 1,264 milligrams | Fiber: 0 grams | Carbohydrates: 7 grams | Sugar: 4 grams

Spicy Hoisin Pork

For a less spicy dish, substitute ¼ teaspoon chili sauce with garlic for the chili paste.

INGREDIENTS | SERVES 4

¾ pound pork tenderloin

1 tablespoon soy sauce

2 teaspoons baking soda

1 bunch spinach

2 tablespoons hoisin sauce

1 tablespoon dark soy sauce

¼ cup water

3 tablespoons vegetable oil, divided

¼ teaspoon chili paste

How to Season a Carbon Steel Wok

It's important to properly season a wok before using it for the first time. First, wash the wok in soapy water; this should be the only time you use soap on your wok. Dry it thoroughly, then lightly coat the inside surface with vegetable oil, using a paper towel and tilting the wok to ensure even coverage. Heat the wok on low-medium heat for 10 minutes. Remove to a cool burner and wipe off the inside with a paper towel. Repeat this process several times. The wok is ready to use when the paper towel doesn't pick up any black residue.

1. Cut the pork into thin slices and place in a medium bowl. Marinate in the soy sauce and baking soda for 30 minutes.

2. Blanch the spinach briefly in boiling water and drain thoroughly.

3. In a small bowl, combine the hoisin sauce, dark soy sauce, and water. Set aside.

4. Add 2 tablespoons of oil to a preheated wok or skillet. When the oil is hot, add the pork and stir-fry until it changes color and is nearly cooked through, 4–5 minutes. Remove and drain on paper towels.

5. Add 1 tablespoon of oil to the wok. When the oil is hot, add the chili paste and stir-fry until aromatic. Add the spinach. Stir-fry for 1 minute, adding sugar or soy sauce to season if desired. Add the prepared sauce in the middle of the wok and bring to a boil. Add the pork. Turn down the heat, mix everything through, and serve hot.

PER SERVING Calories: 210 | Fat: 12 grams | Protein: 19 grams | Sodium: 1,549 milligrams | Fiber: 0 grams | Carbohydrates: 4 grams | Sugar: 2 grams

Char Siu (Chinese Barbecue Pork)

Use pork belly if you like a moist, fatty barbecue, pork loin if you prefer a leaner dish, and pork butt if you want something in between.

INGREDIENTS | SERVES 6

3 tablespoons maltose

3 tablespoons honey

3 tablespoons hoisin sauce

3 tablespoons soy sauce

1 teaspoon Chinese five-spice powder

1 teaspoon white pepper

2 tablespoons sesame oil

6 cloves garlic, minced

2 pounds lean pork butt, pork belly, or pork loin

The Secret of Maltose

Maltose is a kind of sugar syrup that is found in many Asian markets. It's the secret behind the sticky sweetness in Chinese barbecues.

1. Combine all the ingredients except the pork in a small saucepan. The maltose may be a bit lumpy, but will smooth out once heated. Simmer on medium heat until all the ingredients are incorporated and the sauce has thickened slightly, 5–7 minutes. Remove from the heat and let cool.

2. Cut the pork into 4 pieces. Place the pieces in a large shallow dish and pour in about ¾ of the sauce to coat the pork thoroughly. Cover the dish and let the pork marinate in the refrigerator overnight. Save the remaining sauce in a separate container in the refrigerator.

3. When you are ready to cook the pork, preheat the oven to 350°F. Shake excess sauce off the pork and roast on a rack over a roasting pan. Cook for 45 minutes, then remove from the oven.

4. Brush the pork with the remaining marinade. Turn the oven up to broil. Return the pork to the oven to char on all sides.

5. Let the meat rest about 10 minutes, and then slice and serve.

PER SERVING Calories: 515 | Fat: 20 grams | Protein: 48 grams | Sodium: 1,438 milligrams | Fiber: 0 grams | Carbohydrates: 35 grams | Sugar: 31 grams

Chinese Sausage and Cabbage Stir-Fry

Shallot makes an interesting change from garlic and ginger in this simple recipe.
Add mushrooms for a complete, one-dish meal.

INGREDIENTS | SERVES 4

2 tablespoons vegetable oil

2 teaspoons minced shallot

4 Chinese sausages, diagonally sliced into bite-size pieces

6 large cabbage leaves, shredded

¾ cup chicken broth

2 teaspoons Chinese rice wine or dry sherry

2 green onions, finely chopped on the diagonal

How to Clean a Carbon Steel Wok

Never scrub the wok with an abrasive cleanser. Instead, remove stubborn food particles with a nonmetallic scrubber. Wash the wok in soapy water. To ensure it dries completely, leave for a few minutes on the stove with the heat turned low. Add a light coating of oil before storing in the cupboard. (You can skip this last step if the wok sees a lot of use.)

1. Add the oil to a preheated wok or skillet. When the oil is hot, add the shallot and stir-fry briefly. Add the sausages. Stir-fry for about 2 minutes, then push the sausages up to the side of the wok.

2. Add the cabbage. Stir-fry for about 2 minutes.

3. Add the chicken broth and rice wine in the middle of the wok and bring to a boil.

4. Simmer, covered, for 3–4 minutes; stir in the green onions, and serve hot.

PER SERVING Calories: 257 | Fat: 19 grams | Protein: 12 grams | Sodium: 896 milligrams | Fiber: 1 gram | Carbohydrates: 10 grams | Sugar: 3 grams

Pork with Wood's Ear Mushrooms

Wood's ear mushrooms do not have a lot of flavor on their own, but they absorb sauces well. They are also valued for their texture.

INGREDIENTS | SERVES 4

½ pound boneless pork, sliced into strips

2 teaspoons Xiaoshing wine

2 teaspoons cornstarch

4 ounces dried wood's ear mushrooms

2 tablespoons peanut oil

1" piece ginger, julienned

1 small carrot, julienned

½ green pepper, julienned

1 teaspoon sugar

1 teaspoon light soy sauce

1 teaspoon oyster sauce

½ cup water or stock of your choosing

2 scallions, cut into thin strips on the diagonal

1 teaspoon sesame oil

1. In a medium bowl, combine the pork with the wine and cornstarch. Mix with your fingertips to coat the pork thoroughly and set aside.

2. Soak the wood ear mushrooms in water for about 20 minutes to soften. Drain, discarding the soaking liquid.

3. Heat a wok over medium-high heat and swirl in the peanut oil. Add the ginger and stir-fry about 30 seconds. Add the mushrooms, carrot, and green pepper. Stir-fry 2–3 minutes, or until the vegetables turn bright in color.

4. Add pork strips, stirring so that they do not clump. Cook another 2–3 minutes. Add sugar, soy sauce, and oyster sauce. Stir to combine, then add the water or stock. Bring to a boil. The sauce will thicken almost immediately. Stir in the scallions, finish with the sesame oil, and serve.

PER SERVING Calories: 248 | Fat: 10 grams | Protein: 15 grams | Sodium: 174 milligrams | Fiber: 3 grams | Carbohydrates: 26 grams | Sugar: 3 grams

CHAPTER 9

Chicken, Turkey, and Duck Dishes

Basic Chicken Stir-Fry

Simmering the chicken in broth and seasonings brings out its flavors. Serve with Stir-Fried Baby Bok Choy (see recipe in Chapter 12) for a quick and easy meal.

INGREDIENTS | SERVES 4

2 tablespoons vegetable oil

1 garlic clove, minced

2 thin slices ginger

1 pound boneless, skinless chicken breast, cut into cubes or thin slices

½ cup chicken stock or broth

1 tablespoon Chinese rice wine or dry sherry

1 teaspoon sugar

¼ teaspoon salt

1. Add the oil to a preheated wok or skillet. When the oil is hot, add the garlic and ginger. Stir-fry briefly until aromatic. Add the chicken and stir-fry until it changes color, 4–5 minutes.

2. Add the chicken stock, rice wine, sugar, and salt, and bring to a boil. Simmer, covered, until the chicken is cooked, another 1–2 minutes.

PER SERVING Calories: 203 | Fat: 8 grams | Protein: 23 grams | Sodium: 258 milligrams | Fiber: 0 grams | Carbohydrates: 4 grams | Sugar: 2 grams

Chicken Curry Thighs

Leaving the potatoes unpeeled gives a deeper flavor to the curry and provides additional nutrients. Serve these thighs with steamed rice.

INGREDIENTS | SERVES 6

1 tablespoon peanut oil

6 bone-in chicken thighs

2 garlic cloves, minced

1 tablespoon minced ginger

1 teaspoon curry powder

1 teaspoon turmeric

1 medium onion, peeled and finely chopped

1 medium carrot, peeled and diced

1 medium potato, peeled or unpeeled, cut into 1" cubes

1 cup chicken stock

1 tablespoon soy sauce

1 cup fresh or frozen peas

1. Heat the peanut oil in a wok over medium-high heat. Brown the chicken thighs, 5 minutes per side.

2. Add the garlic, ginger, curry powder, and turmeric to the wok. Cook about 30 seconds, stirring. Add the onion, carrot, and potato and stir to coat.

3. Add the chicken stock and soy sauce. Reduce the heat to a medium-low and cook until the vegetables are tender and the chicken is cooked through, about 30 minutes. Add the peas 10 minutes before the end of cooking time.

PER SERVING Calories: 196 | Fat: 11 grams | Protein: 12 grams | Sodium: 230 milligrams | Fiber: 2 grams | Carbohydrates: 11 grams | Sugar: 2 grams

Moo Goo Gai Pan

The combination of chicken and mushrooms is central to this dish. Moo goo refers to mushrooms, and gai pan means chicken stir-fry. However, feel free to substitute other vegetables for the bamboo shoots.

INGREDIENTS | SERVES 4

2 (6-ounce) boneless, skinless chicken breasts, cut into thin slices

4 tablespoons oyster sauce, divided

2 teaspoons cornstarch, divided

½ cup chicken stock or broth

1 teaspoon sugar

⅛ teaspoon white pepper

4 tablespoons vegetable oil, divided

1 clove garlic, minced

½ cup fresh mushrooms, thinly sliced

½ (8-ounce) can bamboo shoots, rinsed

1. Place the chicken in a medium bowl. Mix in 2 tablespoons of oyster sauce and 1 teaspoon of cornstarch. Marinate the chicken for 30 minutes.

2. In a small bowl, mix together the chicken stock, sugar, white pepper, 2 tablespoons of oyster sauce, and 1 teaspoon of cornstarch. Set aside.

3. Add 2 tablespoons of oil to a preheated wok or skillet. When the oil is hot, add the garlic and stir-fry briefly until aromatic. Add the chicken and stir-fry until it changes color and is nearly cooked through, 3–4 minutes. Remove the chicken from the wok and set aside.

4. Wipe the wok clean and add 2 more tablespoons of oil. When the oil is hot, add the mushrooms and stir-fry for about 1 minute. Add the bamboo shoots.

5. Give the prepared sauce a quick stir. Make a well in the middle of the wok by pushing the vegetables up to the sides. Add the sauce in the middle, stirring vigorously to thicken. Add the chicken and mix through. The chicken will be cooked through in about 1–2 minutes.

PER SERVING Calories: 248 | Fat: 15 grams | Protein: 20 grams | Sodium: 555 milligrams | Fiber: 1 gram | Carbohydrates: 7 grams | Sugar: 2 grams

Chicken Glazed in Bean Sauce

This recipe produces a tender chicken lightly glazed with savory bean sauce.
For added protein, try stirring in cashews or peanuts before serving.

INGREDIENTS | SERVES 4

2 tablespoons Chinese rice wine or dry sherry

1 tablespoon soy sauce

2½ green onions, thinly sliced on the diagonal, divided

2 (6-ounce) boneless, skinless chicken breasts, cut into bite-size pieces

½ cup chicken stock or broth

1 tablespoon dark soy sauce

1 tablespoon bean sauce

2 tablespoons brown sugar

1 clove garlic, chopped

2 tablespoons vegetable oil

1 teaspoon cornstarch mixed with 4 teaspoons water

1. Mix together the rice wine, soy sauce, and half of a green onion in a medium bowl. Add the chicken. Marinate the chicken for 1 hour.

2. In a small bowl, combine the chicken stock, dark soy sauce, bean sauce, brown sugar, and garlic. Set aside.

3. Add the oil to a preheated wok or skillet. When the oil is hot, add the chicken and stir-fry until it is nearly cooked through, 3–4 minutes. Remove from the wok and set aside.

4. Add the sauce into the wok. Add the cornstarch-and-water mixture in the middle, stirring vigorously to thicken. Add the chicken, mixing in and letting the sauce reduce until it forms a glaze. The chicken will cook through in another 1–2 minutes. Stir in the 2 sliced green onions.

PER SERVING Calories: 221 | Fat: 0 grams | Protein: 22 grams | Sodium: 1,099 milligrams | Fiber: 1 gram | Carbohydrates: 14 grams | Sugar: 9 grams

New Year's Chicken

This chicken is traditionally served whole—with head and feet included—to symbolize completeness for the lunar new year.

INGREDIENTS | SERVES 4

1 (3-pound) whole chicken

2 tablespoons salt

4 (1") pieces of ginger, smashed lightly with a cleaver

1 bunch scallions, cut into large pieces

1. Clean the chicken, removing the thick ridges of excess fat. Rinse well under cold water, inside and out and pat dry.

2. Rub the salt over the chicken, including the inside cavity. Let sit for 1 hour. Place the ginger and scallions into the chicken cavity. Place the chicken on a platter for steaming.

3. Bring several inches of water to boil in a pot or wok large enough to hold the chicken. It should have a snug-fitting lid. Set a rack in the pot or wok, and place the platter with the chicken on top. Cover. Reduce the heat to low. Steam 45 minutes, not disturbing the lid. Pierce the chicken with a toothpick to test for doneness. Juices should run clear.

4. Remove the garlic and ginger from the cavity. Chop and serve with Ginger Scallion Sauce from Chapter 2.

PER SERVING Calories: 300 | Fat: 16 grams | Protein: 35 grams | Sodium: 1,055 milligrams | Fiber: 0 grams | Carbohydrates: 0 grams | Sugar: 0 grams

Chicken Cantonese

Adding garlic to the egg-and-milk soaking mixture imparts a subtle, mysterious flavor to the chicken.

INGREDIENTS | SERVES 4

2 eggs

1 cup milk

2 cloves garlic, lightly smashed

1 (3-pound) whole chicken, cut into pieces

⅓ cup soy sauce

⅓ cup sugar

1 tablespoon grated ginger

⅓ cup whiskey

1½ cups flour

4 cups vegetable oil

1 scallion, green part only, cut into 1" lengths on the diagonal

1. Mix together the eggs and milk in a large bowl. Add the smashed garlic cloves. Place the chicken in the mixture, turning to ensure it is thoroughly coated. Let sit about 15 minutes.

2. Meanwhile, in a small saucepan, stir together the soy sauce, sugar, ginger, and whiskey. Bring to a gentle boil over medium-high heat, then reduce the heat to low, and simmer until the sauce has thickened so that it will cling to the back of a spoon. Turn off the heat.

3. One by one, remove the chicken pieces from the egg mixture and dredge them in the flour.

4. Heat the oil in a wok until it is very hot but not smoking. Add the chicken pieces, being careful not to overcrowd the wok; work in batches if you have to. Deep-fry the pieces until the crust is a golden brown and very crispy, about 5 minutes. Remove from the wok and drain on paper towels.

5. Heat the sauce through once again, stirring to keep it smooth. Serve the chicken coated in the sauce and garnished with scallions.

PER SERVING Calories: 660 | Fat: 29 grams | Protein: 40 grams | Sodium: 1,497 milligrams | Fiber: 1 gram | Carbohydrates: 44 grams | Sugar: 19 grams

Baked Oyster-Sauce Chicken

Scoring the chicken thighs makes it easier for the marinade to penetrate the meat.
This dish tastes delicious served with Snow Pea Stir-Fry (see recipe in Chapter 12).

INGREDIENTS | SERVES 4

1½ pounds bone-in chicken thighs

1 tablespoon dark soy sauce

2 tablespoons oyster sauce

1 tablespoon Chinese rice wine or dry sherry

1½ teaspoons sugar

4 tablespoons water

½ teaspoon sesame oil

2 garlic cloves, minced

1 teaspoon minced ginger

Bagging It

Don't have a large enough bag to hold the chicken thighs? Place them on a plate and rub the marinade over, making sure to coat all the chicken. Cover with plastic wrap and refrigerate for 2–3 hours. Reserve any leftover marinade to pour over the chicken while baking.

1. Remove the skin from the chicken thighs and make 2 diagonal cuts on each side of the thigh.

2. Mix together the dark soy sauce, oyster sauce, rice wine, sugar, water, and sesame oil. Place the sauce in a gallon-size zip-top plastic bag. Add the chicken, shaking the bag lightly to make sure the sauce coats all the chicken. Seal the bag and place in the refrigerator. Marinate the chicken for 2–3 hours, turning the bag occasionally.

3. Preheat the oven to 400°F.

4. Remove the chicken thighs from the bag, reserving the sauce. Place the chicken thighs on a baking sheet sprayed with cooking spray. Pour half of the sauce over, making sure both sides of the thighs are covered. Add the minced garlic and ginger. Bake the thighs for 15 minutes.

5. Add the remaining half of the sauce and cook for another 15 minutes, or until the thighs are cooked.

PER SERVING Calories: 228 | Fat: 7 grams | Protein: 34 grams | Sodium: 676 milligrams | Fiber: 0 grams | Carbohydrates: 4 grams | Sugar: 2 grams

Soy Sauce Chicken

For a fancier presentation, chop the chicken legs into pieces and place on a platter. Pour the sauce over the chopped chicken.

INGREDIENTS | SERVES 2

1 teaspoon five-spice powder

1 tablespoon cornstarch

2 chicken legs

½ cup soy sauce

¾ cup water

2 tablespoons Chinese rice wine or dry sherry

4 teaspoons brown sugar

3 cups oil

1 large clove garlic, minced

1 slice ginger, minced

From Marinade to Sauce

When a marinade does double duty as a sauce, it's important to ensure that it is thoroughly cooked. As an added precaution, you can bring the marinade to boil in a saucepan before adding it to the wok.

1. In a medium bowl, mix the five-spice powder and the cornstarch. Add the chicken and marinate for 30 minutes.

2. In a small bowl, mix together the soy sauce, water, rice wine, and brown sugar, and set aside.

3. Heat the oil in a wok. When the oil reaches 325°F, deep-fry the chicken legs until they are browned, 5–10 minutes, depending on size. Remove with a slotted spoon and drain on paper towels.

4. Drain all but 2 tablespoons of oil out of the wok. Add the garlic and ginger, and stir-fry briefly until aromatic. Add the prepared sauce. Add the chicken, cover, and simmer for 15–20 minutes, until the chicken is cooked.

PER SERVING Calories: 677 | Fat: 54 grams | Protein: 25 grams | Sodium: 4,229 milligrams | Fiber: 0 grams | Carbohydrates: 23 grams | Sugar: 14 grams

Hoisin Chicken

To avoid the growth of harmful bacteria, always refrigerate any dish while it is marinating.

INGREDIENTS | SERVES 4

1½ pounds bone-in chicken thighs
2 tablespoons hoisin sauce
1 tablespoon dark soy sauce
4 tablespoons water
1 teaspoon sugar
⅛ teaspoon white pepper, or to taste
1 large garlic clove, chopped

1. Remove the skin from the chicken thighs and make 2 diagonal cuts on each side of the thigh.

2. Mix together the hoisin sauce, dark soy sauce, water, sugar, white pepper, and garlic. Place the sauce in a gallon-size zip-top plastic bag. Add the chicken, shaking the bag slightly to make sure the sauce coats all the chicken. Seal the bag and place in the refrigerator. Marinate the chicken for 2–3 hours, turning the bag occasionally.

3. Preheat the oven to 400°F.

4. Remove the chicken thighs from the bag, reserving the sauce. Place the thighs on a baking sheet sprayed with cooking spray. Brush on half of the sauce, making sure both sides of the thighs are covered. Bake the thighs for 15 minutes.

5. Brush on the remainder of the sauce, and bake for another 15 minutes, or until the thighs are cooked.

PER SERVING Calories: 227 | Fat: 7 grams | Protein: 34 grams | Sodium: 525 milligrams | Fiber: 0 grams | Carbohydrates: 5 grams | Sugar: 3 grams

Lemony Chicken Stir-Fry

Sweet brown sugar nicely balances tart lemon juice in this recipe. Serve with Tomato Egg-Flower Soup (see recipe in Chapter 4) for an interesting flavor combination.

INGREDIENTS | SERVES 4

2 (6-ounce) boneless, skinless chicken breasts, cut into thin strips

2 tablespoons Chinese rice wine or dry sherry, divided

3 teaspoons soy sauce, divided

3 tablespoons plus ½ teaspoon freshly squeezed lemon juice, divided

1 teaspoon cornstarch

½ cup water

2 tablespoons brown sugar

1 teaspoon honey

3½ tablespoons vegetable oil, divided

1 clove garlic, minced

1 teaspoon minced ginger

1 teaspoon cornstarch mixed with 4 teaspoons water

Why Marinate?

Although it can seem time-consuming, never forgo marinating meat if a recipe calls for it. Besides lending flavor, a good marinade tenderizes the meat as well. It's rare to find a Chinese recipe that doesn't call for marinating meat prior to stir-frying.

1. Place the chicken in a medium bowl. Add 1 tablespoon of rice wine, 1 teaspoon of soy sauce, ½ teaspoon of lemon juice, and 1 teaspoon of cornstarch to the chicken, adding the cornstarch last. Marinate the chicken for 30 minutes.

2. In a small bowl, mix together 3 tablespoons of lemon juice, the water, 1 tablespoon of rice wine, 2 teaspoons of soy sauce, the brown sugar, and honey. Set aside.

3. Add 2 tablespoons of oil to a preheated wok or skillet. When the oil is hot, add the chicken and stir-fry until it changes color and is nearly cooked. Remove from the wok and set aside.

4. Clean out the wok with a paper towel. Preheat and add 1½ tablespoons of oil. When the oil is hot, add the garlic and ginger. Stir-fry briefly until aromatic. Add the prepared sauce, bringing it to a boil.

5. Give the cornstarch-and-water mixture a quick stir. Add to the sauce, stirring vigorously to thicken. Add the chicken and heat through.

PER SERVING Calories: 255 | Fat: 13 grams | Protein: 20 grams | Sodium: 327 milligrams | Fiber: 0 grams | Carbohydrates: 14 grams | Sugar: 10 grams

Steamed Lemon Chicken

This recipe provides a generous helping of sauce to mix with rice and other vegetables.

INGREDIENTS | SERVES 1

1 (6-ounce) boneless, skinless chicken breast

1 tablespoon minced ginger

1½ tablespoons freshly squeezed lemon juice

¼ cup water

2 teaspoons Chinese rice wine or dry sherry

1 teaspoon soy sauce

1½ teaspoons sugar

½ teaspoon black rice vinegar

1 teaspoon cornstarch

1. Place the chicken on a heatproof plate on a bamboo steamer. Add the ginger. Steam for 20 minutes, or until the chicken turns white and is cooked.

2. While the chicken is steaming, mix together the lemon juice, water, rice wine, soy sauce, sugar, black rice vinegar, and cornstarch in a small saucepan. Heat the sauce to boiling over medium-high heat. Pour over the steamed chicken.

PER SERVING Calories: 218 | Fat: 2 grams | Protein: 40 grams | Sodium: 478 milligrams | Fiber: 0 grams | Carbohydrates: 7 grams | Sugar: 1 gram

Basic Chicken Velvet

To make sure the raw chicken does not contaminate other foods, prepare it in a separate work area and wash your hands thoroughly afterward.

INGREDIENTS | SERVES 4

2 (6-ounce) boneless, skinless chicken breasts

2 tablespoons rice vinegar

¼ teaspoon five-spice powder

2 teaspoons cornstarch

1 egg white

1. Using a sharp knife or a food processor, mince the chicken.

2. Mix together the rice vinegar, five-spice powder, and cornstarch. Add to the minced chicken, separating the individual chicken pieces.

3. Beat the egg white until creamy but not stiff. Fold into the chicken mixture.

PER SERVING Calories: 103 | Fat: 1 gram | Protein: 20 grams | Sodium: 69 milligrams | Fiber: 0 grams | Carbohydrates: 1 gram | Sugar: 0 grams

Deep-Fried Chicken Velvet

Deep-Fried Chicken Velvet nearly melts in your mouth. The possibilities for pairing this dish are endless—look for contrasts in texture and color.

INGREDIENTS | SERVES 4

½ cup chicken stock

2 tablespoons Chinese rice wine or dry sherry

½ teaspoon salt (or to taste)

4 cups plus 2 tablespoons vegetable oil, divided

2 leeks, cut diagonally into 1" sections

1 tablespoon soy sauce

Basic Chicken Velvet (see recipe in this chapter)

2 teaspoons cornstarch

4 teaspoons water

1. In a small bowl, mix together the chicken stock, rice wine, and salt in a small bowl. Set aside.

2. In a wok, heat 4 cups of oil to 350°F. While the oil is heating, heat 2 tablespoons of oil in a second skillet or wok. When the oil in the second skillet is hot, add the leeks. Stir-fry for about 1 minute, then add the soy sauce. Stir-fry until the leeks turn a bright green, and remove from the pan. Wipe out the pan with a paper towel and set aside.

3. When the oil for deep-frying is ready, carefully slide in the Basic Chicken Velvet pieces and deep-fry until the chicken turns white and is cooked. (This will take 1 minute at most.) Remove from the wok and drain on paper towels.

4. Heat the chicken-broth mixture in the second skillet or wok over medium-high heat. When it is boiling, add the Basic Chicken Velvet and mix. If necessary, break up the chicken with chopsticks or a spatula. Push the chicken up to the sides of the pan.

5. Mix the cornstarch and water and add to the middle of the pan, stirring vigorously to thicken. Mix thoroughly with the chicken. Serve the chicken with the leeks.

PER SERVING Calories: 435 | Fat: 36 grams | Protein: 21 grams | Sodium: 689 milligrams | Fiber: 1 gram | Carbohydrates: 11 grams | Sugar: 4 grams

Chicken with Red and Green Peppers

Serve with a sweet-and-sour vegetable dish such as Sweet-and-Sour Chinese Greens (see recipe in Chapter 12) for an interesting juxtaposition of flavors.

INGREDIENTS | SERVES 4

2 (6-ounce) boneless, skinless chicken breasts, cut into 1½" cubes

1 tablespoon soy sauce

1 egg white

2½ teaspoons cornstarch, divided

¼ cup water

1½ teaspoons sugar

1 tablespoon black bean sauce

¼ teaspoon chili paste

4 tablespoons vegetable oil, divided

2 garlic cloves, chopped

1 green bell pepper, seeded and cut into chunks

½ cup chopped red onion

1 red bell pepper, seeded and cut into chunks

Quick Red Bell Peppers

Although they are both members of the capsicum family, red peppers have a shorter cooking time than green peppers. For best results, add them at a later stage in stir-frying.

1. Place the chicken in a medium bowl. Mix in the soy sauce, egg white, and 1½ teaspoons of cornstarch, being sure to add the cornstarch last. Marinate the chicken for 30 minutes.

2. To make the sauce, mix together the water, sugar, black bean sauce, chili paste, and remaining cornstarch in a small bowl and set aside.

3. Add 2 tablespoons of oil to a preheated wok or skillet. When the oil is hot, add the garlic and stir-fry briefly until aromatic. Add the marinated chicken to the wok. Stir-fry until the chicken turns white and is nearly cooked through, 3–4 minutes. Remove from the wok and set aside.

4. Add 2 tablespoons of oil to the wok. When the oil is hot, add the green pepper and onion. Stir-fry for about 1 minute, and then add the red pepper. Stir-fry until the peppers turn a bright color and the onion is softened.

5. Give the prepared sauce a quick stir. Push the vegetables to the side of the wok and add the sauce in the middle, stirring vigorously to thicken. Mix with the vegetables. Add the chicken. Mix all the ingredients and serve hot.

PER SERVING Calories: 245 | Fat: 15 grams | Protein: 21 grams | Sodium: 332 milligrams | Fiber: 1 gram | Carbohydrates: 7 grams | Sugar: 3 grams

Bang Bang Chicken

To use Chinese noodles instead of bean curd sheets, cook the noodles according to instructions, drain well, and lay over the cucumber slices.

INGREDIENTS | SERVES 4

1 pound boneless, skinless chicken breasts

1 large dried bean curd sheet

2 small cucumbers, peeled and sliced

½ teaspoon salt

Spicy Szechwan Peanut Sauce (see recipe in Chapter 2)

1. Boil the chicken breasts in water for 15–20 minutes. Drain well.

2. Cut the bean curd sheet into 4 squares. Soak the sheets in cold water to soften.

3. Toss the cucumbers with salt and set aside for 15 minutes.

4. Cut the chicken into thin slices. Lay the cucumber slices on a plate and top with a bean curd sheet. Top with the chicken and the sauce.

PER SERVING Calories: 136 | Fat: 1 gram | Protein: 26 grams | Sodium: 232 milligrams | Fiber: 0 grams | Carbohydrates: 2 grams | Sugar: 1 gram

Spicy Chicken with Cashews

Native to Brazil, cashews made their way east via seventeenth-century Portuguese explorers and are now commonly featured in Asian dishes.

INGREDIENTS | SERVES 4

2 tablespoons dark soy sauce

1 tablespoon Chinese rice wine or dry sherry

1 teaspoon sugar

¼ teaspoon sesame oil

¼ teaspoon chili paste

3 tablespoons vegetable oil, divided

2 (6-ounce) boneless, skinless chicken breasts, cut into 1" cubes

½ cup cashews

PER SERVING Calories: 283 | Fat: 18 grams | Protein: 23 grams | Sodium: 593 milligrams | Fiber: 0 grams | Carbohydrates: 7 grams | Sugar: 3 grams

1. In a small bowl, mix together the dark soy sauce, rice wine, sugar, sesame oil, and chili paste, and set aside.

2. Add 2 tablespoons of oil to a preheated wok or skillet. Stir-fry the chicken until it is nearly cooked through, about 3–4 minutes. Remove, and drain on paper towels.

3. Wipe the wok clean with a paper towel and add 1 tablespoon of oil. Stir-fry the cashews very briefly, until they are golden.

4. Add the prepared sauce to the wok and bring to a boil. Turn down the heat and add the chicken back into the wok. Mix through and serve hot.

General Tso's Chicken

To serve a vegetable with this dish, stir-fry while you are waiting for the oil to heat for deep-frying.

INGREDIENTS | SERVES 4

1 pound boneless, skinless chicken thighs, cut into 1" cubes

2 tablespoons soy sauce

3 teaspoons Chinese rice wine or dry sherry, divided

⅛ teaspoon white pepper

1 tablespoon cornstarch

4 tablespoons dark soy sauce

2 teaspoons sugar

½ teaspoon sesame oil

4 cups vegetable oil

1 large clove garlic, minced

1 teaspoon minced ginger

2 green onions, thinly sliced

6 dried red chilies, seeded and chopped

Food Fit for a General

General Tso's Chicken is named after a famous military leader who helped quash China's Taiping Rebellion in the mid-1800s. How the dish came to be named after General Tso is lost to history, although he was rumored to have a penchant for fiery foods.

1. Place the chicken in a medium bowl. Mix in the soy sauce, 2 teaspoons of rice wine, the white pepper, and cornstarch, adding the cornstarch last. Marinate the chicken for 30 minutes.

2. In a small bowl, combine the dark soy sauce, sugar, sesame oil, and 1 teaspoon of rice wine. Set aside.

3. Heat the vegetable oil to 350°F. When the oil is hot, add the chicken cubes and deep-fry until they are lightly browned, about 5 minutes. Remove from the wok and drain on paper towels.

4. Raise the temperature of the wok to 400°F. Deep-fry the chicken a second time briefly, until the chicken turns golden brown, another 5 minutes. Remove from the wok and drain on paper towels.

5. Drain the wok, leaving 2 tablespoons of oil for stir-frying. When the oil is hot, add the garlic, ginger, and green onions. Stir-fry briefly until aromatic. Add the chilies and cook for 1 minute.

6. Add the prepared sauce in the middle of the wok and bring to a boil. Add the chicken and mix through.

PER SERVING Calories: 439 | Fat: 32 grams | Protein: 25 grams | Sodium: 1,701 milligrams | Fiber: 0 grams | Carbohydrates: 11 grams | Sugar: 5 grams

Quick and Easy Orange Chicken

Serve with rice and a steamed vegetable for a quick and easy dish on busy weeknights.

INGREDIENTS | SERVES 4

2 (6-ounce) boneless, skinless chicken breasts, cut into 1" cubes

2 tablespoons Chinese rice wine or dry sherry

1 egg white

5 teaspoons cornstarch, divided

¼ cup water

5 teaspoons freshly squeezed orange juice

1 tablespoon soy sauce

1½ teaspoons brown sugar

¼ teaspoon chili paste

¼ teaspoon sesame oil

2 tablespoons vegetable oil

1 teaspoon minced ginger

1 clove garlic, minced

1. Place the chicken in a medium bowl. Mix in the rice wine, egg white, and 3 teaspoons of cornstarch, adding the cornstarch last. Marinate the chicken for 15 minutes.

2. In a small bowl, mix together the water, orange juice, soy sauce, brown sugar, chili paste, sesame oil, and 2 teaspoons of cornstarch.

3. Add the vegetable oil to a preheated wok or skillet. When the oil is hot, add the ginger and garlic. Stir-fry briefly until aromatic.

4. Add the chicken and stir-fry until the chicken changes color and is nearly cooked through, about 3–4 minutes.

5. Give the prepared sauce a quick stir. Push the chicken up the sides of the wok and add the sauce, stirring vigorously to thicken. Mix the sauce with the chicken and cook the chicken for another minute.

PER SERVING Calories: 200 | Fat: 8 grams | Protein: 21 grams | Sodium: 386 milligrams | Fiber: 0 grams | Carbohydrates: 9 grams | Sugar: 4 grams

Kung Pao Chicken

This version of this classic dish does not contain nuts, as it is said to be more authentic this way.

INGREDIENTS | SERVES 4

1 pound skinless, boneless chicken thighs, cut into 1" cubes

1½ teaspoons plus 1 tablespoon cornstarch, divided

2 teaspoons light soy sauce

½ teaspoon salt

1 teaspoon sugar

1 teaspoon rice wine vinegar

1 cup water

2½ teaspoons peanut oil

1 teaspoon chili paste with garlic

2 thin slices fresh ginger

2 garlic cloves, thinly sliced

1 teaspoon Shaoxing rice wine or medium-dry sherry

3 tablespoons garlic chives or other chives, cut into 2" segments

1. Mix the chicken with 1½ teaspoons of cornstarch, the soy sauce, and salt in a medium bowl. Stir well and set aside.

2. In a small bowl, mix together the sugar, vinegar, remaining cornstarch, and water. Set aside.

3. Heat the wok over high heat. Add 1 tablespoon of oil and swirl to coat the pan. When the oil is thoroughly heated, add the chicken and stir-fry until seared, about 2 minutes. Transfer the chicken to paper towels to drain.

4. Wipe the wok clean. Return to medium-high heat. Add the remaining 1½ teaspoons of oil, chili paste, ginger, and garlic. Stir-fry for 30 seconds. Add the chicken, wine, vinegar-cornstarch mixture, and chives. Stir-fry until chicken is thoroughly cooked, about 2 more minutes. Serve hot.

PER SERVING Calories: 228 | Fat: 11 grams | Protein: 22 grams | Sodium: 599 milligrams | Fiber: 0 grams | Carbohydrates: 7 grams | Sugar: 2 grams

Sesame Hoisin Surprise

Hoisin sauce, chili paste, and brown sugar make an intriguing taste combination.
Serve with steamed vegetables and rice or noodles.

INGREDIENTS | SERVES 6

3 (6-ounce) boneless, skinless chicken breasts

2 tablespoons soy sauce

1 tablespoon Chinese rice wine or dry sherry

3 tablespoons cornstarch, divided

1 cup water

2 teaspoons hoisin sauce

2 tablespoons brown sugar

4 teaspoons dark soy sauce

2 teaspoons chili paste

2 teaspoons vegetable oil

2 garlic cloves, minced

2 tablespoons vegetable oil

1 green onion, thinly sliced

2 tablespoons toasted sesame seeds

1. Place the chicken in a medium bowl. Mix in the soy sauce, rice wine, and 1 tablespoon of cornstarch, adding the cornstarch last. Marinate the chicken for 30 minutes. Slice into pieces.

2. In a small saucepan, bring the water, hoisin sauce, brown sugar, dark soy sauce, chili paste, vegetable oil, garlic cloves, and 2 tablespoons of cornstarch to a boil over high heat. Reduce the heat to low and keep warm while stir-frying the chicken.

3. Add the oil to a preheated wok or skillet. When the oil is hot, add the marinated chicken pieces and stir-fry until they change color and are nearly cooked through. Remove the chicken from the wok and set aside.

4. As you finish stir-frying the chicken, bring the sauce back up to a boil. Mix in the green onion. Pour the sauce over the chicken and mix through. Garnish with the toasted sesame seeds.

PER SERVING Calories: 196 | Fat: 7 grams | Protein: 21 grams | Sodium: 775 milligrams | Fiber: 0 grams | Carbohydrates: 11 grams | Sugar: 5 grams

Garlic Chicken

This dish is a garlic lover's delight. To increase its potent aroma,
add more cloves or mince them instead of chopping.

INGREDIENTS | SERVES 8

4 (6-ounce) boneless, skinless chicken breasts, cut into 1½" cubes

2 egg whites

¼ teaspoon salt

2 teaspoons cornstarch

2 tablespoons vegetable oil

3 large garlic cloves, chopped

½ tablespoon chili paste

¼ cup soy sauce

2 tablespoons Chinese rice wine or dry sherry

2 green onions, cut into 1½" pieces

½ teaspoon sesame oil

2 cups cooked white rice

1 tomato, cut into wedges

Water-Poached Chicken

Poaching poultry in water gives it a soft and tender texture. For best results, keep the water at a low simmer and not strongly bubbling. It helps to have a colander set up before you poach the chicken, since it should be drained immediately. On its own, the whitish color of water-poached chicken can be a little disconcerting. This technique works best when you have a darker cut of meat or plan to cook the chicken in a dark-colored sauce.

1. Place the chicken in a medium bowl. Add the egg whites, salt, and cornstarch, adding the cornstarch last. Marinate the chicken for 1 hour.

2. Bring a large pot of water to a very low boil. Add the chicken, stirring to separate the pieces, and remove as soon as it is just turning white (about 60–90 seconds). Drain immediately.

3. Add the oil to a preheated wok or skillet. When the oil is hot, add the garlic and chili paste and stir-fry until the garlic is aromatic. Add the chicken and stir-fry briefly.

4. Add the soy sauce and rice wine. Bring to a boil and cook for a few minutes until everything is heated through. Stir in the green onions and drizzle with the sesame oil. Serve over rice, garnished with the tomato wedges.

PER SERVING Calories: 200 | Fat: 5 grams | Protein: 22 grams | Sodium: 675 milligrams | Fiber: 0 grams | Carbohydrates: 15 grams | Sugar: 1 gram

Chicken with Walnuts

The crunchy texture of walnuts goes well with velvety chicken cooked in a savory sauce.

INGREDIENTS | SERVES 4

2 (6-ounce) boneless, skinless chicken breasts, cut into 1" cubes

1 egg white

¼ teaspoon salt

2 teaspoons cornstarch

1½ tablespoons dark soy sauce

3 tablespoons oyster sauce

1½ tablespoons Chinese rice wine or dry sherry

2¼ teaspoons sugar

⅓ cup water

½ cup walnut halves

1 cup vegetable oil

1 garlic clove, smashed

1 teaspoon cornstarch mixed with 4 teaspoons water

1. Place the chicken in a medium bowl. Mix in the egg white, salt, and cornstarch, adding the cornstarch last. Marinate the chicken for 30 minutes.

2. In a small bowl, combine the dark soy sauce, oyster sauce, rice wine, sugar, and water. Set aside.

3. Boil the walnuts in water for at least 5 minutes. Drain and dry.

4. Add the oil to a preheated wok or skillet. When the oil is hot, add the chicken cubes. Velvet the chicken cubes by submerging them in the hot oil just until they change color. Remove immediately and drain on paper towels.

5. Remove all but 1 tablespoon of oil. When the oil is hot, add the garlic and stir-fry until aromatic. Add the walnuts and stir-fry for about 1 minute. Push up to the side of the wok and add the prepared sauce in the middle. Bring to a boil.

6. Give the cornstarch-and-water mixture a quick stir. Add to the middle of the wok, stirring quickly to thicken. Add the chicken. Mix everything together. Cover and simmer for 3–5 minutes until the chicken is cooked through.

PER SERVING Calories: 310 | Fat: 22 grams | Protein: 21 grams | Sodium: 958 milligrams | Fiber: 0 grams | Carbohydrates: 6 grams | Sugar: 2 grams

Chengdu Chicken

Chengdu Chicken is named after Chengdu, the capital city of the Szechwan province in western China.

INGREDIENTS | SERVES 8

2 stalks celery, cut diagonally into 1"
slices

3 teaspoons red or black rice vinegar

1 teaspoon sugar

¾ teaspoon salt, divided

½ cup hot water

1 teaspoon Chinese rice wine or dry
sherry

3 tablespoons vegetable oil, divided

1 tablespoon chopped ginger

2 garlic cloves, chopped

4 (6-ounce) boneless, skinless chicken
breasts, cut into 1½" cubes

2 tablespoons hot bean sauce

2 teaspoons cornstarch mixed with
¼ cup water

1. Blanch or parboil the celery in a pot of boiling water for 2–3 minutes. Drain.

2. In a small bowl, combine the rice vinegar, sugar, ½ teaspoon of salt, the hot water, and rice wine. Set aside.

3. Add 1 tablespoon of oil to a preheated wok or skillet. When the oil is hot, add the celery. Stir-fry briefly and add ¼ teaspoon of salt. Stir-fry until the celery changes color and is tender but still firm. Remove from the wok.

4. Wipe the wok clean with a paper towel. Add 2 tablespoons of oil. When the oil is hot, add the ginger and garlic and stir-fry briefly until aromatic. Add the chicken cubes. Stir-fry for 2–3 minutes, then add the hot bean sauce. Stir-fry until the chicken changes color and is nearly cooked through, about 3–4 minutes.

5. Add the prepared sauce and bring to a boil. Add the cornstarch-water mixture to the middle of the wok, stirring vigorously to thicken. Add the celery. Mix everything through and serve hot.

PER SERVING Calories: 205 | Fat: 13 grams | Protein: 17 grams | Sodium: 296 milligrams | Fiber: 0 grams | Carbohydrates: 2 grams | Sugar: 1 gram

Mango Chicken

Turmeric is a distant relative of ginger. In this recipe, it gives the chicken a nice yellow color.

INGREDIENTS | SERVES 8

4 (6-ounce) boneless, skinless chicken breasts, cut into 1½" cubes

1 egg white

1 tablespoon Chinese rice wine or dry sherry

¼ teaspoon salt

2 teaspoons cornstarch

2 tablespoons rice vinegar

2 tablespoons plus 1 teaspoon brown sugar

1 can mango slices, drained, juice reserved

1 cup vegetable oil

1 tablespoon minced ginger

1 teaspoon curry paste

½ teaspoon turmeric

Velveting Meat

Velveting meat is a handy trick restaurants use to tenderize meat such as chicken, pork, or beef. Why does it work? The initial contact with hot oil shocks the muscles, causing them to relax. The muscles remain relaxed when they are stir- or deep-fried according to the recipe instructions. The result is a piece of meat that is both firm and juicy.

1. Place the chicken in a medium bowl. Mix in the egg white, rice wine, salt, and cornstarch. Marinate the chicken for 30 minutes.

2. In a small saucepan, bring the rice vinegar, brown sugar, and ¾ cup of reserved mango juice to a boil over medium-high heat. Reduce the heat to low and keep warm.

3. Add the oil to a preheated wok or skillet. When the oil is hot, velvet the chicken by cooking very briefly in the hot oil, until it changes color and is nearly cooked through (about 30 seconds). Use tongs or cooking chopsticks to separate the individual pieces of chicken while it is cooking.

4. Remove all but 2 tablespoons of oil from the wok. (Wipe out the wok with a paper towel if necessary.) When the oil is hot, add the ginger, curry paste, and turmeric. Stir-fry for about 1 minute until aromatic. Add the chicken and mix with the curry paste.

5. Add the sauce and bring to a boil. Stir in the mango slices. Mix all the ingredients and serve hot.

PER SERVING Calories: 202 | Fat: 8 grams | Protein: 20 grams | Sodium: 228 milligrams | Fiber: 0 grams | Carbohydrates: 11 grams | Sugar: 9 grams

Quick and Easy Curry Chicken

Worried your curry powder is too strong? Add 1–2 teaspoons while stir-frying the ginger and garlic, and then add more with the chicken, if desired.

INGREDIENTS | SERVES 4

2 tablespoons vegetable oil

1 heaping teaspoon minced ginger

1 clove garlic, minced

1 tablespoon mild curry powder

2 (6-ounce) boneless, skinless chicken breasts, cut into 1½" cubes

¼ cup sliced water chestnuts

¼ cup sliced bamboo shoots

¼ cup chicken broth

2 green onions, minced

Curry—More Than a Powder

Although we tend to think of curry as a spice or blend of spices, the word has its origins in the Tamil word *kahri*, a spicy sauce. We have a British official to thank for the association of curry with a dry powder. The story is that, when leaving India, the official ordered his servant to prepare a compilation of spices so that he could enjoy his favorite Indian dishes upon returning home to Britain. Freshly made curry powder is preferable to commercially prepared brands. Still, in today's busy world it's not always possible to find time for chopping herbs and grinding fresh spices. Although this recipe uses a mild curry powder, the hotter Madras curry powders generally work best in Chinese dishes.

1. Add the oil to a preheated wok or skillet. When the oil is hot, add the ginger, garlic, and curry powder, and stir-fry until there is a strong odor of curry. Add the chicken and stir-fry for about 5 minutes, until the chicken is well mixed with the curry powder. Remove and set aside.

2. Add the water chestnuts and bamboo shoots to the wok and bring to a boil.

3. Return the chicken to the wok and add the chicken broth. Bring to a boil, cover, and simmer until the dish is cooked through, about 15 minutes. Stir in the green onions.

PER SERVING Calories: 124 | Fat: 7 grams | Protein: 11 grams | Sodium: 182 milligrams | Fiber: 0 grams | Carbohydrates: 2 grams | Sugar: 1 gram

Princess Chicken

Princess Chicken is a variation on General Tso's Chicken, made with light instead of dark chicken meat.

INGREDIENTS | SERVES 4

1 pound boneless, skinless chicken breast, cut into 1½" cubes

6 tablespoons soy sauce, divided

4 teaspoons Chinese rice wine or dry sherry, divided

1 tablespoon cornstarch

2 teaspoons sugar

¼ teaspoon sesame oil

3 tablespoons vegetable oil, divided

1 large clove garlic, minced

1 teaspoon minced ginger

2 green onions, thinly sliced

6 dried red chilies, seeded and chopped

1. Place the chicken in a medium bowl. Mix in 2 tablespoons of soy sauce, 3 teaspoons of rice wine, and the cornstarch, adding the cornstarch last. Marinate the chicken for 30 minutes.

2. In a small bowl, combine 4 tablespoons of soy sauce, 1 teaspoon of rice wine, the sugar, and the sesame oil. Set aside.

3. Add 2 tablespoons of vegetable oil to a preheated wok or skillet. When the oil is hot, add the chicken cubes and stir-fry until they are nearly cooked through, 3–4 minutes. Remove from the wok and drain on paper towels.

4. Add 1 tablespoon of oil to the wok. When the oil is hot, add the garlic, ginger, and green onions. Stir-fry briefly until aromatic. Add the chilies and cook for 1 minute.

5. Add the prepared sauce in the middle of the wok and bring to a boil. Add the chicken and mix through.

PER SERVING Calories: 263 | Fat: 12 grams | Protein: 28 grams | Sodium: 1,628 milligrams | Fiber: 0 grams | Carbohydrates: 8 grams | Sugar: 4 grams

Tea-Smoked Chicken

For a different flavor, try simmering the chicken prior to steaming in the black tea leaves.

INGREDIENTS | SERVES 6

2 tablespoons dark soy sauce

1 teaspoon sugar

1½ teaspoons Chinese rice wine or dry sherry

½ green onion, minced

1 (3-pound) whole chicken

3 tablespoons black tea leaves

½ cup brown sugar

¼ teaspoon Szechwan Salt and Pepper Mix (see recipe in Chapter 2)

½ cup uncooked rice

Tea-Smoked Food

There is no need to purchase a wood smoker to make Chinese favorites such as Tea-Smoked Chicken or Duck. Along with steaming and stir-frying, the versatile wok also functions as a smoker. Chinese cooks make a further departure from traditional smoking methods by using smoking solely to impart flavor to the food, not to cook it. (The food to be cooked is usually steamed or simmered first.) The smoking ingredient of choice in Chinese cooking is tea leaves; black are most popular, although green tea leaves are also used. Other spices and seasonings that may be added to the smoking mix include star anise, and brown or white sugar.

1. Mix together the dark soy sauce, sugar, rice wine, and green onion. Rub over the chicken and marinate for 1 hour.

2. In a medium bowl, mix together the tea leaves, brown sugar, Szechwan Salt and Pepper Mix, and rice. Set aside.

3. Prepare a bamboo steamer and steam the chicken for about 45 minutes, until it is cooked.

4. Cover the bottom and the inside of the wok with several layers of aluminum foil. Place the smoking spices at the bottom of the wok. Place a cake rack inside the wok and place the chicken on the rack. Turn the heat up. When smoke appears in a few places (about 10–15 minutes), cover the chicken with the lid and adjust the heat so that the stream of smoke remains steady. Continue smoking until the chicken turns a deep brown (about 15 minutes).

PER SERVING Calories: 378 | Fat: 17 grams | Protein: 22 grams | Sodium: 773 milligrams | Fiber: 0 grams | Carbohydrates: 32 grams | Sugar: 18 grams

Sesame Chicken

The secret to this popular restaurant dish lies in the sauce—adjust the sweetness level by increasing or decreasing the ratio of vinegar to sugar.

INGREDIENTS | SERVES 6

3 (6-ounce) boneless chicken breasts, cut into 1½" cubes

2 tablespoons soy sauce

1 tablespoon Chinese rice wine or dry sherry

⅛ teaspoon sesame oil

2 tablespoons flour

¼ teaspoon baking powder

¼ teaspoon baking soda

2 tablespoons plus ½ cup water, divided

6 tablespoons cornstarch, divided

1 teaspoon plus 4 cups vegetable oil

1 cup chicken stock or broth

2 tablespoons dark soy sauce

½ cup vinegar

2 teaspoons chili sauce with garlic

1 large clove garlic, minced

1 teaspoon rice vinegar

¾ cup sugar

2 tablespoons sesame seeds

Double Deep-Frying

Deep-frying meat twice is another technique Chinese restaurant chefs have in their cooking repertoire. Besides adding a crispier coating, the second frying seals in the meat's juices. Replacing egg in the batter with vegetable oil helps increase the crispiness.

1. Place the chicken in a medium bowl. Mix in the soy sauce, rice wine, sesame oil, flour, baking powder, baking soda, 2 tablespoons of water, 2 tablespoons of cornstarch, and 1 teaspoon of vegetable oil. Marinate the chicken for 30 minutes.

2. In a small saucepan, combine ½ cup of water, the chicken stock, dark soy sauce, vinegar, chili sauce, garlic, rice vinegar, sugar, and remaining cornstarch. Set aside.

3. Heat 4 cups of oil in a wok to 350°F. Add the marinated chicken and deep-fry until golden brown, about 5 minutes. Remove from the wok with a slotted spoon and drain on paper towels.

4. Raise the oil temperature in the wok to 400°F. Deep-fry the chicken a second time, until it turns golden brown. Remove and drain.

5. Give the sauce a quick stir. Bring to a boil over high heat. Pour over the deep-fried chicken. Garnish with the sesame seeds.

PER SERVING Calories: 360 | Fat: 16 grams | Protein: 19 grams | Sodium: 720 milligrams | Fiber: 1 gram | Carbohydrates: 33 grams | Sugar: 23 grams

Spicy Braised Chicken Wings

Madras—a hot curry paste made with turmeric, chili, cumin, and coriander, works well in this recipe. Yogurt is not typically found in Chinese cooking, but it tempers the heat of the curry.

INGREDIENTS | SERVES 6

12 chicken wings
¼ cup chicken broth
½ cup plain yogurt
1 tablespoon Chinese rice wine or dry sherry
1 tablespoon soy sauce
1 teaspoon honey
1 tablespoon curry paste
4 cups vegetable oil

1. Chop the chicken wings into pieces. In a large saucepan, blanch the chicken-wing pieces in boiling water for 2 minutes. Drain.

2. Combine the chicken broth, yogurt, rice wine, soy sauce, honey, and curry paste in a small bowl. Set aside.

3. Heat the oil for deep-frying. When the oil reaches 350°F, carefully slide the chicken-wing pieces into the wok. Deep-fry until they turn light brown. Remove with a slotted spoon and drain on paper towels.

4. Bring the sauce to a boil in a skillet or wok. Add the chicken pieces, cover, and simmer for 10–15 minutes, or until the chicken is cooked through.

PER SERVING Calories: 213 | Fat: 18 grams | Protein: 9 grams | Sodium: 235 milligrams | Fiber: 0 grams | Carbohydrates: 4 grams | Sugar: 3 grams

Oyster-Sauce Chicken Wings

To make an appealing appetizer, serve the wings cold, with a few sprigs of cilantro for a garnish.

INGREDIENTS | SERVES 8

⅓ cup soy sauce

1 tablespoon dark soy sauce

3 tablespoons oyster sauce

1 tablespoon Chinese rice wine or dry sherry

2 teaspoons sugar

2 tablespoons water

2 teaspoons sesame oil

16 chicken wings

3 garlic cloves, minced

How to Reduce Splattering During Deep-Frying

Make sure the food to be deep-fried is at room temperature. If deep-frying foods are coated in a sauce or batter, use a slotted spoon to drain off any excess before adding the food to the wok.

1. Combine the soy sauce, dark soy sauce, oyster sauce, rice wine, sugar, water, and sesame oil. Place the sauce in a gallon-size zip-top plastic bag. Add the chicken, shaking the bag lightly to make sure the sauce coats all the chicken. Seal the bag and place in the refrigerator. Marinate the chicken for 2–3 hours, turning the bag occasionally.

2. Preheat the oven to 350°F.

3. Remove the chicken wings from the bag, reserving the sauce. Place the wings on a baking sheet sprayed with cooking spray. Pour ½ the sauce over. Add the minced garlic. Bake the wings for 20 minutes.

4. Add the remaining half of the sauce and cook for another 15 minutes, or until the wings are cooked.

PER SERVING Calories: 181 | Fat: 12 grams | Protein: 14 grams | Sodium: 917 milligrams | Fiber: 0 grams | Carbohydrates: 3 grams | Sugar: 1 gram

Stuffed Chicken Wings

Serve this hearty appetizer on a bed of lettuce leaves garnished with cilantro.

INGREDIENTS | SERVES 10

10 chicken wings

2 Chinese dried mushrooms

½ cup ground pork

½ tablespoon soy sauce

½ tablespoon Chinese rice wine or dry sherry

¼ teaspoon sesame oil

½ teaspoon sugar

½ teaspoon salt

¼ teaspoon pepper

½ (8-ounce) can bamboo shoots, drained and julienned

1. Cut through the middle section of each wing and discard the drumette. Take a paring knife and, starting with the end of the midsection that was attached to the drumette, carefully scrape the meat away from the 2 bones in the middle section, taking care not to cut the skin. When the meat is scraped away, pull and remove the 2 bones in the midsection. This will give you a pouch to stuff.

2. Soak the dried mushrooms in hot water for at least 20 minutes to soften. Gently squeeze the mushrooms to remove excess water. Cut into thin slices.

3. Place the pork in a medium bowl. Use your hands to mix the soy sauce, rice wine, sesame oil, sugar, salt, and pepper in with the pork.

4. Take a small ball of pork and place it inside the chicken skin. Add 2 slices of bamboo and 2 slices of mushroom. Continue with the remainder of the chicken wings.

5. Steam the chicken wings on a heatproof plate on a bamboo steamer in the wok for about 20 minutes, or until the pork is cooked through.

PER SERVING Calories: 110 | Fat: 8 grams | Protein: 9 grams | Sodium: 207 milligrams | Fiber: 0 grams | Carbohydrates: 1 gram | Sugar: 0 grams

Drunken Chicken Wings

A dry white wine such as a Chardonnay works best in this recipe.

INGREDIENTS | SERVES 4

8 cups water

8 chicken wings

¼ teaspoon salt

⅛ teaspoon pepper

1 green onion, chopped

2 slices ginger

6 cups dry white wine

Out of Chicken Wings?

You can also make this dish using a whole chicken. Increase the amount of seasonings if desired. When ready to serve, place the whole chicken on a platter and garnish with sprigs of cilantro or green onion brushes. Carve up the chicken in front of guests.

1. In a large pot, bring 8 cups of water to a boil. While waiting for the water to boil, chop the chicken wings through the middle so that you have a drumette and the midsection. Chop off and discard the wing tips.

2. Cook the chicken wings in the boiling water for 5 minutes.

3. Add the salt, pepper, green onion, and ginger. Cover and simmer the chicken for 45 minutes. Cool.

4. Place the chicken wings in a sealed container and cover with the wine. Refrigerate for at least 12 hours before serving.

PER SERVING Calories: 174 | Fat: 10 grams | Protein: 12 grams | Sodium: 195 milligrams | Fiber: 0 grams | Carbohydrates: 1 gram | Sugar: 0 grams

Turkey with Water Chestnuts

For extra flavor, add ¼ teaspoon of chili paste to the sauce. Serve with a spicy dish such as Cold Szechwan Sesame Noodles (see recipe in Chapter 5).

INGREDIENTS | SERVES 4

2 tablespoons hoisin sauce

2 tablespoons soy sauce

3 tablespoons water

3 teaspoons brown sugar

3 tablespoons vegetable oil, divided

2 garlic cloves, minced

2 slices ginger, minced

1½ pounds boneless, skinless turkey breast, cut into 1½" cubes

1 can water chestnuts, rinsed

¼ teaspoon salt

1. In a small bowl, combine the hoisin sauce, soy sauce, water, and brown sugar. Set aside.

2. Add 2 tablespoons of oil to a preheated wok or skillet. When the oil is hot, add the garlic and ginger and stir-fry briefly until aromatic. Add the turkey and stir-fry in batches on medium to medium-high heat for about 4–5 minutes, until the meat is tender. Remove from the wok and set aside.

3. Add 1 tablespoon of oil to the wok. When the oil is hot, add the water chestnuts and stir-fry for about 1 minute. Add the salt and stir-fry until the water chestnuts turn light brown. Push the water chestnuts up to the sides of the wok.

4. Add the prepared sauce in the middle of the wok and bring to a boil. Add the turkey cubes and stir-fry for 2–3 minutes, until all the ingredients are mixed together.

PER SERVING Calories: 326 | Fat: 12 grams | Protein: 43 grams | Sodium: 863 milligrams | Fiber: 0 grams | Carbohydrates: 9 grams | Sugar: 6 grams

Peking Duck

Peking Duck is a featured dish at many Beijing restaurants. The trick to preparing this impressive dish is to make sure the duck is completely dry before roasting. Serve the duck on Mu Shu Pancakes (see recipe in Chapter 6) brushed with hoisin sauce.

INGREDIENTS | SERVES 4

1 (5-pound) whole duck

8 cups water

3 tablespoons honey

1½ tablespoons rice vinegar

1 tablespoon Chinese rice wine or dry sherry

1. Thaw the duck and remove the inner organs. Rinse through with cold water, and pat dry.

2. Take a long piece of string and tie a knot at the end of each of the duck's legs to form a loop. (This will make it easy to hang the duck from a hook or nail.)

3. Bring the water to a boil in a large pot or a wok. Stir in the honey, rice vinegar, and rice wine. Turn down the heat and simmer the sauce, covered, for about 20 minutes, stirring occasionally.

4. Ladle the honey and water mixture over the skin of the duck several times, making sure the skin is completely coated. Dry the duck by hanging in a cool place for at least 4 hours, keeping a pan underneath to catch any drippings.

5. When the duck is done drying, preheat the oven to 375°F. Fill the bottom of a roasting pan with water (this prevents the fat from splattering when you remove the duck from the oven). Place the duck on the roasting pan, breast-side up. Roast for 30 minutes, turn over, and roast for 30 minutes on the other side, and then turn and roast a final 10 minutes on the breast side, or until the duck is cooked. Cool and carve into thin slices.

PER SERVING Calories: 1,172 | Fat: 105 grams | Protein: 30 grams | Sodium: 222 milligrams | Fiber: 0 grams | Carbohydrates: 23 grams | Sugar: 22 grams

CHAPTER 10

Fish and Other Seafood

Clams in Black Bean Sauce

Many foods have symbolism for the Chinese. Clams represent prosperity.

INGREDIENTS | SERVES 4

3 pounds littleneck clams

3 tablespoons peanut oil

5 cloves garlic, minced

1 tablespoon minced ginger

4 scallions, cut into ½" slices

1½ tablespoons fermented black beans, rinsed and coarsely chopped

2 tablespoons Xiaoshing wine

½ cup water or stock

2 tablespoons soy sauce

PER SERVING Calories: 381 | Fat: 14 grams | Protein: 46 grams | Sodium: 1,077 milligrams | Fiber: 1 gram | Carbohydrates: 15 grams | Sugar: 2 grams

1. Scrub the clamshells thoroughly and make sure they are tightly closed, to ensure freshness.

2. Preheat a wok over medium-high heat and swirl in the oil. Add the garlic, ginger, and scallions. Stir-fry 30 seconds. Add the black beans and stir to mix.

3. Add the clams, stirring constantly. Toss for about 1 minute, and then add the wine, stock or water, and soy sauce. Continue stirring. The clams should begin to open after about 3 minutes of cooking. Lower the heat to medium and cook until the liquid is reduced to half, another 3–4 minutes.

Butter Prawns

Butter prawns taste delicious served with steamed rice or stir-fried noodles.

INGREDIENTS | SERVES 4

1 pound large tiger prawns, shelled and deveined

½ teaspoon Chinese rice wine or dry sherry

¼ teaspoon salt

1 teaspoon cornstarch

½ cup chicken broth

1 tablespoon plus 1 teaspoon oyster sauce

½ teaspoon sugar

2 tablespoons vegetable oil

1 tablespoon butter

1 small garlic clove, minced

½ teaspoon chili sauce with garlic

PER SERVING Calories: 193 | Fat: 11 grams | Protein: 18 grams | Sodium: 397 milligrams | Fiber: 0 grams | Carbohydrates: 4 grams | Sugar: 1 gram

1. Place the prawns in a medium bowl. Add the rice wine, salt, and cornstarch and marinate for 15 minutes.

2. In a small bowl, combine the chicken broth, oyster sauce, and sugar and set aside.

3. Add the oil to a preheated wok or skillet. When the oil is hot, add the prawns and stir-fry briefly, until they turn pink. Remove and drain on paper towels.

4. Add the butter, garlic, and chili sauce. Stir-fry briefly, then add the prawns. Stir-fry for about 1 minute, mixing the prawns in with the butter, then add the prepared sauce. Bring the sauce to a boil. Mix the sauce with the prawns and serve hot.

Spicy Fish Fry

Young ginger, which has a light color and is quite tender, works well in this dish.

INGREDIENTS | SERVES 2

½ cup chicken broth

1 teaspoon brown sugar

1 teaspoon black rice vinegar

3 tablespoons vegetable oil, divided

½ pound fish fillets, cut into slices approximately 2" × ½"

½ tablespoon minced ginger

¼ teaspoon chili paste

1 cup fresh mushrooms, sliced

1 green onion, diagonally sliced into 1" slices

1. In a small bowl, combine the chicken broth, brown sugar, and black rice vinegar. Set aside.

2. Add 2 tablespoons of oil to a preheated wok or skillet. When the oil is hot, add the fish pieces. Stir-fry until browned. Remove from the wok and drain on paper towels.

3. Add 1 tablespoon of oil to the wok. Add the ginger and chili paste and stir-fry until aromatic. Add the mushrooms. Stir-fry until tender, then push up to the sides of the wok.

4. Add the prepared sauce in the middle of the wok and bring to a boil. Add the fish and stir in the green onion. Mix through and serve hot.

PER SERVING Calories: 311 | Fat: 22 grams | Protein: 21 grams | Sodium: 78 milligrams | Fiber: 1 gram | Carbohydrates: 7 grams | Sugar: 4 grams

Stir-Fried Fish Fillets

Cod fillets work well in this dish. Serve with rice and stir-fried vegetables.

INGREDIENTS | SERVES 2

½ pound fish fillets

1 teaspoon Chinese rice wine or dry sherry

1 tablespoon soy sauce

1 green onion, minced

½ cup chicken broth

2 tablespoons oyster sauce

2 teaspoons brown sugar

¼ teaspoon sesame oil

2 tablespoons vegetable oil

½ tablespoon minced ginger

1 green onion, sliced into 1" pieces

1. Place the fish fillets in a medium bowl. Marinate in the rice wine, soy sauce, and the minced green onion for 30 minutes.

2. In a small bowl, combine the chicken broth, oyster sauce, brown sugar, and sesame oil. Set aside.

3. Add the vegetable oil to a preheated wok or skillet. When the oil is hot, add the ginger. Stir-fry briefly until aromatic. Add the fish fillets and cook until they are browned on both sides (2–3 minutes on each side).

4. Add the prepared sauce in the middle of the wok and bring to a boil. Stir in the sliced green onion. Reduce the heat, cover, and simmer for about 10 minutes. Serve hot.

PER SERVING Calories: 272 | Fat: 14 grams | Protein: 21 grams | Sodium: 1,104 milligrams | Fiber: 1 gram | Carbohydrates: 12 grams | Sugar: 7 grams

Lumpy Brown Sugar

One of the less attractive features of brown sugar is its tendency to form lumps. This happens when the sugar loses moisture and hardens. There are several ways to remove lumps. First, if the sugar is being used in a hot sauce, simply melt it to remove the lumps before adding to the sauce. Stir constantly while the sugar is melting in the saucepan. If the recipe calls for dry sugar, use a strainer to squeeze out the lumps. Several techniques exist for adding the moisture back into the sugar, but these normally take several days.

Cantonese Ketchup Shrimp

Cooking the shrimp with shells on will provide a deeper sauce flavor but requires extra effort to eat. If shelling the shrimp before cooking, consider storing the shells in the freezer for use in seafood stocks and stews.

INGREDIENTS | SERVES 4

2 tablespoons ketchup

1 tablespoon soy sauce

½ cup chicken stock

1 tablespoon cornstarch

3 tablespoons peanut oil

3 cloves garlic, minced

1 teaspoon minced fresh ginger

4 scallions, chopped into ¼" lengths

1 pound medium shrimp, shells on or off

Chopped scallions for garnish (optional)

1. In a small bowl, stir together ketchup, soy sauce, stock, and cornstarch. Set aside.

2. Preheat the wok over medium-high heat. Swirl in the peanut oil to heat through. Add the garlic, ginger, and scallions. Stir-fry 30 seconds.

3. Reduce the heat to medium. Add the shrimp and cook until they are bright pink and firm to the touch, about 3 minutes.

4. Give the ketchup mixture a quick stir to make sure that the cornstarch is fully mixed in. Pour the mixture into the wok and bring to a boil to thicken. Garnish with chopped scallions.

PER SERVING Calories: 240 | Fat: 12 grams | Protein: 23 grams | Sodium: 508 milligrams | Fiber: 0 grams | Carbohydrates: 7 grams | Sugar: 2 grams

Kung Pao Shrimp

This dish pairs well with the lighter flavors of stir-fried bok choy.

INGREDIENTS | SERVES 4

½ teaspoon salt

2 teaspoons light soy sauce

1 teaspoon Shaoxing rice wine or medium-dry sherry

1½ teaspoons plus 1 tablespoon cornstarch, divided

1 tablespoon plus 1 cup water, divided

1 pound medium shrimp, shelled and deveined

1 teaspoon sugar

1 teaspoon rice wine vinegar

2 teaspoons peanut oil

1 teaspoon chili paste with garlic

2 thin slices fresh ginger

2 garlic cloves, thinly sliced

3 tablespoons garlic chives or other chives, cut into 2" segments

1. In a medium bowl, mix together the salt, soy sauce, wine, 1½ teaspoons of cornstarch, and 1 tablespoon of water. Add the shrimp and marinate at least 30 minutes.

2. In a small bowl, mix together the sugar, vinegar, 1 tablespoon of cornstarch, and 1 cup of water. Set aside.

3. Heat the wok over medium-high heat. Add the peanut oil, chili paste, ginger, and garlic. Stir-fry for 30 seconds. Add the shrimp, cooking until they turn bright pink, 3–4 minutes.

4. Add the vinegar mixture and chives to the wok. Bring to a boil and let the sauce thicken.

PER SERVING Calories: 160 | Fat: 4 grams | Protein: 23 grams | Sodium: 658 milligrams | Fiber: 0 grams | Carbohydrates: 5 grams | Sugar: 2 grams

Butterfly Prawns

This dish tastes delicious with stir-fried spinach or Chinese greens.
For added flavor, serve with a dipping sauce.

INGREDIENTS | SERVES 10

½ teaspoon Szechwan peppercorns, roasted and ground

5 tablespoons bread crumbs

3 cups vegetable oil

10 large tiger prawns, shelled, with tails intact

1 large egg, lightly beaten

1. In a small bowl, mix the Szechwan peppercorns with the bread crumbs.

2. Add the oil to a preheated wok and heat to at least 350°F. To prepare prawns for deep-frying, hold them by the tail and dip them into the beaten egg, and then coat with the bread crumbs.

3. When the oil is hot, deep-fry the prawns until they turn golden brown (about 1 minute). Remove and drain on paper towels. Serve warm.

PER SERVING Calories: 89 | Fat: 8 grams | Protein: 2 grams | Sodium: 452 milligrams | Fiber: 0 grams | Carbohydrates: 2 grams | Sugar: 0 grams

Pepper-Salt Shrimp

This quick and easy dish makes an excellent party appetizer. Serve garnished with lemon wedges.

INGREDIENTS | SERVES 6

2 cups vegetable oil

2 egg whites

¼ cup cornstarch

1 pound large shrimp, peeled and deveined

2 tablespoons Szechwan Salt and Pepper Mix (see recipe in Chapter 2)

1. Heat the oil in a preheated wok to 375°F.

2. While oil is heating, mix the egg whites with cornstarch in a small bowl to form a smooth batter.

3. Lightly coat the shrimp with the Szechwan Salt and Pepper Mix. Dip shrimp into the batter. Place a few shrimp at a time into the wok. Deep-fry until they turn golden brown (about 3 minutes). Remove and drain on paper towels.

PER SERVING Calories: 234 | Fat: 15 grams | Protein: 16 grams | Sodium: 3,000 milligrams | Fiber: 0 grams | Carbohydrates: 7 grams | Sugar: 0 grams

Lobster Cantonese

The secret to preparing this popular Cantonese dish is not to overcook the lobster tails.

INGREDIENTS | SERVES 2

1 teaspoon fermented black beans

1 clove garlic, minced

¾ cup chicken broth

2 tablespoons Chinese rice wine or dry sherry, divided

1 tablespoon soy sauce

2 tablespoons vegetable oil

¼ pound ground pork

3 slices ginger, minced

1 green onion, thinly sliced

1 tablespoon cornstarch mixed with 4 tablespoons water

2 lobster tails, shelled and cut into ½" pieces

1 teaspoon sugar

1 egg, lightly beaten

Preparing Fermented Black Beans

Fermented black beans need a little preparation before using. Soak the beans until they are softened, about 30 minutes. Mash the beans under the blade of a knife or cleaver, and then mince or chop as called for in the recipe.

1. Soak the beans in warm water and rinse. Mash, chop finely, and mix with the garlic.

2. In a small bowl, combine the chicken broth, 1 tablespoon of rice wine, and the soy sauce. Set aside.

3. Add the oil to a preheated wok or skillet. When the oil is hot, add the black bean mixture. Stir-fry briefly until aromatic. Add the pork and stir-fry for 2–3 minutes, until cooked through.

4. Push the ingredients up to the side of the wok. Add the ginger and green onion in the middle. Stir-fry briefly. Add the sauce and bring to a boil.

5. Give the cornstarch-and-water mixture a quick stir and add to the wok, stirring quickly to thicken.

6. Add the lobster, sugar, and 1 tablespoon of rice wine. Stir-fry for about 2 minutes, then stream in the egg. Mix together and serve.

PER SERVING Calories: 509 | Fat: 29 grams | Protein: 40 grams | Sodium: 1,207 milligrams | Fiber: 1 gram | Carbohydrates: 20 grams | Sugar: 8 grams

Whole Steamed Fish

Although Westerners may not be accustomed to seeing a fish head on the serving plate, a whole fish has important symbolism for the Chinese. It is common to serve a whole fish on special occasions, as it symbolizes wealth and abundance. If entertaining, the head is pointed toward the guest of honor.

INGREDIENTS | SERVES 6

1 (4-pound) white-fleshed whole fish (such as sea bass or red snapper)
1 teaspoon salt
2 scallions, cut into 3" pieces
1" piece ginger, sliced thinly
2 tablespoons soy sauce
½ teaspoon rice wine vinegar

PER SERVING Calories: 225 | Fat: 3 grams | Protein: 40 grams | Sodium: 848 milligrams | Fiber: 0 grams | Carbohydrates: 0 grams | Sugar: 0 grams

1. Rinse and drain the fish. Score the skin in a diagonal pattern on both sides.

2. Place the fish on a large plate. Sprinkle with salt inside and out. Let rest for 10 minutes. Place the scallions and ginger on top of the fish.

3. Steam 10 minutes using a bamboo steamer if you have one. Otherwise, heat several inches of water in a wok, place a rack inside, and place the plate on top. When steaming, be sure that the water is at a simmer, not a boil.

4. In a small bowl, mix together the soy sauce and rice wine vinegar for a dipping sauce.

Deep-Fried Fish

Serve with the dipping sauce of your choice, accompanied with rice and a bitter green, like Chinese broccoli (gai lan).

INGREDIENTS | SERVES 2

½ pound fish fillets, cut into bite-size squares
1 egg white
2 teaspoons soy sauce
1 tablespoon cornstarch
4 cups vegetable oil

1. Place the fish in a medium bowl. Add the egg white, soy sauce, and cornstarch, adding the cornstarch last. Marinate the fish for 30 minutes.

2. Heat the oil in a preheated wok to 375°F. When the oil is hot, add the fish. Fry until golden brown. Remove and drain on paper towels.

PER SERVING Calories: 367 | Fat: 28 grams | Protein: 22 grams | Sodium: 424 milligrams | Fiber: 0 grams | Carbohydrates: 4 grams | Sugar: 0 grams

Hot-and-Sour Prawns

This hot dish is a great way to enliven plain stir-fried or boiled noodles or steamed rice.

Yin and Yang Harmony

The philosophy of yin and yang permeates every aspect of Chinese culture, including the kitchens of its cooks. Yin and yang represent all the forces in the universe. Things that are feminine, cold, dark, or submissive are said to be yin in nature, while masculinity, heat, light, and dominance are yang forces. Chinese physicians frequently treat illness as an imbalance between yin and yang in the body. For example, since heartburn is thought to come from consuming too many spicy yang foods, a physician might prescribe a soup featuring yin ingredients like walnuts as a tonic.

1. Place the prawns in a large bowl. Add the rice wine, salt, and cornstarch to the bowl and marinate the fish for 15 minutes.

2. In a small saucepan, bring the water, black rice vinegar, Hot Chili Oil, and Worcestershire sauce to a boil. Add the cornstarch-and-water mixture, stirring quickly to thicken. Turn the heat to low and keep warm.

3. Add the oil to a preheated wok or skillet. When the oil is hot, add the prawns and stir-fry briefly, until they turn pink. Push up to the side and add the prepared sauce in the middle of the wok. Mix the prawns with the sauce. Serve hot.

PER SERVING Calories: 116 | Fat: 8 grams | Protein: 6 grams | Sodium: 223 milligrams | Fiber: 0 grams | Carbohydrates: 3 grams | Sugar: 0 grams

Prawns with Snow Peas

Serve on a bed of steamed rice mixed with chopped green onion.

INGREDIENTS | SERVES 8

20 large prawns, shelled and deveined
1 teaspoon sugar
1 teaspoon cornstarch
1 cup (about 25) snow peas, trimmed
½ cup mung bean sprouts
2 tablespoons vegetable oil
1 slice ginger, finely chopped
1½ teaspoons Chinese rice wine or dry sherry

1. Place the prawns in a large bowl. Marinate in the sugar and cornstarch for 15 minutes.

2. Blanch the snow peas and bean sprouts by plunging them briefly into boiling water. Drain thoroughly.

3. Add the oil to a preheated wok or skillet. When the oil is hot, add the ginger and stir-fry briefly until aromatic. Add the prawns and stir-fry briefly until they turn a pinkish-red color.

4. Add the snow peas to the wok. Stir-fry briefly, then add the bean sprouts. Splash with the 1½ teaspoons of rice wine. Serve hot.

PER SERVING Calories: 62 | Fat: 4 grams | Protein: 4 grams | Sodium: 44 milligrams | Fiber: 0 grams | Carbohydrates: 2 grams | Sugar: 1 gram

Spicy Shrimp with Hot Shanghai Noodles

Adding the hot bean sauce after the noodles helps reduce its strength.
Use sparingly at first, and add more to taste if desired.

INGREDIENTS | SERVES 4

10 ounces medium shrimp, shelled and deveined

¼ teaspoon five-spice powder

½ teaspoon cornstarch

2 stalks bok choy

4 tablespoons vegetable oil, divided

2 leaves cabbage, shredded

1 teaspoon soy sauce

2 garlic cloves, finely chopped

2 slices ginger, finely chopped

¾ pound fresh Shanghai noodles

1 tablespoon hot bean sauce

1. Place the shrimp in a medium bowl. Add the five-spice powder and cornstarch and marinate the shrimp for at least 15 minutes.

2. Separate the bok choy stalks and leaves. Cut across the leaves and cut the stalks into 1" pieces on the diagonal.

3. Add 2 tablespoons of oil to a preheated wok or skillet. When the oil is hot, add the shrimp and stir-fry briefly until they turn pink.

4. Push the shrimp up to the side of the wok and add the bok choy stalks and cabbage. Stir-fry briefly, then add the bok choy leaves. Add the soy sauce and stir-fry until the vegetables turn a bright color and are tender. Remove from the wok and set aside.

5. Add 2 tablespoons of oil to the wok or skillet. When the oil is hot, add the garlic and ginger. Stir-fry briefly until aromatic. Add the noodles. Stir-fry for 1–2 minutes, then mix in the hot bean sauce. If necessary, add 2 tablespoons of water, so that the noodles do not stick to the bottom of the pan.

6. Add the shrimp and vegetables. Mix everything through and serve hot.

PER SERVING Calories: 375 | Fat: 16 grams | Protein: 24 grams | Sodium: 701 milligrams | Fiber: 4 grams | Carbohydrates: 34 grams | Sugar: 5 grams

Shrimp with Lobster Sauce

For a fancier presentation, remove the shell from the shrimp but leave the tail intact. Prepare the sauce separately and pour over the shrimp.

INGREDIENTS | SERVES 4

4 tablespoons vegetable oil, divided

½ pound medium shrimp, shelled and deveined

1 teaspoon fermented black beans

1 clove garlic, minced

¾ cup chicken broth

2 tablespoons Chinese rice wine or dry sherry, divided

1 tablespoon soy sauce

¼ pound ground pork

1 tablespoon cornstarch

4 tablespoons water

1 teaspoon sugar

1 egg, lightly beaten

1. Add 2 tablespoons of oil to a preheated wok or skillet. When the oil is hot, add the shrimp. Stir-fry until they turn pink and are nearly cooked. Remove from the wok and drain on paper towels.

2. To prepare the lobster sauce: Soak the fermented black beans about 30 minutes in warm water and rinse. Mash them, chop finely, and mix with the garlic clove in a small bowl. Add the chicken broth, 1 tablespoon of rice wine, and the soy sauce. Set aside.

3. Add 2 tablespoons of oil to the wok. When the oil is hot, add the black bean mixture. Stir-fry briefly until aromatic. Add the pork and stir-fry for 2–3 minutes, until cooked through.

4. Push the ingredients up to the side of the wok. Add the lobster sauce and bring to a boil.

5. Mix the cornstarch and water in a small bowl and add to the wok, stirring quickly to thicken.

6. Mix in the sugar and 1 tablespoon rice wine to the wok. Stream in the egg. Add the shrimp. Mix together and serve hot.

PER SERVING Calories: 327 | Fat: 22 grams | Protein: 21 grams | Sodium: 537 milligrams | Fiber: 0 grams | Carbohydrates: 10 grams | Sugar: 4 grams

Quick and Easy Salt and Pepper Squid

The trick to this dish is not to overcook the seafood. When cooked too long, squid turns rubbery.

INGREDIENTS | SERVES 4

2 teaspoons Szechwan Salt and Pepper Mix (see recipe in Chapter 2)

¼ cup cornstarch

2 tablespoons soy sauce

1 tablespoon Chinese rice wine or dry sherry

½ teaspoon sesame oil

½ teaspoon Hot Chili Oil (see recipe in Chapter 2)

3 cups vegetable oil

2 slices ginger, minced

1 pound cleaned squid, cut into 1" pieces

1 clove garlic, minced

1. In a small bowl, mix the Szechwan Salt and Pepper Mix with the cornstarch. In a separate bowl, combine the soy sauce, rice wine, sesame oil, and Hot Chili Oil. Set aside.

2. Add the vegetable oil to a preheated wok or skillet. While the oil is heating, dip the squid pieces in the salt-and-pepper mixture.

3. When the oil is hot, drop in the squid pieces, a few at a time. Deep-fry for about 2 minutes, until they change color. Remove and drain on paper towels.

4. Remove all but 2 tablespoons of oil from the wok. Add the ginger and garlic, and stir-fry briefly until aromatic.

5. Add the soy sauce mixture in the middle of the wok and bring to a boil. Add the squid and cook very briefly, about 1 minute. Mix through and serve hot.

PER SERVING Calories: 346 | Fat: 23 grams | Protein: 18 grams | Sodium: 2,731 milligrams | Fiber: 0 grams | Carbohydrates: 13 grams | Sugar: 1 gram

CHAPTER 11

Tofu

Crispy Tofu

These tofu cubes may be eaten as a snack with the dipping sauce of your choice, or be used as part of another recipe.

INGREDIENTS | SERVES 6

½ cup rice flour
1 teaspoon salt
1 teaspoon ground white pepper
1 (12.3-ounce) block tofu of desired texture
½ cup peanut oil

1. In a medium bowl, combine the flour, salt, and pepper. Cut the tofu into segments of desired size. Coat with the flour mixture.

2. Add the oil to a preheated wok and heat to 350°F. When the oil is hot, add the tofu pieces. Fry until they turn golden. Drain on paper towels.

PER SERVING Calories: 206 | Fat: 15 grams | Protein: 5 grams | Sodium: 391 milligrams | Fiber: 0 grams | Carbohydrates: 12 grams | Sugar: 0 grams

Slow-Fried Tofu

Use the tofu in this recipe as a basis for other dishes!

INGREDIENTS | SERVES 6

1 (12.3-ounce) block firm tofu
2–3 cups vegetable oil

1. Press the tofu and cut into cubes.

2. Add the oil to a preheated wok and heat to 350°F. When the oil is hot, add the tofu.

3. Fry until the cubes turn a golden brown. (This will take about 10 minutes.) Add more oil if necessary. Drain the fried tofu on paper towels.

PER SERVING Calories: 172 | Fat: 16 grams | Protein: 5 grams | Sodium: 2 milligrams | Fiber: 0 grams | Carbohydrates: 1 gram | Sugar: 0 grams

Deep-Fried Tofu with Garlic and Chilies

Serve this dish with Hot Chili Oil (see recipe in Chapter 2) or a dipping sauce of your choice.

INGREDIENTS | SERVES 6

1 (12.3-ounce) block medium tofu
½ cup rice flour
1 teaspoon salt
2 teaspoons red chili flakes
1 tablespoon minced garlic
½ cup peanut oil

1. Drain the tofu and cut into 1" cubes.

2. In a shallow bowl, combine the rice flour, salt, chili flakes, and minced garlic.

3. Heat the oil in a wok over medium-high heat. Coat the tofu cubes in the flour mixture and immediately set them in the hot oil. Fry until golden on all sides. Drain on paper towels.

PER SERVING Calories: 263 | Fat: 21 grams | Protein: 6 grams | Sodium: 389 milligrams | Fiber: 0 grams | Carbohydrates: 12 grams | Sugar: 0 grams

Sesame Celery Sauté with Pressed Tofu

Surprised to find celery at center stage? For the Chinese, celery is more than a garnish.

INGREDIENTS | SERVES 4

2 teaspoons peanut oil
2 cups celery, cut on the diagonal into 1" pieces
1 shallot, chopped fine
2 cloves garlic, minced
6 ounces pressed tofu, sliced thinly
1 teaspoon salt
½ teaspoon ground white pepper
2 teaspoons sesame oil
1 tablespoon minced cilantro

1. Preheat a wok over high heat. Swirl in the peanut oil. Add the celery, shallots, and garlic all at once. Stir-fry quickly until celery takes on a bright green color, about 2–3 minutes.

2. Add the tofu, stirring to coat thoroughly. Lower the heat to medium and add the salt and white pepper. Stir-fry another minute or so, adding the sesame oil toward the end to finish. Serve garnished with cilantro.

PER SERVING Calories: 88 | Fat: 7 grams | Protein: 4 grams | Sodium: 622 milligrams | Fiber: 1 gram | Carbohydrates: 2 grams | Sugar: 1 gram

Kung Pao Tofu

Serve with a vegetable stir-fry for a hearty and balanced meal.

INGREDIENTS | SERVES 6

16 ounces firm tofu

½ teaspoon salt

2 teaspoons light soy sauce

1 teaspoon Shaoxing rice wine or medium-dry sherry

1½ teaspoons plus 1 tablespoon cornstarch

1 tablespoon plus 1 cup water

1 teaspoon sugar

1 teaspoon rice wine vinegar

2 teaspoons peanut oil

1 teaspoon chili paste with garlic

2 thin slices fresh ginger

2 garlic cloves, thinly sliced

3 tablespoons garlic chives or other chives, cut into 2" segments

1. Press tofu if you like. Cut into 1" cubes.

2. In a medium bowl, mix together the salt, light soy sauce, rice wine, 1½ teaspoons of cornstarch, and 1 tablespoon of water. Add the tofu, stir to coat, and set aside.

3. In small bowl, mix together the sugar, vinegar, 1 tablespoon of cornstarch, and 1 cup of water. Set aside.

4. Heat a wok over medium-high heat. Add the oil, chili paste, ginger, and garlic. Stir-fry for 30 seconds.

5. Add the marinated tofu, stirring gently so that the cubes don't break apart. Cook 2–3 minutes, until the tofu is heated through and has absorbed the seasonings.

6. Add the vinegar mixture and the chives. Bring to a boil and let the sauce thicken.

PER SERVING Calories: 92 | Fat: 4 grams | Protein: 7 grams | Sodium: 315 milligrams | Fiber: 0 grams | Carbohydrates: 5 grams | Sugar: 1 gram

Spicy Eggplant and Tofu

This deeply aromatic dish needs little more than rice to make a full meal.

INGREDIENTS | SERVES 6

1 (12.3-ounce) block firm tofu

2 tablespoons peanut oil

2 tablespoons finely minced ginger

2 tablespoons finely minced garlic

2 tablespoons black bean–chili sauce, homemade or store-bought

1 tablespoon soy sauce

¼ teaspoon white pepper

1 pound Chinese eggplant, cut into 1" dice

5 scallions, cut into ¼" pieces

½ cup vegetable stock

1. Drain the tofu. Press to remove excess water if you wish. Cut into 1" cubes.

2. Preheat a wok over high heat. Swirl in the oil. Add the ginger, garlic, and black bean–chili sauce. Stir-fry for 30 seconds. Lower heat to medium.

3. Add the soy sauce and white pepper and stir just to combine. Add the eggplant and stir-fry until tender, about 5 minutes. Add the scallions.

4. Add the tofu and coat in the eggplant-spice mixture, being careful not to break up the tofu cubes. Cook until the tofu has heated through, about 3 minutes.

5. Add the stock and stir to combine. Turn off heat once the sauce has reduced, another 2–3 minutes.

PER SERVING Calories: 131 | Fat: 7 grams | Protein: 6 grams | Sodium: 197 milligrams | Fiber: 2 grams | Carbohydrates: 10 grams | Sugar: 3 grams

Tofu Curry

Tofu absorbs the flavors of every dish it is in. Use the softest tofu that will hold together for this recipe.

INGREDIENTS | SERVES 4

1 (12.3-ounce) block medium tofu
3 tablespoons peanut oil
2 garlic cloves, minced
1 tablespoon minced ginger
1 teaspoon curry powder
1 teaspoon turmeric
2 star anise
1 medium onion, peeled and finely chopped
1 medium carrot, peeled and diced
1 tablespoon soy sauce
½ cup vegetable stock
¼ cup scallions, cut into ¼" lengths

1. Drain the tofu and cut into 1" cubes.

2. Heat a wok or stockpot over high heat. Swirl in the oil. Add the garlic, ginger, curry powder, turmeric, and star anise. Stir-fry about 30 seconds to release the aromas of the spices.

3. Reduce the heat to medium and add onion and carrots. Stir-fry 3–4 minutes, or until the onion is translucent and the carrots are bright orange. Add the soy sauce; stir to combine.

4. Add the tofu, stirring gently so as not to break up the cubes. Cook another 3–4 minutes to heat the tofu cubes through.

5. Add the stock and cook until most of the liquid is absorbed by the tofu. Sprinkle with scallions and serve with rice.

PER SERVING Calories: 205 | Fat: 14 grams | Protein: 10 grams | Sodium: 285 milligrams | Fiber: 3 grams | Carbohydrates: 9 grams | Sugar: 3 grams

Tofu and Shiitake Stir-Fry

*Shiitake's dense flavor is balanced with tofu in this recipe.
Mushrooms such as cremini or portabella may also be added or substituted.*

INGREDIENTS | SERVES 4

1 (12.3-ounce) block medium tofu

2 cups sliced dried or fresh shiitake mushrooms

1 teaspoon salt

2 tablespoons peanut oil

1 shallot, finely chopped

2 tablespoons minced garlic

2 tablespoons minced ginger

1 tablespoon Xiaoshing wine

1 tablespoon soy sauce

1 teaspoon cornstarch, dissolved in 1 tablespoon water

¼ cup scallions chopped into ¼" lengths

1. Drain the tofu and press to remove excess water if you wish. Cut into 1" cubes.

2. If using dried mushrooms, cover with water and soak for several hours. Reserve the liquid. Remove the stems from the mushrooms and place them in a small saucepan with the soaking liquid. Add more water if necessary to make 2½ cups. If using fresh mushrooms, cut off the stems and place them in a pan with 2½ cups water. Add salt and bring to a boil. Reduce the heat and simmer 20–30 minutes. Cool, strain, and discard the stems.

3. Meanwhile, preheat a wok over medium-high heat and swirl in the peanut oil. Add the shallot, garlic, and ginger. Stir-fry 30–60 seconds, or until the aromas are released and the shallot becomes translucent.

4. Add the mushrooms and stir to coat. Reduce the heat to medium. Stir-fry until the mushrooms release their juice, 3–4 minutes. Add the Xiaoshing wine and soy sauce.

5. Add the tofu, stirring gently so that the cubes do not break up. Add mushroom stock and bring to a boil.

6. Add cornstarch mixture and stir until the sauce thickens. Sprinkle in scallions and serve.

PER SERVING Calories: 166 | Fat: 11 grams | Protein: 9 grams | Sodium: 869 milligrams | Fiber: 1 gram | Carbohydrates: 8 grams | Sugar: 2 grams

Red-Cooked Tofu

*This may be served as a main dish with rice or used in a dim sum dish,
like Bao with Red-Cooked Tofu (see recipe in Chapter 3).*

INGREDIENTS | SERVES 6

1 pound firm tofu

½ cup peanut oil

2 tablespoons coarsely chopped garlic

8 scallions, trimmed and cut into 1"
lengths on a slant

1 tablespoon light soy sauce

1 tablespoon dark soy sauce

2 tablespoons Xiaoshing wine

1 tablespoon Chinese rock sugar,
crushed

2 star anise

1 cup vegetable stock

1. Press the tofu to expel excess water if you wish. Cut into 1" cubes. Preheat a wok over high heat and pour in the oil. Test to see when the oil has heated through by sticking the tip of a chopstick in it. Bubbles will form around the chopstick when it is hot. Fry the tofu in the oil until it is golden brown on all sides. Remove the tofu and drain on paper towels.

2. Discard all but 1 tablespoon of oil. Stir-fry the garlic and scallions for about 1 minute.

3. Add the light soy sauce, dark soy sauce, wine, sugar, star anise, and stock. Bring to a boil, then lower the heat so that the liquid is at a simmer.

4. Add the tofu to the sauce and stir gently so that the tofu is covered. Simmer until the tofu has absorbed most of the sauce.

PER SERVING Calories: 130 | Fat: 8 grams | Protein: 7 grams | Sodium: 534 milligrams | Fiber: 1 gram | Carbohydrates: 7 grams | Sugar: 4 grams

Ma Po Tofu

Most restaurants use ground pork in their Ma Po Tofu dishes. This recipe includes pork, but it can easily be excluded, and vegetable stock substituted for a delicious vegan option.

INGREDIENTS | SERVES 4

1 (12.3-ounce) block medium tofu

1 tablespoon fermented black beans

4 tablespoons peanut oil

2½ tablespoons Szechwan chili bean paste

¼–½ teaspoon ground Szechwan pepper

2 teaspoons ground red chilies (optional)

1 tablespoon finely chopped ginger

1 tablespoon finely chopped garlic

6 ounces ground pork

¾ cup chicken stock

1 teaspoon cornstarch

¼ teaspoon ground white pepper

1 teaspoon salt

4 scallions, diagonally cut into 1" slices

The Legend of Ma Po Tofu

One of the most iconic Chinese dishes, Ma Po Tofu is said to be named after the pock-marked old woman who served it. In some stories, she was redeemed by the dish, despite her disfigurement; in others, her fame was independent of her physical appearance. Traditional Chinese culture tends to be more blunt than Westerners are accustomed to. Being identified as a pockmarked old lady is less offensive than an American might imagine.

1. Drain the tofu and cut into 1" cubes. If you like, you may set these into hot—but not boiling—water to warm through while you work.

2. Rinse and drain the black beans; crush slightly with the side of a cleaver.

3. Preheat a wok or skillet on high. Pour in the peanut oil and swirl to heat through. Reduce the heat to medium, add the chili bean paste and stir-fry until the oil has turned red and smells of chili.

4. Add the black beans, Szechwan pepper, and ground chilies and stir-fry for a few seconds, until their scent combines with the other ingredients. Add the ginger and garlic and stir-fry for 30 seconds.

5. Add the ground pork, breaking up any clumps as it cooks for 2–3 minutes.

6. Remove the tofu from the hot water with a slotted spoon and place into the wok. Stir the cubes gently so that they are coated in the seasoning mixture but do not break.

7. In a small bowl, stir together the chicken stock and cornstarch. Add to the wok, stirring gently until it boils and thickens. Season with white pepper and salt.

8. Sprinkle with scallions and serve.

PER SERVING Calories: 324 | Fat: 27 grams | Protein: 16 grams | Sodium: 824 milligrams | Fiber: 1 gram | Carbohydrates: 4 grams | Sugar: 0 grams

Bean Curd with Bean Sauce and Noodles

Slow-Fried Tofu (see recipe in this chapter) works well in this recipe.
You can substitute other fresh noodles for the Peking noodles.

INGREDIENTS | SERVES 4

8 ounces fresh Peking-style noodles

1 (12.3-ounce) block firm tofu

3 large stalks bok choy

⅓ cup dark soy sauce

2 tablespoons black bean sauce

2 teaspoons Chinese rice wine or dry sherry

2 teaspoons black rice vinegar

2¼ teaspoons sugar, divided

½ teaspoon salt, divided

¼ teaspoon chili paste with garlic

1 teaspoon Hot Chili Oil (see recipe in Chapter 2)

¼ teaspoon sesame oil

½ cup water

2 tablespoons vegetable oil

2 slices ginger, minced

2 garlic cloves, minced

2 green onions, diagonally sliced into 1" slices

¼ red onion, peeled and chopped

1. Cook the noodles in boiling water until they are tender. Drain thoroughly. Drain the tofu and cut into cubes.

2. Parboil the bok choy by plunging it briefly into boiling water and draining thoroughly. Separate the stalks and leaves.

3. In a small bowl, combine the dark soy sauce, black bean sauce, rice wine, black rice vinegar, 2 teaspoons of sugar, ¼ teaspoon of salt, the chili paste, Hot Chili Oil, sesame oil, and water. Set aside.

4. Add the vegetable oil to a preheated wok or skillet. When the oil is hot, add the ginger, garlic, and green onions. Stir-fry briefly until aromatic. Add the red onion and stir-fry briefly. Push up to the sides and add the bok choy stalks. Add the leaves and stir-fry until the bok choy is a bright green and the onion tender. Season with remaining salt and sugar.

5. Add the prepared sauce in the middle of the wok and bring to a boil. Add the tofu. Simmer for a few minutes to allow the tofu to absorb the sauce. Add the noodles. Mix everything through and serve hot.

PER SERVING Calories: 346 | Fat: 14 grams | Protein: 22 grams | Sodium: 2,106 milligrams | Fiber: 8 grams | Carbohydrates: 37 grams | Sugar: 12 grams

Peppery Bean Sprouts with Pressed Tofu

This is an interesting dish where bean sprouts take center stage.

INGREDIENTS | SERVES 4

1 tablespoon peanut oil

1 shallot, finely chopped

1 teaspoon minced ginger

2 cups mung bean sprouts

8 ounces pressed tofu

1 teaspoon soy sauce

2 teaspoons ground white pepper

1. Heat a wok over medium-high heat and swirl in the oil. Add the shallot and ginger. Stir-fry 20 seconds. Add the bean sprouts. Stir-fry 2–3 minutes.

2. Add the tofu, soy sauce, and pepper. Cook another 1–2 minutes to heat through.

PER SERVING Calories: 96 | Fat: 6 grams | Protein: 7 grams | Sodium: 94 milligrams | Fiber: 0 grams | Carbohydrates: 4 grams | Sugar: 2 grams

Spicy Broccoli and Cauliflower with Pressed Tofu

Serve with rice as a main dish or as a side for a larger meal.

INGREDIENTS | SERVES 4

2 tablespoons peanut oil

2 cloves garlic, minced

1 teaspoon minced ginger

2 teaspoons red chili flakes

2 cups broccoli florets

2 cups cauliflower florets

8 ounces pressed tofu, sliced into thin strips

1 teaspoon sesame oil

½ cup vegetable stock

1 teaspoon cornstarch mixed with 1 tablespoon water

1. Heat a wok over medium-high heat. Swirl in the oil. Add the garlic, ginger, and red chili flakes. Stir-fry 30 seconds, then add the broccoli and cauliflower. Stir-fry until the broccoli turns bright green, 3–4 minutes.

2. Add the tofu and sesame oil. Stir to coat. Add the vegetable stock. When it comes to a boil, add the cornstarch mixture. The sauce should thicken immediately.

PER SERVING Calories: 161 | Fat: 11 grams | Protein: 8 grams | Sodium: 33 milligrams | Fiber: 3 grams | Carbohydrates: 8 grams | Sugar: 2 grams

Braised Tofu with Three Vegetables

This recipe can easily be doubled to serve as a main dish for four people.

INGREDIENTS | SERVES 2

4 dried mushrooms

⅔ cup fresh mushrooms

½ cup chicken broth

1½ tablespoons oyster sauce

1 teaspoon Chinese rice wine or dry sherry

2 tablespoons vegetable oil

1 garlic clove, minced

1 cup baby carrots, halved

2 teaspoons cornstarch mixed with 4 teaspoons water

12 ounces pressed tofu, cut into ½" cubes

1. Soak the dried mushrooms in hot water for at least 20 minutes. Drain and reserve ¼ cup of the soaking liquid. Slice the dried and fresh mushrooms.

2. In a small bowl, combine the reserved mushroom liquid, chicken broth, oyster sauce, and rice wine. Set aside.

3. Add the oil to a preheated wok or skillet. When the oil is hot, add the garlic and stir-fry briefly until aromatic. Add the carrots. Stir-fry for 1 minute, then add the mushrooms and stir-fry.

4. Add the prepared sauce and bring to a boil. Stir the cornstarch-and-water mixture and add to the sauce, stirring quickly to thicken.

5. Add the tofu cubes. Mix everything together, turn down the heat, and simmer for 5–6 minutes. Serve hot.

PER SERVING Calories: 381 | Fat: 23 grams | Protein: 19 grams | Sodium: 468 milligrams | Fiber: 5 grams | Carbohydrates: 26 grams | Sugar: 6 grams

Pressed Bean Curd with Preserved Szechwan Vegetable

*Find preserved Szechwan vegetable a little too salty? Try soaking it in warm water
for 15 minutes prior to stir-frying, or substitute blanched spinach leaves.*

INGREDIENTS | SERVES 4

4–5 cups oil for frying

½ cup vegetable stock

1 teaspoon Chinese rice wine or dry sherry

2 (7-ounce) blocks pressed bean curd, cut into ½" cubes

¼ cup preserved Szechwan vegetable, cut into cubes

½ teaspoon sugar

½ teaspoon soy sauce

For Salt Lovers

Who said vegetables are bland? Preserved Szechwan vegetable is famous for its salty taste. The round green vegetable with the reddish trim is one of the ingredients that gives Szechwan cuisine its distinctive flavor. Preserved Szechwan vegetable is sold in cans in Asian markets. Stored in a covered jar after opening, it should last for several months. Pickled first in salt and then in chili paste, it can be a bit overpowering, so use sparingly at first.

1. Heat 4 cups of oil in a preheated wok to 350°F. In a small bowl, combine the vegetable stock and rice wine. Set aside.

2. When the oil is hot, add the bean curd cubes, and deep-fry until they turn light brown. Remove from the wok with a slotted spoon and set aside.

3. Remove all but 2 tablespoons of oil from the wok. Add the preserved Szechwan vegetable. Stir-fry for 1–2 minutes, then push up to the side of the wok.

4. Add the vegetable stock mixture in the middle of the wok and bring to a boil. Mix in the sugar and the soy sauce. Add the pressed bean curd. Mix everything together, simmer for a few minutes, and serve hot.

PER SERVING Calories: 338 | Fat: 27 grams | Protein: 12 grams | Sodium: 146 milligrams | Fiber: 0 grams | Carbohydrates: 10 grams | Sugar: 3 grams

Twice-Cooked Tofu

These tofu cubes make a flavorful addition to stir-fries, cooked noodles, and salad. Cooked Szechwan peppercorns give them an intriguing aroma reminiscent of cinnamon.

INGREDIENTS | SERVES 4

½ pound firm tofu

2 tablespoons hoisin sauce

2 tablespoons water

½ teaspoon sugar

1 teaspoon ground Szechwan peppercorns, toasted

3 cups vegetable oil

1 tablespoon cornstarch

1. Preheat the oven to 325°F.

2. Drain the tofu and cut into ½" cubes. Place the tofu cubes on a baking dish.

3. In a small bowl, combine the hoisin sauce, water, and sugar. Spread half the mixture over the tofu cubes. Sprinkle with the toasted peppercorns. Bake for 15 minutes.

4. Spread the remaining sauce over the tofu and bake for another 15 minutes or until the tofu is browned and cooked.

5. Add the oil to a preheated wok and heat to 350°F. While the oil is heating, coat the tofu cubes in the cornstarch.

6. When the oil is hot, carefully add the tofu cubes into the wok. Deep-fry until browned (this will take 1–2 minutes). Remove and drain on paper towels.

PER SERVING Calories: 241 | Fat: 21 grams | Protein: 5 grams | Sodium: 138 milligrams | Fiber: 0 grams | Carbohydrates: 7 grams | Sugar: 3 grams

Fermented Bean Curd with Spinach

Don't like spinach? Try substituting amaranth, also known as Chinese spinach.
The red and green leaves contain even more nutrients.

INGREDIENTS | SERVES 4

5 cups spinach leaves

4 cubes fermented bean curd with chilies

Pinch of five-spice powder (less than ⅛ teaspoon)

2 tablespoons vegetable oil

2 garlic cloves, minced

½ teaspoon sugar

Fermented Bean Curd

These small cubes of bean curd preserved in rice and spicy seasonings have a pungent aroma reminiscent of strong cheese. Sold in glass jars in Asian markets, fermented bean curd marries well with other savory foods such as garlic and salted black beans. Usually 1 or 2 cubes is enough.

1. Blanch the spinach by plunging the leaves briefly into boiling water. Drain thoroughly.

2. In a small bowl, mash the fermented bean curd and mix in the five-spice powder.

3. Add the oil to a preheated wok or skillet. When the oil is hot, add the garlic and stir-fry briefly until aromatic. Add the spinach and stir-fry for 1–2 minutes. Add the sugar.

4. Add the mashed bean curd in the middle of the wok and mix with the spinach. Cook through and serve hot.

PER SERVING Calories: 130 | Fat: 10 grams | Protein: 6 grams | Sodium: 32 milligrams | Fiber: 1 gram | Carbohydrates: 4 grams | Sugar: 1 gram

CHAPTER 12

Chinese Vegetables

Easy Vegetable Stir-Fry

Create your own stir-fry with your favorite vegetables! Serve over rice or noodles.

INGREDIENTS | SERVES 4

1 teaspoon cornstarch

½ cup vegetable stock

1 tablespoon peanut oil

2 cups fresh snow peas, whole or sliced

1 cup thinly sliced carrots

1 cup sliced mushrooms

½ cup sliced scallions

1 tablespoon soy sauce

1. In a small bowl, dissolve the cornstarch in the vegetable stock. Set aside.

2. Preheat the wok over medium-high heat. Swirl in the peanut oil. Add snow peas and carrots. Stir-fry until the carrots turn bright orange. Add mushrooms and scallions. Cook until mushrooms soften. Add soy sauce.

3. Stir the cornstarch mixture and add to the wok. The liquid should come to a boil quickly and thicken. Remove from heat and serve.

PER SERVING Calories: 71 | Fat: 3 grams | Protein: 2 grams | Sodium: 293 milligrams | Fiber: 2 grams | Carbohydrates: 8 grams | Sugar: 3 grams

Stir-Fried Bok Choy and Mustard Greens

This flavorful stir-fry may be served with rice as a main course or used as the filling in Bao with Bok Choy and Mustard Greens (see recipe in Chapter 3).

INGREDIENTS | SERVES 4

1 tablespoon peanut oil

6 garlic cloves, minced

2 large shallots, minced

½ pound bok choy, chopped

½ pound mustard greens, chopped

1 teaspoon salt

Pinch red chili flakes

1. Preheat a wok over high heat. Swirl in the oil. Add the garlic and shallots. Stir-fry no more than 30 seconds.

2. Add the bok choy and mustard greens to the wok, making sure they are fully coated in the cooking oil. The bok choy and greens should wilt and collapse within 1 minute.

3. Add the salt and chili flakes and continue stir-frying another 2–3 minutes.

PER SERVING Calories: 67 | Fat: 3 grams | Protein: 2 grams | Sodium: 634 milligrams | Fiber: 2 grams | Carbohydrates: 7 grams | Sugar: 1 gram

Snow Pea Stir-Fry

Serve as a side dish or use where snow peas are called for in recipes.

INGREDIENTS | SERVES 4

2 cups snow peas, trimmed

1½ tablespoons vegetable oil

¾ teaspoon sugar

1½ tablespoons Chinese rice wine or dry sherry

1. Wash and remove the fibrous string from the back of the snow peas by snapping the hook-like end and pulling. Add the oil to a frying pan or preheated wok.

2. When the oil is hot, begin stir-frying the snow peas. Add the sugar and rice wine.

3. Stir-fry until the snow peas turn a bright green and are hot.

PER SERVING Calories: 72 | Fat: 5 grams | Protein: 1 gram | Sodium: 51 milligrams | Fiber: 1 gram | Carbohydrates: 5 grams | Sugar: 3 grams

Leek Stir-Fry with Broccoli and Carrots

You can also use broccoli stems in your stir-fry. Prepare them by peeling the tough outer part and slicing thinly. Serve with rice as a main course.

INGREDIENTS | SERVES 4

1 tablespoon peanut oil

1 teaspoon finely minced ginger

1 teaspoon finely minced garlic

2 cups broccoli florets

2 cups carrots sliced into coins on the diagonal

2 cups sliced leeks, white parts only

¼ cup vegetable stock

1 teaspoon soy sauce

1 teaspoon sesame oil

1. Heat a wok over medium-high heat and swirl in the peanut oil. Add the ginger and garlic and stir-fry 30 seconds.

2. Add the broccoli, carrots, and leeks. Cook until the vegetables are brightly colored, about 5 minutes.

3. Add the stock, soy sauce, and sesame oil. Cook several minutes more, until the stock is reduced and the vegetables are tender.

PER SERVING Calories: 115 | Fat: 5 grams | Protein: 2 grams | Sodium: 169 milligrams | Fiber: 4 grams | Carbohydrates: 16 grams | Sugar: 5 grams

Buddha's Feast

*Also known as Buddha's Delight, this hearty vegetarian dish is
a Chinese New Year tradition, but it can be enjoyed anytime.*

INGREDIENTS | SERVES 4

1 bundle glass noodles

8 large dried shiitake mushrooms

½ cup dried cloud ear mushrooms

2 teaspoons dark sesame oil

1 teaspoon ground white pepper

2 tablespoons soy sauce

⅔ cup vegetable stock

2 tablespoons peanut oil

1 clove garlic, minced

1 teaspoon grated fresh ginger

3 scallions, cut into 1" pieces on the diagonal

1 medium carrot, thinly sliced on the diagonal

8 ounces snow peas, strings removed

8 ounces napa cabbage, roughly chopped

8 ounces firm tofu, drained and cut into 1" cubes

1. Soak the glass noodles in warm water for about 10 minutes to soften. Drain and set aside.

2. Soak the shiitake mushrooms in water to cover until soft, about 20 minutes. Drain, reserving the liquid. It may be used in place of the vegetable stock in this recipe or saved for future use. Remove the shiitake stems and cut the caps into strips. Soak the cloud ear mushrooms in water to cover until soft. Drain.

3. In a small bowl, mix together the sesame oil, pepper, soy sauce, and stock. Set aside.

4. Heat a wok over medium-high heat. Swirl in the peanut oil. Add the garlic, ginger, and scallions. Stir-fry 30 seconds. Add the carrots, snow peas, and cabbage. Stir-fry for about 2 minutes. Add both kinds of mushrooms and stir-fry 1 minute.

5. Add the stock mixture, reduce the heat to medium, and cook, covered, for 5 minutes.

6. Add the tofu, stirring gently so the cubes do not break. Add the noodles and stir to coat. Reduce the heat to low and cook until most of the sauce is absorbed.

PER SERVING Calories: 275 | Fat: 10 grams | Protein: 8 grams | Sodium: 494 milligrams | Fiber: 4 grams | Carbohydrates: 37 grams | Sugar: 4 grams

Spicy Green Beans

If you like tender green beans, you may also blanch them in boiling water before stir-frying.

INGREDIENTS | SERVES 4

1 tablespoon peanut oil

2 garlic cloves, minced

2 tablespoons minced ginger

1 teaspoon red chili flakes

1 pound fresh green beans, trimmed and cut into 2" lengths

1 teaspoon soy sauce

¼ teaspoon white pepper

1. Heat a wok over medium-high heat. Swirl in the peanut oil. Add the garlic, ginger, and red chili flakes. Stir-fry 30 seconds.

2. Add the green beans, soy sauce, and white pepper. The beans will be al dente but cooked through after 5–6 minutes.

PER SERVING Calories: 71 | Fat: 3 grams | Protein: 2 grams | Sodium: 91 milligrams | Fiber: 4 grams | Carbohydrates: 9 grams | Sugar: 1 gram

Stir-Fried Spinach

This dish is easy to prepare and can be served hot or cold. The sharpness of the spinach flavor makes a nice accompaniment to Sweet-and-Sour Shrimp (see recipe in Chapter 6).

INGREDIENTS | SERVES 4

18 spinach leaves

1 tablespoon vegetable oil

¼ teaspoon salt

1. Blanch the spinach in boiling water briefly, just until the leaves begin to wilt. Drain well.

2. Add the oil to a preheated wok or skillet. When the oil is hot, add the spinach. Add the salt and stir-fry briefly, for less than 1 minute. Serve hot.

PER SERVING Calories: 41 | Fat: 3 grams | Protein: 1 gram | Sodium: 181 milligrams | Fiber: 1 gram | Carbohydrates: 1 gram | Sugar: 0 grams

Stir-Fried Bok Choy

Serve as a side dish, or use in combination with a meat or tofu entrée.

INGREDIENTS | SERVES 4

1 bunch bok choy
2 tablespoons vegetable oil
¼ teaspoon salt
1½ tablespoons water

Better Bok Choy

For best results, always separate bok choy stalks from the leaves prior to stir-frying, as the thick stalks take longer to cook.

1. Separate the bok choy stalks and leaves. Cut the stalks diagonally into 1" pieces. Cut the leaves crosswise into 1" pieces.

2. Add the oil to a preheated wok or skillet. When the oil is hot, add the bok choy stalks. Stir-fry for about 1 minute and then add the leaves. Add the salt, sprinkle the water over, and cover and cook on medium heat, until the bok choy is tender but still firm and not mushy.

PER SERVING Calories: 89 | Fat: 7 grams | Protein: 3 grams | Sodium: 281 milligrams | Fiber: 2 grams | Carbohydrates: 4 grams | Sugar: 2 grams

Steamed Broccoli

Looking for an alternative to beef and broccoli with oyster sauce? Try this side dish with a beef stir-fry. Experiment with substituting seasonal vegetables.

INGREDIENTS | SERVES 4

1 pound broccoli
2 tablespoons light soy sauce
1 tablespoon rice wine or dry sherry
1 teaspoon minced ginger
1 tablespoon finely chopped green onion, green part only
¼ teaspoon sesame oil

1. Break off the broccoli florets and cut in half. Cut the spears on the diagonal into thin slices. Steam the broccoli until tender.

2. Mix together the remaining ingredients and pour over the broccoli.

PER SERVING Calories: 53 | Fat: 1 gram | Protein: 4 grams | Sodium: 572 milligrams | Fiber: 3 grams | Carbohydrates: 10 grams | Sugar: 3 grams

Sweet-and-Sour Chinese Greens

Both bok choy and napa cabbage can be found in the produce section of most supermarkets.

INGREDIENTS | SERVES 4

½ pound bok choy

2 tablespoons oil for stir-frying

½ pound napa cabbage, cut into 1" pieces

¼ teaspoon salt

2¼ teaspoons sugar, divided

¼ cup water

3 tablespoons black rice vinegar

Substituting Vinegar

To replace the rice vinegar in this recipe with white distilled vinegar, use 3 table-spoons of distilled vinegar to 2 teaspoons of brown sugar. Increase the amount of brown sugar if the vinegar flavor is a little too overpowering.

1. Separate the bok choy stalks and leaves. Cut the stalks diagonally into 1" pieces. Cut the leaves crosswise into 1" pieces.

2. Add the oil to a preheated wok or skillet. When the oil is hot, add the bok choy stalks. Stir-fry for 1 minute, then add the bok choy leaves and the cabbage. Stir-fry for 1 more minute.

3. Add the salt, ¼ teaspoon of sugar, and the water. Cover and cook for 2–3 minutes on medium heat, until the vegetables are tender but still firm.

4. Remove the cover and add the black rice vinegar and 2 teaspoons of sugar. Mix thoroughly with the bok choy and cabbage.

PER SERVING Calories: 95 | Fat: 7 grams | Protein: 2 grams | Sodium: 197 milligrams | Fiber: 2 grams | Carbohydrates: 7 grams | Sugar: 4 grams

Mushrooms and Bamboo Shoots

This dish is commonly called "Fried Two Winters," because the Cantonese words for mushrooms and bamboo shoots are similar to the word for winter.

INGREDIENTS | SERVES 2

8 dried mushrooms

2 tablespoons dark soy sauce

2 teaspoons sugar

2 tablespoons vegetable oil

1 (8-ounce) can bamboo shoots, rinsed, drained, and cut in half

1 tablespoon cornstarch mixed with 4 tablespoons water

Don't Discard the Soaking Liquid

The soaking liquid from reconstituted (softened) ingredients like dried mushrooms and wood fungus makes a flavorful substitute for water in recipes. It can also be used in place of a meat stock. Before using, strain the water to remove any gritty particles.

1. Soak the mushrooms in hot water for 20 minutes to soften or reconstitute. Reserve the soaking liquid. Gently squeeze the mushrooms to remove excess water and thinly slice.

2. In a small bowl, mix together the dark soy sauce and sugar. Set aside.

3. Add the oil to a preheated wok or heavy skillet. When the oil is hot, add the bamboo shoots. Stir-fry for 1 minute and add the mushrooms.

4. Add the dark soy sauce mixture and ½ cup of reserved mushroom liquid. Turn the heat down to low, cover, and simmer the vegetables for 10 minutes.

5. Give the cornstarch-and-water mixture a quick stir. Turn the heat up and push the vegetables up to the side of the wok. Add the cornstarch mixture in the middle, stirring quickly to thicken. Mix through and serve hot.

PER SERVING Calories: 230 | Fat: 14 grams | Protein: 5 grams | Sodium: 1,015 milligrams | Fiber: 3 grams | Carbohydrates: 23 grams | Sugar: 7 grams

Mushrooms and Cabbage

*The combination of fresh and dried mushrooms gives this dish a more elegant appearance.
Feel free to use either napa or other types of cabbage.*

INGREDIENTS | SERVES 2

4 dried mushrooms

2 cabbage leaves

2 tablespoons light soy sauce

1 tablespoon dark soy sauce

3 teaspoons sugar

2 tablespoons vegetable oil

1 (8-ounce) can bamboo shoots, drained, rinsed, and cut in half

6 fresh mushrooms, sliced

½ cup water

1 tablespoon cornstarch mixed with 4 tablespoons water

1. Soak the dried mushrooms in hot water for 20 minutes to reconstitute. Reserve the soaking liquid. Gently squeeze the mushrooms to remove excess water and thinly slice.

2. Blanch the cabbage leaves by plunging them briefly into boiling water. Drain thoroughly and shred.

3. In a small bowl, mix together the light soy sauce, dark soy sauce, and sugar. Set aside.

4. Add the oil to a preheated wok or heavy skillet. When the oil is hot, add the bamboo shoots and stir-fry. Add all the mushrooms and stir-fry. Add the cabbage leaves.

5. Add the soy sauce and sugar mixture and the reserved mushroom liquid. Add the water. Turn the heat down to low, cover, and simmer the vegetables for 10 minutes.

6. Turn the heat up and push the vegetables up to the side of the wok. Give the cornstarch/water mixture a quick stir and add in the middle, stirring quickly to thicken. Mix through and serve hot.

PER SERVING Calories: 243 | Fat: 14 grams | Protein: 7 grams | Sodium: 1,535 milligrams | Fiber: 4 grams | Carbohydrates: 23 grams | Sugar: 9 grams

Stir-Fried Spinach with Roasted Garlic

*Although roasting garlic is not a typical Chinese preparation,
it gives this dish a delightful sweet and complex flavor.*

INGREDIENTS | SERVES 4

3 garlic cloves

¼ cup chicken stock

1 tablespoon oil for stir-frying

18 fresh spinach leaves, trimmed

1 tablespoon soy sauce

½ teaspoon sugar

1. Begin preparing the garlic 1 hour ahead of time. Preheat the oven to 350°F. Peel the garlic, place in a small baking dish, and drizzle with the chicken stock. Bake 1 hour or until the cloves are golden. Cool. Press down on cloves to release the garlic (it should come out easily).

2. Add the oil to a preheated wok or skillet. When the oil is hot, add the spinach leaves. Stir-fry for about 1 minute, then add the soy sauce and sugar. Continue stir-frying until the spinach turns a bright green. Serve with the garlic.

PER SERVING Calories: 52 | Fat: 3 grams | Protein: 2 grams | Sodium: 291 milligrams | Fiber: 1 gram | Carbohydrates: 4 grams | Sugar: 1 gram

Wild Mushrooms in Vegetarian Brown Sauce

This dish may be prepared using fresh or dried mushrooms.

INGREDIENTS | SERVES 2

2 tablespoons peanut oil

1 shallot, finely chopped

1 tablespoon minced ginger

3 garlic cloves, minced

3 cups sliced assorted mushrooms (shiitake, oyster, cremini, etc.)

1 tablespoon soy sauce

½ cup vegetable stock

1 teaspoon cornstarch, dissolved in 1 tablespoon water

¼ cup sliced scallions

1. Preheat a wok over medium-high heat. Swirl in the peanut oil. Add shallot, ginger, and garlic and stir-fry 30–60 seconds, so that their aromas are released and the shallot begins to turn translucent.

2. Add the mushrooms and stir to coat. Reduce the heat to medium. Continue cooking, stirring frequently, until the mushrooms soften and release their liquid.

3. Add the soy sauce and stock. Bring to a boil.

4. Stir in the cornstarch mixture. Turn the heat off once the sauce has thickened. Sprinkle with scallions and serve.

PER SERVING Calories: 181 | Fat: 14 grams | Protein: 4 grams | Sodium: 552 milligrams | Fiber: 1 gram | Carbohydrates: 9 grams | Sugar: 2 grams

Stir-Fried Baby Bok Choy

For best results, wash bok choy and mung bean sprouts earlier in the day
so that they have plenty of time to drain before stir-frying.

INGREDIENTS | SERVES 4

2 tablespoons vegetable oil

2 garlic cloves, chopped

4 bunches baby bok choy

1 tablespoon rice vinegar

1 teaspoon sugar

¼ teaspoon salt

1 teaspoon sesame oil

1. Add the oil to a preheated wok or skillet. When the oil is hot, add the garlic and stir-fry until aromatic. Add the baby bok choy and stir-fry briefly.

2. Add the rice vinegar, sugar, and salt. Cook for 1 minute. Drizzle the sesame oil over and serve.

PER SERVING Calories: 91 | Fat: 8 grams | Protein: 1 gram | Sodium: 209 milligrams | Fiber: 1 gram | Carbohydrates: 3 grams | Sugar: 2 grams

Pickled Carrots

Pickled vegetables are very popular in Cantonese cuisine; look for them
on the menu the next time you dine at a Cantonese restaurant.

INGREDIENTS | MAKES 1½ CUPS

1½ cups (12 ounces) baby carrots

⅓ cup rice vinegar

⅓ cup sugar

¼ teaspoon salt

2 cups water

1. Place carrots in a glass jar.

2. In a medium saucepan, bring the vinegar, sugar, salt, and water to a boil, stirring to dissolve the sugar.

3. Pour the liquid over the carrots, seal the jar, and refrigerate for at least 2 days.

PER SERVING (½ CUP) Calories: 25 | Fat: 0 grams | Protein: 2 grams | Sodium: 172 milligrams | Fiber: 2 grams | Carbohydrates: 7 grams | Sugar: 3 grams

Broccoli with Oyster Sauce

Broccoli and savory oyster sauce make a perfect combination. Serve with stir-fried chicken and rice.

INGREDIENTS | SERVES 4

1 pound broccoli
2 tablespoons vegetable oil
3 teaspoons oyster sauce
1 teaspoon sugar
¼ cup water plus 4 teaspoons water
1 teaspoon cornstarch

Colorless Vegetables

Covering and cooking firm green vegetables in a bit of water will help make them more tender. Do not lift the wok lid to check on covered green vegetables more than once during cooking. If you do, the vegetables will turn yellow.

1. Break off the broccoli florets and cut in half. Cut the spears on the diagonal into thin slices.

2. Add the oil to a skillet or a preheated wok. When the oil is hot, add the broccoli, adding the spears first and then the florets.

3. Add the oyster sauce, sugar, and ¼ cup of water. Cover and cook about 3 minutes, or until the broccoli turns a brilliant green.

4. In a small bowl, mix the cornstarch and remaining water. Uncover the wok, make a well in the middle, and add the cornstarch mixture, stirring quickly to thicken. Mix through.

PER SERVING Calories: 95 | Fat: 7 grams | Protein: 3 grams | Sodium: 160 milligrams | Fiber: 3 grams | Carbohydrates: 5 grams | Sugar: 1 gram

Braised Ridged Gourd with Mushrooms

Like tofu, this gourd acts like a sponge, soaking up the flavors of the food it is cooked with.

INGREDIENTS | SERVES 4

1 ridged gourd (also called angled luffa)

3 tablespoons vegetable oil

1 clove garlic, minced

5 mushrooms, sliced

¼ teaspoon salt

¼ cup chicken broth

2 tablespoons Chinese rice wine or dry sherry

2 teaspoons soy sauce

1 teaspoon brown sugar

1 teaspoon cornstarch

4 teaspoons water

Too Much Cornstarch

If the mixture of cornstarch and water in a recipe produces a soggier sauce than you would like, try reducing the amount of cornstarch while keeping the ratio of cornstarch to water constant. For example, instead of 1 tablespoon of cornstarch mixed with 4 tablespoons of water, use ½ tablespoon of cornstarch and 2 tablespoons of water.

1. Peel the gourd, leaving a few strips of green if desired to add a bit of color. Cut diagonally into thin slices.

2. Add the oil to a preheated wok or skillet. When the oil is hot, add the garlic. When the garlic is aromatic, add the ridged gourd, and stir-fry for about 1 minute. Add the mushrooms and the salt.

3. Add the chicken broth and stir-fry for another minute. Add the rice wine, soy sauce, and brown sugar.

4. In a small bowl, mix the cornstarch and water and then add it to the middle of the wok, stirring quickly to thicken. Mix through.

PER SERVING Calories: 131 | Fat: 10 grams | Protein: 1 gram | Sodium: 383 milligrams | Fiber: 0 grams | Carbohydrates: 9 grams | Sugar: 3 grams

Braised Chinese Broccoli (*Gai Lan*) in Oyster Sauce

*Chinese broccoli or gai lan has an attractive appearance
and an earthy flavor—plus, it's rich in vitamins A and C.*

INGREDIENTS | SERVES 4

½ pound Chinese broccoli

1 tablespoon plus 1 teaspoon oyster sauce

2 teaspoons soy sauce

½ teaspoon sugar

¼ cup water

2 tablespoons vegetable oil

2 slices ginger

1 teaspoon tapioca starch mixed with 4 teaspoons water

Revamping Recipes

Want to adjust a recipe to suit your family? Doubling a recipe can turn a side dish into an entrée. Just make sure the ingredients are not crowded in your wok or frying pan, so that everything cooks evenly. Tofu can often be substituted for meat, or the amount of meat in a dish increased. Be prepared to increase the amount of marinade and sauce as well, and take into account the overall volume when cooking in the wok or frying pan.

1. Blanch the Chinese broccoli by plunging it briefly into boiling water until the stalks turn a bright green. Drain thoroughly. Separate the stalks and leaves. Cut the leaves across, and cut the stalks thinly on the diagonal.

2. In a small bowl, combine the oyster sauce, soy sauce, sugar, and water. Set aside.

3. Add the oil to a preheated wok or skillet. When the oil is hot, add the ginger slices. Stir-fry briefly until aromatic. Add the Chinese broccoli stalks. Stir-fry for 1 minute, then add the leaves. Stir-fry until the leaves turn a bright green.

4. Add the oyster sauce mixture. Turn down the heat and cook, covered, for 4–5 minutes.

5. Add the tapioca mixture to the middle of the wok, stirring to thicken. Mix well and serve hot.

PER SERVING Calories: 85 | Fat: 7 grams | Protein: 1 gram | Sodium: 335 milligrams | Fiber: 1 gram | Carbohydrates: 4 grams | Sugar: 1 gram

Stir-Fried Young Bamboo Shoots

Blanching fresh young bamboo shoots lessens their acidic flavor. Serve with a sweet dish such as Sweet-and-Sour Spareribs (see recipe in Chapter 6).

INGREDIENTS | SERVES 4

4 pieces (1 cup) peeled young bamboo shoots

1½ tablespoons vegetable oil

1 tablespoon soy sauce

1 teaspoon Chinese rice wine or dry sherry

1 teaspoon rice vinegar

1 green onion, diagonally cut into 1" pieces

1. Blanch the bamboo shoots in boiling water for at least 5 minutes. Drain thoroughly and chop into 1" pieces.

2. Add the oil to a preheated wok or skillet. When the oil is hot, add the bamboo shoots. Stir-fry for about 2 minutes, then add the soy sauce, rice wine, and rice vinegar. Stir in the green onion. Simmer for 5 more minutes. Chill.

PER SERVING Calories: 62 | Fat: 1 gram | Protein: 3 grams | Sodium: 266 milligrams | Fiber: 1 gram | Carbohydrates: 3 grams | Sugar: 1 gram

Ridged Gourd with Red Pepper

Sweet red pepper contrasts nicely with the gourd. Serve with chicken for a balanced meal.

INGREDIENTS | SERVES 4

1 ridged gourd

2 tablespoons vegetable oil

1 slice ginger

1 red bell pepper, seeded and thinly sliced

½ cup chicken broth

2 tablespoons Chinese rice wine or dry sherry

1 tablespoon soy sauce

1 teaspoon sugar

1. Peel the gourd, leaving a few strips of green if desired to add a bit of color. Cut diagonally into thin slices.

2. Add the oil to a preheated wok or skillet. When the oil is hot, add the ginger slice and stir-fry until aromatic. Add the ridged gourd and stir-fry for about 1 minute. Add the red pepper and stir-fry until it is bright red.

3. Add the chicken broth and bring to a boil. Add the rice wine, soy sauce, and sugar. Serve hot.

PER SERVING Calories: 106 | Fat: 7 grams | Protein: 1 gram | Sodium: 325 milligrams | Fiber: 1 gram | Carbohydrates: 10 grams | Sugar: 5 grams

Three-Vegetable Stir-Fry

*The combination of shiitake mushrooms, snow peas, and baby corn provides
an interesting contrast in color and texture. Serve with a more highly seasoned dish.*

INGREDIENTS | SERVES 4

1½ tablespoons vegetable oil

1 (15-ounce) can baby corn, rinsed and drained

4 ounces snow peas, trimmed

6 shiitake mushrooms, sliced

1 tablespoon dark soy sauce

¼ teaspoon sesame oil

1. Add the oil to a preheated wok or frying pan. Add the baby corn and stir-fry briefly, then add the snow peas. Stir-fry until the snow peas turn a bright green. Push them up to the side of the wok and stir-fry the mushrooms.

2. Add the dark soy sauce and mix thoroughly. Finish with a drizzle of sesame oil.

PER SERVING Calories: 79 | Fat: 5 grams | Protein: 1 gram | Sodium: 254 milligrams | Fiber: 1 gram | Carbohydrates: 7 grams | Sugar: 2 grams

Spicy Eggplant Stir-Fry

*This dish can be made with truncheon-shaped Chinese eggplant
or the thicker eggplant commonly available in local supermarkets.*

INGREDIENTS | SERVES 4

3 tablespoons vegetable oil

1 eggplant, sliced diagonally into 1" pieces

2 tablespoons red rice vinegar

½ teaspoon brown sugar

2 tablespoons soy sauce

1 tablespoon chopped garlic

½ teaspoon chili paste

¼ teaspoon sesame oil

1. Add the oil to a preheated wok or skillet. When the oil is hot, add the eggplant slices, stir-frying in batches if necessary. Stir-fry for about 2–3 minutes.

2. Add the red rice vinegar, brown sugar, soy sauce, garlic, and chili paste, and mix through. Drizzle the sesame oil over and give a final stir.

PER SERVING Calories: 145 | Fat: 11 grams | Protein: 2 grams | Sodium: 502 milligrams | Fiber: 2 grams | Carbohydrates: 11 grams | Sugar: 5 grams

Szechwan Eggplant with Black Rice Vinegar

In order not to waste any oil, strain the oil from stir-frying the eggplant so that it can be used again.

INGREDIENTS | SERVES 4

2 teaspoons soy sauce

½ teaspoon black rice vinegar

½ teaspoon sugar

1 teaspoon dark soy sauce

¼ teaspoon salt

5 tablespoons vegetable oil, divided

2 Chinese eggplants, chopped into tiny pieces

1 tablespoon chopped ginger

1 garlic clove, chopped

1 teaspoon hot bean sauce

¼ cup chicken stock or broth

¼ teaspoon sesame oil

2 green onions, chopped into thirds

1. In a small bowl, mix together the soy sauce, black rice vinegar, sugar, dark soy sauce, and salt. Set aside.

2. Add 4 tablespoons of oil to a preheated wok or skillet. When the oil is hot, add the eggplant. Stir-fry about 5 minutes, until the eggplant is soft. Gently press the eggplant with a spatula to remove any excess oil. Remove from the wok.

3. Remove the oil from the wok, and wipe the wok clean with a paper towel. Add 1 tablespoon of oil back into the wok. When the oil is hot, add the ginger, garlic, and hot bean sauce and stir-fry briefly. Add the sauce and the chicken stock. Bring to a boil. Add the eggplant back to the wok and stir-fry until the sauce is nearly gone.

4. Add the sesame oil and green onions. Stir and serve.

PER SERVING Calories: 170 | Fat: 14 grams | Protein: 1 gram | Sodium: 399 milligrams | Fiber: 3 grams | Carbohydrates: 10 grams | Sugar: 4 grams

Bitter Melon Stir-Fry

Bitter melon is one of those foods that people either love or hate. Native to China, it works best with pungent ingredients such as chilies and black bean sauce that can hold their own against its strong flavor.

INGREDIENTS | SERVES 6

2 bitter melons, seeded and thinly sliced

1 teaspoon salt

2 tablespoons vegetable oil

1 clove garlic, chopped

2 tablespoons hoisin sauce

4 tablespoons water

1 tablespoon Chinese rice wine or dry sherry

½ teaspoon brown sugar

PER SERVING Calories: 78 | Fat: 4 grams | Protein: 2 grams | Sodium: 487 milligrams | Fiber: 1 gram | Carbohydrates: 8 grams | Sugar: 3 grams

1. Place the bitter melon slices in a large bowl and toss with salt. Leave for 15 minutes and place on paper towels to drain excess water.

2. Bring a large pot of water to a boil. Boil the bitter melons for 3 minutes. Drain well.

3. Add the oil to a preheated wok or skillet. Add the garlic and stir-fry briefly until aromatic. Add the bitter melon and stir-fry for 2–3 minutes.

4. Add the hoisin sauce, water, rice wine, and brown sugar. Mix thoroughly and serve hot.

Braised Baby Bok Choy

Baby bok choy has a sweeter flavor and is more tender than regular bok choy.

INGREDIENTS | SERVES 4

4 bunches baby bok choy

½ cup chicken stock or broth

½ cup water

1½ teaspoons rice vinegar

2 tablespoons vegetable oil

2 garlic cloves, finely chopped

½ teaspoon sesame oil

PER SERVING Calories: 89 | Fat: 7 grams | Protein: 1 gram | Sodium: 72 milligrams | Fiber: 1 gram | Carbohydrates: 4 grams | Sugar: 2 grams

1. Cut off the baby bok choy roots and separate the stalks and leaves.

2. In a small bowl, combine the chicken stock, water, and rice vinegar. Set aside.

3. Add the oil to a preheated wok or skillet. When the oil is ready, add the garlic. Stir-fry until aromatic.

4. Add the bok choy stalks and stir-fry until they turn a bright green. While stir-frying the stalks, add the leaves.

5. Add the chicken stock mixture. Turn down the heat and simmer, covered, for 5 minutes. Turn off the heat and drizzle with the sesame oil.

CHAPTER 13

Desserts and Snacks

Almond Cookies

Delicately flavored with a hint of almond, these cookies make a satisfying light afternoon snack or finale to a dim sum brunch.

INGREDIENTS | MAKES 30 COOKIES

2 cups flour

½ teaspoon baking powder

½ teaspoon baking soda

½ cup butter

½ cup shortening

¾ cup white sugar

2 eggs

2 teaspoons almond extract

¼ pound whole, blanched almonds

1 egg, lightly beaten

Aromatic Almonds

Cooks have been exploiting the almond's rich flavor for thousands of years. In China of days past, peddlers traveled from door to door selling almond tea, a sweet concoction made with almonds ground into a paste. Today, almonds are featured in desserts and some restaurant dishes.

1. Preheat oven to 325°F.

2. In a large bowl, sift the flour, baking powder, and baking soda.

3. In a medium bowl, use an electric mixer to beat the butter, shortening, and sugar. Add the eggs and almond extract and beat until well blended.

4. Add the butter mixture to the flour mixture, stirring.

5. Knead the dough into a roll or log. If you find 1 long roll too difficult to work with, split the dough into 2 equal pieces.

6. Cut the dough into 30 pieces. Roll each piece into a ball and place on a lightly greased cookie tray, approximately 2" apart. Place an almond in the center of each cookie and press down lightly.

7. Brush each cookie lightly with beaten egg before baking. Bake for 15 minutes or until golden brown. Cool and store in a sealed container.

PER SERVING (2 COOKIES) Calories: 268 | Fat: 17 grams | Protein: 4 grams | Sodium: 67 milligrams | Fiber: 1 gram | Carbohydrates: 24 grams | Sugar: 10 grams

Walnut Cookies

These sweet cookies are a popular feature in Chinese bakeries.
Food coloring is sometimes used to give them a yellow color.

INGREDIENTS | MAKES 30 COOKIES

2 teaspoons baking powder

3 cups flour

¾ cup vegetable shortening

½ cup finely chopped walnuts

2 teaspoons vanilla extract

1¼ cups white sugar

4 eggs, divided

Chinese Bakery

Need a little inspiration before you're ready to get out the rolling pin and start mixing and measuring? Try visiting a Chinese bakery. Classics like Egg Custard Tarts share space with sticky rice dumplings, foot-long doughnuts, and buns filled with everything from pineapple and taro to red bean paste. All reflect the Chinese belief that no one flavor should upstage any other. Indulge, and you'll leave feeling pleasantly satisfied but without a case of "sugar hangover."

1. Preheat oven to 325°F.

2. In a large bowl, sift the baking powder into the flour. Cut the shortening into the flour and mix with your fingers until it forms the texture of fine crumbs.

3. Add the walnuts, vanilla extract, sugar, and 3 eggs. Mix into the dough to form a paste.

4. Take a piece of dough and form into a round ball the size of a large golf ball. Place the ball in the palm of one hand and press down with the palm of the other hand to form a flat circle about 2" in diameter. Continue with the remainder of the dough. Place the dough circles on a greased baking tray.

5. In a small bowl, lightly beat the remaining egg. Brush the dough lightly with the beaten egg. Bake for about 20–25 minutes, or until a toothpick stuck in the center comes out clean. Cool and store in a sealed container.

PER SERVING (2 COOKIES) Calories: 292 | Fat: 14 grams | Protein: 5 grams | Sodium: 69 milligrams | Fiber: 1 gram | Carbohydrates: 36 grams | Sugar: 17 grams

Egg Custard Tarts

Egg tarts are a popular dim sum treat. Make sure that the tart pans are well greased so that the pastry does not stick.

INGREDIENTS | SERVES 18

2 cups flour

¾ teaspoon salt

⅔ cup lard

½ teaspoon vanilla extract

3 tablespoons hot water

2 large eggs

½ cup evaporated milk

½ cup milk

¼ cup sugar

1. Preheat oven to 300°F.

2. In a large bowl, sift together the flour and salt. Cut in the lard, and then use your fingers to mix it in. When the mixture has the consistency of bread crumbs, add the vanilla extract and hot water and mix together to form a dough. Add another tablespoon of water if necessary. Cut the dough into thirds.

3. On a lightly floured surface, roll each piece of dough out until it is ⅛" thick. Cut 6 circles that are each 3" in diameter, so that you have a total of 18 circles.

4. Place the circles into greased tart pans or muffin tins, carefully shaping the sides so that they reach the rim.

5. In a medium bowl, lightly beat the eggs, and stir in the evaporated milk, milk, and sugar.

6. Add up to 2 tablespoons of the custard into each tart shell, so that it nicely fills the shell but does not overflow.

7. Bake for about 25 minutes or until the custard is cooked through and a knife stuck in the middle comes out clean.

PER SERVING Calories: 151 | Fat: 9 grams | Protein: 2 grams | Sodium: 115 milligrams | Fiber: 0 grams | Carbohydrates: 14 grams | Sugar: 3 grams

Almond Jelly

This dim sum dessert classic may be served with familiar American fruits, such as peaches and strawberries, or typical Chinese ones, such as lychees.

INGREDIENTS | SERVES 6

1½ packages Knox unflavored gelatin

1 cup cold water

3 tablespoons sugar

1 cup boiling water

1 cup evaporated milk

2 teaspoons almond extract

1 cup fresh lychees

Lychee Lore

Native to southern China, lychees hold a special place in Chinese food culture. Successions of emperors prized the small, heart-shaped fruit for its sweet flavor. An exiled Chinese poet is reputed to have consoled himself by consuming 300 lychees daily. Nutritionally, lychees are low in calories and a good source of vitamin C. Fresh lychees come into season during the summer months; they are available canned in syrup year-round. Both are sold in Asian markets.

1. In a small bowl, pour the gelatin over the cold water and wait about 3 minutes for it to soften.

2. In a separate bowl, add the sugar to the boiling water, stirring to dissolve. Add the evaporated milk to the sugar-and-water mixture. Wait a few minutes for the mixture to cool slightly and stir in the almond extract.

3. Add the evaporated milk mixture to the gelatin and water. Stir well and pour into a shallow pan or a serving mold. Chill until firm.

4. Cut into diamond shapes and place on a serving tray. Garnish with lychees.

PER SERVING Calories: 125 | Fat: 3 grams | Protein: 9 grams | Sodium: 58 milligrams | Fiber: 0 grams | Carbohydrates: 15 grams | Sugar: 11 grams

Annin Tofu

This version of almond jelly varies in texture, depending on the thickener used.

INGREDIENTS | SERVES 6

3 cups almond milk, divided
⅓ cup crushed Chinese rock sugar
2 teaspoons agar-agar powder or pectin
½ teaspoon almond extract

The Jiggle Factor

The traditional dessert Almond Jelly is sometimes called Annin Tofu, due to its texture. This may come as a surprise for anyone who has only seen it in gelatin-like form. Depending on the thickener, the jelly can be solid or soft. Agar-agar will produce a firmer texture, pectin a softer one.

1. Put 1 cup of almond milk in a medium saucepan, and stir the sugar into it until dissolved.

2. Sprinkle the agar-agar powder or pectin over the surface of the almond milk and stir. Bring the mixture to a slow boil over medium heat and cook, stirring constantly, until the agar is completely dissolved.

3. Add the remaining 2 cups of almond milk, stir well, and pour into 6 lightly oiled molds or a single large mold about 4 cups in size. Cover and refrigerate until set, about 1 hour.

PER SERVING Calories: 76 | Fat: 0 grams | Protein: 0 grams | Sodium: 74 milligrams | Fiber: 0 grams | Carbohydrates: 16 grams | Sugar: 14 grams

Grass Jelly Dessert

The flavor of this gelatin, which is blackish in color, can be a little overpowering, but it works well when balanced with sweet, syrupy fruits like canned lychees.

INGREDIENTS | SERVES 4

1 (19-ounce) can grass jelly
1 cup canned lychees in syrup

Eating for Health

Grass jelly, like many Chinese foods, is said to have curative powers. It is made from an herb that is in the mint family, although more bitter and much less familiar to the Western palate. Traditionally, the jelly is served with a sweet syrup.

1. Remove the grass jelly from the can, slice, and cut into cubes.

2. Place the grass jelly cubes in a large bowl. Add the lychees and syrup.

PER SERVING Calories: 96 | Fat: 0 grams | Protein: 0 grams | Sodium: 2 milligrams | Fiber: 0 grams | Carbohydrates: 24 grams | Sugar: 14 grams

Steamed Fruit with a Surprise

The world's first sweetener, honey has been used in China since ancient times. When sugarcane was introduced, the Chinese originally called it "stone honey."

INGREDIENTS | SERVES 4

4 pears
2 tablespoons honey
4 Chinese honey dates

Guilt-Free Indulging
This healthy dessert lets you indulge and fight off illness at the same time. According to traditional Chinese medicine, pears lower cholesterol and reduce high blood pressure, while honey dates build up the blood.

1. Slice off the top of each pear and set the top piece aside. Core the pear from the top, being careful not to go through to the bottom.

2. Spoon ½ tablespoon of honey into each pear. Add a Chinese honey date. Replace the tops of the pears.

3. Steam until tender. Remove the pears from the pot immediately so they don't keep cooking and become mushy. Serve hot.

PER SERVING Calories: 201 | Fat: 0 grams | Protein: 1 gram | Sodium: 2 milligrams | Fiber: 7 grams | Carbohydrates: 54 grams | Sugar: 41 grams

Sweet Red Bean Paste

Use in Sesame Seed Dumplings with Red Bean Paste and Fried Pancakes with Red Bean Paste (see recipes in this chapter), or as a filling for steamed buns.

INGREDIENTS | MAKES 1½ CUPS

½ cup dried red beans
1½ cups water
¼ cup sugar
1¼ tablespoons vegetable oil

1. Rinse the beans and soak overnight in water to cover, adding more water if necessary. Drain.

2. In a medium saucepan bring the water to a boil. Add the beans and simmer for at least 2 hours or until they are tender. Drain.

3. Place the beans and the sugar in a blender and process until smooth. Heat the oil in a preheated wok or saucepan. Add the bean paste and stir-fry until it is dry. Store in a sealed container in the refrigerator. The bean paste will last for approximately 1 week.

PER SERVING (1 TABLESPOON) Calories: 27 | Fat: 0 grams | Protein: 1 gram | Sodium: 0 milligrams | Fiber: 1 gram | Carbohydrates: 4 grams | Sugar: 2 grams

Red Bean Bao

These lightly sweetened steamed buns can be eaten as snacks as well as dessert at the end of dim sum.

INGREDIENTS | SERVES 10

Bao Dough (see recipe in Chapter 3)
1¼ cups Sweet Red Bean Paste (see recipe in this chapter)

Precious Packages

The word *bao* in Chinese has multiple meanings, not only "bun" but "gift." When the word is repeated, *bao bao*, the meaning is "something precious."

1. Divide the dough into 10 equal pieces. Flatten a piece of dough between your hands to form a circle about 5" or 6" in diameter.

2. Place 2 tablespoons of the bean paste in the center of the circle. Bring up the edges of the dough and twist together to form a pouch around the filling. Place each bun on a 3" square of parchment paper.

3. Once you have finished forming all the buns, cover them with a clean towel and place in a warm, draft-free place to rise for 30 minutes.

4. Heat water to simmer in a wok and set a rack on top. Place the buns inside a bamboo steamer or on a plate, about 1" apart, and steam with the lid on for 15 minutes. Do not lift the lid to check. Let cool to room temperature and serve.

PER SERVING Calories: 234 | Fat: 4 grams | Protein: 6 grams | Sodium: 100 milligrams | Fiber: 3 grams | Carbohydrates: 41 grams | Sugar: 7 grams

Sesame Seed Dumplings with Red Bean Paste

Glutinous rice flour, also known as sweet rice flour, is used mainly for desserts and dim sum snacks. It is sold in bags in Asian markets.

INGREDIENTS | SERVES 12

¾ cup packed brown sugar

1 cup boiling water

2⅓ cups glutinous rice flour

1 cup Sweet Red Bean Paste (see recipe in this chapter)

¼ cup white sesame seeds

6 cups vegetable oil

1. In a small saucepan add the brown sugar to the boiling water, stirring to dissolve. Cool.

2. Place the flour in a large bowl, making a well in the middle. Give the sugar/water mix a quick stir and slowly pour into the well, stirring to mix with the flour. Continue stirring until well mixed. You should have a sticky, caramel-colored dough at this point.

3. Rub your hands in a bit of the rice flour so that the dough doesn't stick to them. Take a heaping tablespoon of dough and shape into a ball roughly the size of a golf ball.

4. Flatten the ball with the palm of your hand, then use your thumb to make an indentation in the middle. Take no more than 1 teaspoon of red bean paste, and use your hand to shape the paste into a circle. Place the paste in the indentation in the dough. Fold the dough over the paste and roll back into a ball. Continue with the remainder of the dough.

5. Sprinkle the sesame seeds on a sheet of waxed paper. Roll the balls in the seeds.

6. In a wok or large pot, heat the oil to between 330–350°F. Deep-fry the sesame seed balls a few at a time, carefully pushing them against the sides of the wok when they float to the top. The sesame balls are cooked when they expand to approximately 3 times their size and turn golden brown. Drain on paper towels. Serve warm.

PER SERVING Calories: 334 | Fat: 16 grams | Protein: 3 grams | Sodium: 5 milligrams | Fiber: 2 grams | Carbohydrates: 44 grams | Sugar: 16 grams

Sesame Seed Dumplings with Peanut Filling

Sesame seed dumplings, or jian dui, *are made for the Chinese New Year to bring luck.*

INGREDIENTS | SERVES 12

⅓ cup plus ¾ cup packed brown sugar, divided

⅔ cup chopped peanuts

1 cup boiling water

2⅓ cups glutinous rice flour

¼ cup white sesame seeds

6 cups vegetable oil

1. In a small bowl, mix ⅓ cup of brown sugar and the peanuts. Set aside.

2. Add ¾ cup of brown sugar to the boiling water, stirring to dissolve. Cool.

3. Place the flour in a large bowl, making a well in the middle. Give the sugar/water mix a quick stir and slowly pour into the well, stirring to mix with the flour. Continue stirring until well mixed. You should have a sticky, caramel-colored dough at this point.

4. Rub your hands in rice flour so the dough doesn't stick to them. Take a tablespoon of dough and shape it into a ball roughly the size of a golf ball.

5. Flatten the ball with the palm of your hand, then use your thumb to make an indentation in the middle. Take no more than 1 teaspoon of the peanut mixture, and use your hand to shape it into a circle. Place the peanut mixture in the indentation in the dough. Fold the dough over the paste and roll back into a ball. Continue with the remainder of the dough.

6. Sprinkle the sesame seeds on a sheet of waxed paper. Roll the balls in the sesame seeds.

7. In a wok or large pot, heat the oil to between 330–350°F. Deep-fry the sesame seed balls a few at a time, carefully pushing them against the sides of the wok when they float to the top. The sesame balls are cooked when they expand to approximately 3 times their size and turn golden brown. Drain on paper towels. Serve warm.

PER SERVING Calories: 367 | Fat: 19 grams | Protein: 4 grams | Sodium: 6 milligrams | Fiber: 1 gram | Carbohydrates: 45 grams | Sugar: 19 grams

Fried Pancakes with Red Bean Paste

*Mu Shu Pancakes, also known as Mandarin Pancakes, are used here as a dessert.
For an added treat, dust the pancakes with sugar or icing sugar after frying.*

INGREDIENTS | SERVES 9

Mu Shu Pancakes (see recipe in Chapter 6)

1 cup Sweet Red Bean Paste (see recipe in this chapter)

2 tablespoons vegetable oil

1. Lay pancakes on a flat surface. Add approximately 1 tablespoon of red bean paste to each pancake and spread it out evenly. Roll up the pancake into a cylinder shape.

2. Heat the oil in a preheated wok or skillet. When the oil is hot, stir-fry the pancakes until golden. Serve warm.

PER SERVING Calories: 222 | Fat: 10 grams | Protein: 4 grams | Sodium: 2 milligrams | Fiber: 2 grams | Carbohydrates: 27 grams | Sugar: 3 grams

Sweet Red Bean Paste Soup

*This simplified version of a famous Chinese wedding soup
can be served as a snack or as a sweet dessert soup.*

INGREDIENTS | SERVES 3

4 cups water

1 piece dried tangerine peel, 2"–3" wide

½ cup Sweet Red Bean Paste (see recipe in this chapter)

⅓ cup sugar

Chinese Wedding Soup

Traditionally, sweet red bean paste soup is made with raw adzuki beans and contains lotus seeds, a symbol of fertility in Chinese culture.

1. In a medium saucepan, add the water and the dried tangerine peel. Bring to a boil and simmer for about 30 minutes.

2. Add the Sweet Red Bean Paste. Continue simmering for another 30 minutes. Add the sugar, stirring to dissolve. Chill before serving.

PER SERVING Calories: 158 | Fat: 2 grams | Protein: 2 grams | Sodium: 1 milligram | Fiber: 2 grams | Carbohydrates: 33 grams | Sugar: 27 grams

Sweet Almond Soup

Traditionally this dessert would be made with Chinese almonds, which—surprisingly enough—are actually apricot pits!

INGREDIENTS | SERVES 4

½ cup unblanched almonds

3 tablespoons long-grain rice

2 tablespoons Chinese dates

2 tablespoons vegetable oil

2½ cups milk

2 tablespoons sugar

1. Process the almonds in a blender or food processor into a fine powder. Combine 3 tablespoons of the processed almonds with the rice and process again. Add water, a few drops at a time, to form a paste.

2. Chop the Chinese dates into small pieces and set aside.

3. Add the oil to a preheated wok or heavy skillet. When the oil is hot, add the milk and heat until it is almost, but not quite, boiling. Add the almond and rice paste and cook for 10 minutes at a near-boil, stirring frequently.

4. Bring the milk mixture to a boil. Stir in the sugar and Chinese date pieces. Remove from the heat and refrigerate. Serve chilled.

PER SERVING Calories: 378 | Fat: 21 grams | Protein: 9 grams | Sodium: 61 milligrams | Fiber: 3 grams | Carbohydrates: 41 grams | Sugar: 31 grams

Sweetened Walnuts

*Watch the oil temperature in the wok—if it gets too high,
the walnuts will turn black before the sugar has a chance to melt.*

INGREDIENTS | MAKES ½ CUP

½ cup chopped walnut pieces

¼ cup sugar

3 cups vegetable oil

1. Blanch the walnut pieces in boiling water for 5 minutes to remove their bitter flavor.

2. Spread the sugar out on a piece of waxed paper. Roll the walnuts in the sugar. Spread out on a tray and leave overnight to dry.

3. Heat the oil to 275°F. When the oil is hot, add the walnuts. Deep-fry until they turn golden brown. Remove and drain. Cool and store in a sealed container.

PER SERVING (2 TABLESPOONS) Calories: 113 | Fat: 9 grams | Protein: 2 grams | Sodium: 2 milligrams | Fiber: 1 gram | Carbohydrates: 8 grams | Sugar: 6 grams

Marinated Cashews

Glazed nuts are a popular Chinese snack food.

INGREDIENTS | SERVES 4

½ cup honey

¼ cup sugar

1 tablespoon orange juice

1 tablespoon Grand Marnier

1 cup unsalted cashews

1. In a medium saucepan, combine the honey, sugar, orange juice, and Grand Marnier. Stir in the cashews. Bring to a boil over high heat.

2. Boil for 2–3 minutes. Remove from the heat and pour onto a baking sheet. Separate the nuts with a slotted spoon. Leave for at least 2 hours to allow the cashews to soak up the sugar and dry. Store in a sealed container.

PER SERVING Calories: 377 | Fat: 16 grams | Protein: 5 grams | Sodium: 7 milligrams | Fiber: 1 gram | Carbohydrates: 59 grams | Sugar: 49 grams

Spicy Roasted Peanuts

*Spicy peanuts are popular during the Chinese New Year season
because peanuts symbolize longevity in Chinese culture.*

INGREDIENTS | SERVES 8

1¼ teaspoons salt

¼ cup hot water

¼ teaspoon five-spice powder

2 cups unblanched peanuts

Five-Flavor Taste Sensation

Five-spice powder contains all five flavors—
sweet, sour, salty, pungent, and bitter. Its
unique taste is achieved through blending
popular baking spices cinnamon, fennel,
and cloves with the more exotic star anise
and Szechwan peppercorns.

1. Preheat the oven to 300°F.

2. In a medium bowl, add the salt to the hot water, stirring to dissolve. Repeat with the five-spice powder.

3. Add the peanuts to the bowl, stirring well to mix.

4. Spread the peanuts out on a roasting pan. Pour any leftover liquid over the peanuts. Roast for about 45 minutes or until the peanuts are a rich golden brown. Stir every 15 minutes to make sure they cook evenly. Cool and store in a sealed container.

PER SERVING Calories: 214 | Fat: 18 grams | Protein: 8 grams | Sodium: 297 milligrams | Fiber: 2 grams | Carbohydrates: 7 grams | Sugar: 1 gram

Quick and Easy Fried Melon

*Deep-frying brings out the melon's natural sweetness.
Watermelon can be substituted for the Chinese winter melon.*

INGREDIENTS | SERVES 6

2 pounds winter melon, peeled, seeded
and cut into bite-size pieces

7 tablespoons flour

4 cups vegetable oil

½ cup flaked coconut

1. Lightly dust the melon with the flour.

2. In a preheated wok or skillet, heat the oil to 250°F. Slide the winter melon into the wok, a few pieces at a time. Deep-fry until light brown, being sure to keep the oil temperature around 250°F.

3. Remove from the wok. Dust with the coconut and serve immediately.

PER SERVING Calories: 270 | Fat: 20 grams | Protein: 2 grams | Sodium: 207 milligrams | Fiber: 5 grams | Carbohydrates: 21 grams | Sugar: 7 grams

Candied Ginger

The combination of ginger's sharp bite and sweet sugar is incomparable. Enjoy alone, or use to enliven salads and desserts such as Szechwan Peppered Fruit (see recipe in this chapter).

INGREDIENTS | MAKES ¾ CUP

6 ounces fresh ginger

1½ cups water

1¾ cups sugar

Versatile Ginger

Queen Elizabeth may have invented the gingerbread man, but Chinese cooks have been putting ginger's subtle flavor to use since ancient times. Fresh ginger is featured in soups, salads, stews, and stir-fries; it is also used to flavor oil and remove fishy odors. And nothing beats a comforting cup of ginger tea when you're feeling run-down.

1. Soak the ginger overnight and drain. Peel the ginger, removing any knobs, and cut into chunks.

2. Fill a large saucepan with water and bring to a boil. Add the ginger and simmer for about 1½ hours. Drain. Repeat again, simmering until the ginger is tender and can be easily pierced with a fork. Drain well.

3. Bring 1½ cups water combined with 1½ cups sugar to a boil in a medium saucepan over high heat. When the sugar and water have formed a thick syrup, reduce the heat to low and add the ginger. Simmer until the water is nearly absorbed and the hardened sugar coats the ginger. Remove and roll the ginger in the remaining ¼ cup of sugar. Cool and store in an air-tight container.

PER SERVING (1 TABLESPOON) Calories: 123 | Fat: 0 grams | Protein: 0 grams | Sodium: 2 milligrams | Fiber: 0 grams | Carbohydrates: 31 grams | Sugar: 29 grams

Szechwan Peppered Fruit

This foolproof dessert combines sweet honey with fiery Szechwan peppercorns.
Feel free to experiment with other canned fruits like lychees.

INGREDIENTS | SERVES 4

2 tablespoons Szechwan peppercorns or pink peppercorns

1 (20-ounce) can Asian jackfruit, drained

1 (20-ounce) can pineapple slices, drained, juice reserved

3 tablespoons honey

2 teaspoons butter

4 slices Candied Ginger (see recipe in this chapter)

Tropical Temptations

Tropical fruits live up to their exotic names. Durian is famous for its unique combination of foul odor and heavenly taste, while a single jackfruit can weigh up to 100 pounds. While fresh Asian fruit is subject to seasonal availability, canned versions can be found in Asian markets.

1. Rub the Szechwan peppercorns onto the jackfruit and pineapple slices.

2. In a small saucepan over medium heat, add the honey and ½ cup of the reserved pineapple juice. Stir until the honey is melted; then turn down the heat to low.

3. Add the butter to a large skillet over low heat. Add the Candied Ginger to the pan and heat through. Remove and set aside.

4. Add the pineapple and jackfruit to the pan. Heat, shaking and turning over the slices to make sure the Szechwan peppercorns are heated through and become aromatic. Turn the heat down to low and add the Candied Ginger back into the pan.

5. Raise the temperature on the honey and pineapple juice and bring it to a boil. Pour over the fruit. Serve immediately.

PER SERVING Calories: 357 | Fat: 2 grams | Protein: 1 gram | Sodium: 5 milligrams | Fiber: 2 grams | Carbohydrates: 88 grams | Sugar: 82 grams

Chinese Cream-Filled Buns

Most Chinese desserts are steamed. This recipe for a baked bun is a delicious exception.

INGREDIENTS | SERVES 12

2 teaspoons dry active yeast

1 tablespoon plus ¼ cup sugar

½ cup lukewarm milk

4 cups flour

4 tablespoons cold butter, cut into chunks

1 cup lukewarm water

1 egg yolk, mixed with 1 teaspoon water

3 cups whipped cream

1. Place the yeast in a small bowl with 1 tablespoon of sugar, and the milk. Set aside in a warm spot until foamy (about 10–15 minutes).

2. Sift the flour and remaining sugar into a bowl. Cut in the butter, using a fork, until the mixture resembles fine bread crumbs.

3. Make a well in the center. Add the yeast mixture and water. Mix to a soft dough and turn out onto a lightly floured surface. Knead until the dough is smooth. Place the dough in a lightly oiled bowl, turning to oil the dough on all sides. Cover and let stand in a warm, draft-free place 1 hour, or until doubled in bulk.

4. Punch down the dough. Turn out onto a lightly floured surface. Knead gently until the dough is one smooth ball. Divide into 12 even portions. Form each into a ball and place on a well-oiled baking sheet. Cover with a clean towel and set in a warm, draft-free place to rise for 10 minutes.

5. Preheat the oven to 400°F. Brush the tops of the buns with the egg yolk mixture.

6. Bake for 10 minutes, then reduce the heat to 350°F and bake 15 minutes more, or until golden brown.

7. Cool thoroughly. Slit the buns open and fill with whipped cream.

PER SERVING Calories: 254 | Fat: 8 grams | Protein: 5 grams | Sodium: 25 milligrams | Fiber: 1 gram | Carbohydrates: 39 grams | Sugar: 6 grams

Almond-Flavored Egg Cake

This treat can serve as a snack or light breakfast. A heartier version, made with seafood or ground pork, is served as a main dish.

INGREDIENTS | SERVES 6

¼ cup milk

1 tablespoon sugar

¼ teaspoon almond extract

3 eggs, lightly beaten

Cooking Tips

For best results, it's important not to let too much air into the egg mixture. Lightly beat the eggs so that, if possible, no air bubbles form. Scalding the milk makes for a shorter cooking time.

1. In a small saucepan, scald the milk.

2. In a small bowl, mix 3 tablespoons of the milk with the sugar, stirring. (You can discard the leftover milk.)

3. Add the almond extract to the milk and sugar mixture, stirring to combine. Add the mixture to the beaten eggs.

4. Pour the mixture into a pie plate, and steam in a wok on medium to medium-high heat until a toothpick comes out clean.

PER SERVING Calories: 45 | Fat: 2 grams | Protein: 3 grams | Sodium: 35 milligrams | Fiber: 0 grams | Carbohydrates: 2 grams | Sugar: 2 grams

New Year's Sticky Cake

Sticky Cake is one of many foods symbolizing good luck that play a large role in Chinese New Year celebrations.

INGREDIENTS | SERVES 8

6 Chinese dates
3 cups glutinous rice flour
1 cup boiling water
1¼ cups brown sugar
2 tablespoons milk
1 egg
1 tablespoon vegetable oil
1 tablespoon sesame seeds

Chinese Dates

Also known as jujubes, these tiny red berries with the crinkly skin have been enjoyed in China since ancient times. Their delicate sweetness makes them a valuable addition to desserts and soups; they can also be enjoyed alone as a snack. Soak in water to soften before using.

1. Soak the Chinese dates in hot water for at least 30 minutes to soften. Cut in half and remove the pits.

2. Place the flour in a large bowl. In a separate bowl, mix the boiling water and the brown sugar until the sugar dissolves.

3. Make a well in the middle of the glutinous rice flour and stir in the sugar-and-water mixture. Add the milk and the egg. Stir until the batter is well mixed.

4. Prepare the wok for steaming. Grease a cake pan with the vegetable oil and pour the cake batter into the pan. Decorate with the dates and sesame seeds.

5. Set the cake pan on a bamboo steamer and place in the wok. Steam the cake for 50 minutes, or until the edges move away from the cake pan. Cool. To serve, cut the cake into wedges.

PER SERVING Calories: 323 | Fat: 3 grams | Protein: 4 grams | Sodium: 11 milligrams | Fiber: 2 grams | Carbohydrates: 68 grams | Sugar: 19 grams

APPENDIX A

Festival Foods

Many foods in Chinese culture have symbolic significance. Oranges signify wealth because they are close to gold in color, eating chicken brings luck because the word for it is similar to the one for fortune, and never break a noodle for cooking, because its length represents lifespan. These folkloric beliefs hold true throughout the year, but are most important during festivals—the cultural holy days.

Chinese New Year, or the Lunar New Year

The traditional Chinese calendar is based on the cycles of the moon, in conjunction with planting and harvest seasons. The Chinese New Year usually falls in early-to-mid-February by the standard calendar now used. A great deal of importance is placed upon the transition from one year to the next, and thus the food eaten during the celebration is particularly important.

Buddha's Feast, or Buddha's Delight

This is a vegetarian dish to be eaten on the first day of the New Year festival, which traditionally lasts two weeks. Many Chinese are from a Buddhist cultural background. Buddhist monks follow a vegetarian diet. For the sake of purification, all Chinese people are to be vegetarian for the first five days of the New Year.

New Year's Chicken or Fish

The whole body of any animal consumed is presented at the meal table to represent completeness, prosperity, and luck. Practically speaking, being able to show the entire animal demonstrates the amount you can afford. Symbolically, wholeness means bringing together the family and community, which the Chinese value beyond the individual. And because the Chinese language consists largely of single syllables whose meaning is determined by inflection or context, words that sound the same have huge significance. The fact that chicken, *gai*, sounds like fortune—again, *gai*—weights the importance of the food. Often, a person will be instructed to take a mouthful of chicken during the New Year, even if the dish is otherwise not wanted.

Peanut Dumplings

Sesame dumplings filled with peanuts represent fortune for the golden color of the nuts and brown sugar. Making them as a family is an added bonus.

Dragon Boat Festival

This occurs on the fifth day of the fifth month of the lunar calendar, and is said to represent masculine energy, whereas everything associated with the moon is feminine. Sticky rice with various fillings in lotus leaves is a traditional food for this festival, as is the drinking of wine. For family-friendly fun, check out your local area for dragon boat races and drumming.

Moon Festival

Although commonly called the August Moon Festival, this event does not always occur in August, but rather during the eighth month of the traditional Chinese calendar. This festival celebrates the autumn full moon. Moon cakes are the food most associated with this holiday. They are muffin-sized circular pastries with a thin crust and mainly consist of sweet red bean paste. A variation of this is the snow-skinned moon cake, in which the crust is made of glutinous rice and is thus more delicate. In either case, the molds used to form the cakes leave both decorative and meaningful imprints on the exterior. The custom is for the head of the household—who may be a grandfather or grand-uncle, due to the Chinese extended family patterns—to cut the moon cakes and hand out the portions. A very fun part of this festival is the lighting of lanterns for a children's procession.

Glossary of Asian Ingredients

agar-agar

Made from seaweed, it takes the place of gelatin in Asian cooking. Agar and gelatin can be substituted for each other in recipes—just remember that agar-agar has different setting properties, requiring less time to set the same amount of liquid.

bean curd

Bean curd is made from curdled soy milk in a process that has a great deal in common with making cheese. Tofu, the name by which bean curd is commonly known, is a Japanese modification of the Chinese word for bean curd, *doufu*. Bean curd comes in a number of different textures, from firm to soft, depending on how firmly the curd is pressed. There is also fermented tofu flavored with spicy seasonings, and dried bean curd sheets and sticks.

bitter melon

A green gourd with a distinctive pockmarked skin, bitter melon has a strong chalky flavor that isn't completely removed by degorging (a manner of drawing out liquid with salt and then a cold water rinse). Bitter melon is normally paired with other strongly flavored ingredients, such as chilies.

black bean sauce and paste

Savory sauces and pastes made from dried black beans. Different varieties include hot bean sauce and yellow bean sauce.

blanch (parboil)

In Chinese cooking, blanching generally refers to plunging vegetables briefly into boiling water and then draining thoroughly. Blanching helps preserve the natural color and texture of vegetables, as well as the nutrients. It also precooks the vegetables slightly for those who prefer their stir-fries more well done. In addition, parboiling is used to clarify beef, chicken, and pork bones when making stock.

bok choy

A large cabbage with dark green leaves that is available in both Western and Asian supermarkets, bok choy is used in soups, stir-fries, and braised dishes. The thicker stalks require a longer cooking time than the more delicate leaves. Shanghai or baby bok choy is a smaller variety of bok choy with a sweeter flavor and more delicate texture.

chili pepper

Szechwan cuisine wouldn't be the same without these small, hot peppers. Chili peppers comes in a number of varieties, from jalapeño to hot habaneros. In general, the smaller the chili, the higher the heat content. Chili peppers are used to make Hot Chili Oil (Chapter 2).

Chinese cabbage

Also known as napa cabbage or Peking cabbage, Chinese cabbage is the other main cabbage besides bok choy used in Chinese cooking. Its pale green leaves readily absorb the flavors of the food it is cooked with. Napa cabbage is used in soups, salads, and stir-fries, and is even eaten raw.

Chinese sausage

Chinese sausages are highly cured, usually with a high proportion of sugar as well as salt, making them sweeter and harder than most sausages in European-American cuisine. They are usually bright red in color, with proportionally large pockets of pure fat, and like all sausages, made from a number of ingredients, including pork and liver. Look for them under their Chinese name, *lop cheong*.

cilantro
Also known as Chinese parsley, cilantro consists of the leaves of the coriander plant. While coriander is a popular Indian spice, the leaves feature more prominently in Chinese cooking. Note that dried coriander and coriander leaves are not interchangeable. Use in sauces and as a garnish.

corn flour
Another term for cornstarch.

deep-fry
Cooking food by completely submerging it in hot oil. This is one of the three main techniques used in Chinese cooking.

dim sum
Literally meaning "touch your heart," dim sum is a meal consisting of numerous small appetizers or snacks that had its origins in Chinese teahouses. Dim sum may have been the inspiration for the Western and European custom of brunch.

dried lily buds
These are the dried unopened buds of day lilies. Their earthy flavor is featured in Restaurant-Style Mu Shu Pork (Chapter 6) and Hot-and-Sour Soup (Chapter 4).

dried mushrooms
In some branches of Chinese cooking, dried mushrooms are favored over fresh, as the drying

process enhances their flavor. They must be softened in water before use.

dried tangerine peel
Dried tangerine peel lends a citrusy aroma to simmered dishes, and can also be used in stir-fries. Soften in water before use.

fuzzy melon
Related to winter melon, fuzzy melon is roughly the size and shape of a cucumber, with a dark green skin covered in light fuzz. It is baked, stuffed, and added to soups and stir-fries. If the recipe does not require peeling the melon skin, be sure to remove the fuzz before cooking.

glutinous rice
Glutinous rice is made from short-grain rice kernels. In Chinese cooking, it is normally, although not always, reserved for sweets and desserts.

groundnut oil
Another term for peanut oil.

hoisin sauce
A thick sauce made from soybean paste, hoisin sauce is a mainstay of northern Chinese regional cuisine and the base for many Chinese satay sauces. Seasonings such as garlic and chilies give hoisin sauce its unique sweet and savory flavor.

kecap manis
The Indonesian version of soy sauce, although it is much more flavorful. *Kecap manis* is made with an assortment of seasonings, including star anise and palm sugar. Kecap is the source of the word *ketchup*.

oil velveting

A technique to tenderize meat or poultry by submerging it in hot oil very briefly, just until it changes color. It is then cooked by conventional methods such as stir-frying or deep-frying. Prior to velveting, the meat is frequently marinated with a mixture of egg white and cornstarch.

oyster sauce

A savory sauce made with boiled oysters and seasonings such as soy sauce and garlic. Oyster sauce is most commonly used in sauces and dips. For vegetarians, Lee Kum Kee offers an oyster sauce using mushrooms in place of oysters.

red cooking

This cooking technique consists of browning food, and then braising or stewing it in soy sauce for a lengthy period of time. Dark soy sauce is frequently used in red cooking.

rice flour

Made from glutinous rice, it is used in a few Chinese desserts, such as New Year's Sticky Cake (Chapter 13).

rice vinegar

Rice vinegar is made from fermented rice. The three main types of rice vinegar used in Chinese cooking are red, white, and black. White rice vinegar comes closest in flavor to Western cider vinegar.

rice wine

A wine made with glutinous short-grained rice, Chinese rice wine is used frequently in marinades and sauces. The most famous rice wine comes from the Shaoxing region in northern China. If rice wine is unavailable, a good quality pale dry sherry can be used as a substitute.

rock sugar

A mixture of refined sugar, honey, and brown sugar, rock sugar is used in desserts and recipes where a different infusion of flavor than regular sugar is required.

sesame oil

A nutty-flavored oil made from toasted sesame seeds, sesame oil is used in sauces, marinades, and dips. It is frequently drizzled over food in the final stages of cooking. Sesame oil's strong flavor and low smoking point generally make it a poor choice as a cooking oil.

sesame paste

A richly flavored paste made from toasted sesame seeds. If unavailable, peanut butter can be used instead. Tahini, the Mediterranean version of sesame paste, is not a good substitute, as it is made from untoasted sesame seeds.

sesame seeds

The seeds that come from the Asian sesame plant, sesame seeds are used in dishes such as Sesame Chicken (Chapter 9). They are frequently toasted before use.

shoyu

The Japanese version of light soy sauce, *shoyu* can be used in Chinese cooking.

soy sauce, dark

A soybean-based sauce that is aged for a longer period of time than regular (light) soy sauce, dark soy sauce is commonly used in marinades and red-cooked dishes. Do not use in place of regular (light) soy sauce, as it has a very different flavor.

soy sauce, light

A soybean-based sauce that is one of the most important ingredients in Chinese cooking, light soy sauce has a lighter color, thinner texture, and saltier flavor than dark soy sauce. Japanese *shoyu* can be used as a substitute.

soy sauce, thick

Used to lend flavor to fried rice and noodle dishes, thick soy sauce has been thickened with molasses.

steaming

Cooking food by placing it over boiling water so that the steam reaches and cooks the food. This is the third most popular Chinese cooking technique.

stir-frying

Cooking food in oil at very high heat for a short period of time, while continuously stirring. It is the cooking technique most commonly associated with Chinese cuisine.

Szechwan peppercorn

Known for the biting sensation it leaves on the tongue, the Szechwan peppercorn gives Szechwan cuisine its distinctive flavor. It is actually not a peppercorn at all, but a berry from the prickly ash tree. Szechwan peppercorns are normally roasted and ground before use.

tapioca starch

A starch made from the tubers of the tapioca plant, tapioca starch is used as a thickener in Chinese cooking. Cornstarch and tapioca starch can be substituted for each other in sauce recipes, but cornstarch takes longer to thicken.

water chestnuts

The name can cause confusion, since water chestnuts come from an aquatic plant and are not related to horse chestnuts, which grow on trees. Fresh water chestnuts have a sweet flavor reminiscent of banana. Canned water chestnuts can be substituted for texture but don't have the same flavor. Jicama is also used as a substitute.

white pepper

A seasoning made from ground white peppercorns. A little-known fact is that white and black pepper both come from the same plant; the main difference between them is that white pepper berries are allowed to ripen before processing. In Chinese cooking, white pepper makes a frequent appearance in soups and spicier stir-fries. Use sparingly as it has a sharp bite.

winter melon

A type of squash with an oblong shape and dark green rind similar to a watermelon. The inside flesh is white and pleasantly sweet. Winter Melon Soup (Chapter 4) is a popular banquet soup.

wok

A bowl-shaped utensil designed to be used in cooking methods requiring high heat, such as deep-frying. A wok is the main piece of Chinese cooking equipment.

Standard U.S./Metric Measurement Conversions

VOLUME CONVERSIONS

U.S. Volume Measure	Metric Equivalent
⅛ teaspoon	0.5 milliliter
¼ teaspoon	1 milliliter
½ teaspoon	2 milliliters
1 teaspoon	5 milliliters
½ tablespoon	7 milliliters
1 tablespoon (3 teaspoons)	15 milliliters
2 tablespoons (1 fluid ounce)	30 milliliters
¼ cup (4 tablespoons)	60 milliliters
⅓ cup	90 milliliters
½ cup (4 fluid ounces)	125 milliliters
⅔ cup	160 milliliters
¾ cup (6 fluid ounces)	180 milliliters
1 cup (16 tablespoons)	250 milliliters
1 pint (2 cups)	500 milliliters
1 quart (4 cups)	1 liter (about)

WEIGHT CONVERSIONS

U.S. Weight Measure	Metric Equivalent
½ ounce	15 grams
1 ounce	30 grams
2 ounces	60 grams
3 ounces	85 grams
¼ pound (4 ounces)	115 grams
½ pound (8 ounces)	225 grams
¾ pound (12 ounces)	340 grams
1 pound (16 ounces)	454 grams

OVEN TEMPERATURE CONVERSIONS

Degrees Fahrenheit	Degrees Celsius
200 degrees F	95 degrees C
250 degrees F	120 degrees C
275 degrees F	135 degrees C
300 degrees F	150 degrees C
325 degrees F	160 degrees C
350 degrees F	180 degrees C
375 degrees F	190 degrees C
400 degrees F	205 degrees C
425 degrees F	220 degrees C
450 degrees F	230 degrees C

BAKING PAN SIZES

U.S.	Metric
8 × 1½ inch round baking pan	20 × 4 cm cake tin
9 × 1½ inch round baking pan	23 × 3.5 cm cake tin
11 × 7 × 1½ inch baking pan	28 × 18 × 4 cm baking tin
13 × 9 × 2 inch baking pan	30 × 20 × 5 cm baking tin
2 quart rectangular baking dish	30 × 20 × 3 cm baking tin
15 × 10 × 2 inch baking pan	30 × 25 × 2 cm baking tin (Swiss roll tin)
9 inch pie plate	22 × 4 or 23 × 4 cm pie plate
7 or 8 inch springform pan	18 or 20 cm springform or loose bottom cake tin
9 × 5 × 3 inch loaf pan	23 × 13 × 7 cm or 2 lb narrow loaf or pâté tin
1½ quart casserole	1.5 liter casserole
2 quart casserole	2 liter casserole

Index